A KING'S
LEGACY

A KING'S LEGACY

The Clyde King Story

CLYDE KING
WITH BURTON ROCKS

MASTERS PRESS

NTC/Contemporary Publishing Group

Library of Congress Cataloging-in-Publication Data

King, Clyde, 1925–.
    A king's legacy : the Clyde King story / Clyde King with Burton Rocks ;
foreword by Yogi Berra.
       p.   cm.
    ISBN 0-8092-2661-8
      1. King, Clyde, 1925–   .   2. Baseball managers—United States—
Biography.   I. Rocks, Burton.   II. Title.
GV865.K516A3   1999
796.357′092—dc21   98-42215
[b]   CIP

Cover photograph: Clyde King, pitcher for the Brooklyn Dodgers, 1951.
AP/Wide World Photos.
Cover design by Nick Panos
Interior design by Impressions Book and Journal Services, Inc.

Published by Masters Press
A division of NTC/Contemporary Publishing Group, Inc.
4255 West Touhy Avenue, Lincolnwood (Chicago), Illinois 60646-1975 U.S.A.
Printed in the United States of America
International Standard Book Number: 0-8092-2661-8
99 00 01 02 03 04 QP 19 18 17 16 15 14 13 12 11 10 9 8 7 6 5 4 3 2 1

To my lovely wife, Norma, who has been with me since day one and who encouraged me to write this book.

To my wonderful daughters, Norma, Princie, and Janet, who, along with their mother, insisted that I leave a legacy for my grandchildren and great-grandchildren. Without these four beautiful ladies, this book would never have been written.

Most important of all, I dedicate this book to God and to His son, Jesus Christ, to be used for their honor and glory.

—Clyde

To Mom and Dad, who have given me life, love, and the greatest support any parents have ever given a son. Thanks, Mom, for your love and friendship, for always comforting me when I needed it, and for encouraging me throughout my law school days at Hofstra University. I would not have been able to sign this book contract at age 25 if it were not for your support. Thanks also, Mom, for the title to this book.

Thanks, Dad. Many sons of ballplayers have pictures of themselves as kids with a bat and glove. Being the son of an author, in my picture I am holding your book in my eight-month-old hands. Thanks, Dad, for everything: your writing knowledge, your love and support, and your friendship.

I think the greatest "team" to take the field is you two: Dr. Lawrence Rocks and Marlene Rocks—30 years of happy marriage.

I thank God every day for everything I have, especially for Mom and Dad.

—Burton

Contents

Foreword

I PLAYED AGAINST CLYDE KING IN BROOKLYN, AND OH, IT WAS GREAT.
We had some great World Series together, 1947 and 1952. We both
had good teams. The Yankees were just fortunate enough to beat the
Dodgers. Clyde and I became good friends when he was a scout,
before he became general manager. While he was a scout, he observed
a lot of stuff; he had to because he was a scout. He had an opinion on
every player, and everybody appreciated his opinions because he's a
pretty level-headed guy. Clyde won't praise himself. He's the kind of
guy who would never criticize anyone in public. He always took a
player aside if he was doing something incorrectly and called him into
the office. He wouldn't take the credit for helping anyone, and he
helped everyone. He's pretty darn good at selecting talent. He's been
at it long enough. He's also a listener. I know that when I used to talk
to Clyde and tell him that I wanted to do this and do that, he'd say
"let's try it." We came together on the issue of making Dave Righetti
a relief pitcher. They thought we couldn't do it, but we did it. As a
baseball man, Clyde did everything well. Every job he had, he did
well. He was quite creative as a baseball executive. Whatever he did,
he paid attention to it. He was really good with me, and we were a
great team together.

Clyde is also a person you can't get mad at. He's a very soft-
spoken man, you know, with that southern drawl. Good old North
Carolina. There are a lot of Yankees fans down in North Carolina. My
granddaughter goes to UNC Chapel Hill and he visits her. They love
him there. North Carolina is a great baseball state. The UNC campus
is beautiful. It's changed over the years. It's bigger. I have been down
there a few times to visit my granddaughter and Clyde would come
up to visit with us, as he belongs to their private club, their alumni
club. They have very nice food. Even there he picks out the good
restaurants. He loves to eat. He's in such great shape. That's another

thing about Clyde King. We always came to spring training together. We always ate ice cream together. He still loves ice cream. He loves to eat. He's very careful about what he eats, but I know he loves that ice cream; boy, he really loves it. In fact, the first thing that comes to mind when Clyde's name is mentioned is "how've you been eating lately, Clyde?"

The game has changed a lot since Clyde and I played. There's Astroturf and there's television. I think the Astroturf takes away from the game. The ball goes faster through the infield and outfield. It's tough to pull-up. You go to catch a fly ball, and if you come in too close the ball jumps over your head. As for television, when I went to coach for Houston, you'd be surprised how many people said to me that there are great Yankee fans down in Texas. Back then, we were on *The Game of the Week* a lot, when Pee Wee Reese was announcing the games with Dizzy Dean. Houston was a minor league club then. Dizzy Dean, as the voice of *The Game of the Week*, brought baseball to the fans in Texas. Television and modern marketing changed the game. But I was happy when I played and so was Clyde. We enjoyed every minute of it.

Nowadays players make so much money, but I blame the owners. If they're willing to give it to them, then it's their fault. If I was playing today and I was making a million, I'd ask for five million, and if they give it to me it's their problem. The problem is that they all want to win today and only one team can win. I think years ago people cared more about the game.

The baseball wives were closer back when Clyde and I played the game. The Dodger wives and the Yankee wives were close. The marriages lasted and everyone was happy. They were much closer back then than they are today, and I think it's because of free agency and large contracts. One year players are in one place, and the next year they're in another. The players are constantly changing teams, which makes it tough with the younger players because they need stability.

By the way, as a pitcher Clyde had a good arm. He had a really good curveball. Now about Clyde's old quick-pitch that he and Roy Campanella developed. I'm surprised they didn't call a balk on him. In the wind-up you couldn't do that quick pitch. In the stretch you could, however.

Clyde's golf game is another story. Clyde's played in my golf tournaments and we've had many great golfing memories over the years. He's not a bad golfer, but he cheats on his handicap. I don't even know his handicap. He won't tell you the truth.

Clyde is also very resilient. When I heard about him falling out of his tree house, I said to myself, "What the heck's he doing up in a tree house?" My kids won't even let me go on a ladder. I quit climbing things. When he cracked a rib in Israel I couldn't believe it. "There he goes!" I thought. "Oh, boy. I've got to give him a buzz and ask him 'what did you do now, Clyde?' "

Clyde has been a great ambassador for baseball. He loves the game. He wouldn't have stayed close to the game this long if he didn't love it. When I first learned of the book I knew that Clyde would have some great things to say, and so does his wife Norma in her chapter, "Norma Gets the Last Word."

Clyde and Norma were meant for each other. She's an old-fashioned dedicated baseball wife. Without Norma, Clyde would be nothing. They are close, good family people. He needs her to organize him and she does a great job of it. She makes him biscuits anytime he wants them. When he goes on the road, she packs for him. He misses her cooking when he's away by himself. They were really meant for each other. She's the boss.

—*Yogi Berra*

Introduction

IT WAS A FINE, CRISP AUTUMN MORNING IN 1942 IN CHAPEL HILL, North Carolina, 75 miles west of a tobacco town called Goldsboro. The young Clyde King, however, had awakened tired and frustrated.

Clyde had graduated from Goldsboro High School that year and had enrolled at the University of North Carolina on the advice of teachers and coaches. Most people in the class of 1942 did not go to college, but Clyde was told that he had the scholastic ability to make it and the athletic skills to earn a scholarship. But he had not yet received any scholarship money, and things were not working out. Clyde dressed, pulled on his only jacket, and stuffed his belongings into his duffel bag.

This Saturday morning in early October was a pivotal day in the life of Clyde King, in a way he could not expect.

With the duffel bag over his shoulder, Clyde walked along South Road toward a spot where students often thumbed rides. He thought of the hardship of these last few weeks and of the joy with which his family would welcome him back.

Clyde had needed to work to earn money for his tuition and living expenses. The university gave him a job at Lenoir Hall that included serving both breakfast and supper. That meant he had to rise before 5 A.M., serve breakfast, attend classes, go to baseball practice, then basketball practice, and then go back to the cafeteria to serve supper. There was too little time for studying and rest, and Clyde had come to doubt that he would get a baseball or basketball scholarship. He had not exactly known what to expect of college, but if he had known it would be as difficult as this, he would never have come. He had tried for weeks to make a go of it, but it seemed hopeless. He had made up his mind to quit.

Clyde put his duffel bag on the curb in front of Woollen Gym and waited for a car to pass so he could signal that he wanted a ride. Soon a car pulled over. The driver turned out to be someone Clyde knew: freshman basketball coach Al Mathes.

The news that his young charge was leaving the university disappointed Mathes. He asked Clyde to get into the car so they could talk. They drove around Chapel Hill for almost an hour while Mathes explained to Clyde that, by leaving, he would be tossing aside athletic talent and scholastic ability that could lead him to a productive and rewarding life. When he got out of the car, Clyde walked back to Steele Dormitory. He had decided to persevere for a while longer.

At that time, freshmen basketball players were not allowed to go home during the first six weeks of the first semester. If anyone else had stopped to give Clyde a ride, his career at the university would have been over. Had Al Mathes not passed by while on his way to a golf game, and had he not cared enough to let the game wait while he counseled a frustrated young student, Clyde's entire life would have been different.

Clyde believes that his life has been in God's plan, and that God sent Al Mathes to talk with him that morning. He does not make a critical decision without prayer, and he is certain that God has touched all of them. His life has been one of such love, joy, and adventure that even now—past his 3 score and 10 years—Clyde reflects on it with the wide-eyed amazement of a boy.

He went on to become baseball's Mr. Nice Guy, a determined competitor but always a gentleman, with the emphasis on gentle. He found joy in playing and considered his ability to earn a living by having fun to be a gift for which he is thankful. As an executive, he worked smoothly—sometimes to the bewilderment of others—with people whose personalities put them at odds with many of their associates. The reason is simple: Clyde King has the inner warmth, security, and confidence of a spiritual man.

His is an inspirational life, and an instructional one. His memories of it are vivid, and he relates them clearly, in the language of a small-town North Carolina boy who made the big time and is tickled to share what it was like.

Here, in his own words, is Clyde's story.

A KING'S
LEGACY

I

The Great Lessons in Life
A King Is Born

I was born on May 23, 1924, in the town of Goldsboro, North Carolina. I came from a hardworking and extremely giving family. They gave me all the love a child could hope and pray for, especially the chance to go to college, which was the best decision I ever made in my life. I had three brothers and three sisters: Estelle, Irene, Norwood, Claude Jr., then me, and then Billy and Marie. We lived in a modest house on North George Street. I remember living on William Street and Brownrigg Street. My father, Claude Sr., was a foreman at A. T. Griffin Lumber Company. He made $42.50 per week and supported us seven children on that salary, which meant that we really did have to watch our pennies. My brothers and I were greatly intrigued by sports and wanted to play sports at an early age. Unfortunately, equipment was rather expensive. We were a modest family and did not have the money to spare to buy things such as baseball equipment or supplies necessary to make sports equipment, and we surely couldn't afford to buy new baseball gloves, shoes, bats, and balls. But this didn't faze us! We were going to play baseball, basketball, and football anyway. We were energetic kids and decided to turn our energy into making our own equipment. Where there's a will, there's a way, as the old saying goes.

I can remember the very day we decided to turn our plan into reality. I was about eight years old at the time and my brother Claude and I had an idea. We saw an old abandoned leather sofa, got out my mother's scissors from the sewing kit, and went to work. We knew exactly what to do with her scissors from watching her. My mother sewed a lot for us. She had to sew in order to clothe all of us. We took a marker and marked out the fingers of a baseball glove on the sofa. Then, we used her scissors to cut out a pattern of a baseball glove. We now had an outline of a hand. We needed another outline to be able to stitch the two "hands" together to form our glove. We went through the whole process once more, cutting more leather off of that sofa. We now had two of these cut-outs. They had to match so that the glove would be of uniform size. Indeed, after all our hard work they did match. We took some cotton and sort of shredded it, which made the cotton softer. Then we placed that soft cotton in the middle of those two leather outlines. We took some twine and sewed those two leather outlines together with the cotton in between and made a baseball glove. I must say, our glove held together quite well over the years. Now remember, this glove wasn't a Spalding glove or anything close to the kind of glove that could be bought at a store. It was a rudimentary glove, but it made us kids very happy because we made it ourselves.

We then took a big round rock and placed it in the middle of the glove and folded the glove around the rock. We wrapped the twine around the glove so that the glove would fit tightly around that big rock. This allowed a "pocket" to be formed in the glove. Then we placed it in a bucket of water and left it there for two days and two nights and it formed the shape of a baseball glove. Some major leaguers use this technique today to break in their gloves, and it's a great method. Now we had our glove, but we had neither a ball nor bat. However, we had come this far so we weren't about to stop now.

As for our homemade baseball, we made it this way. First, we found a small round rock about the size of a golf ball. Second, we took some tobacco twine, which is a little heavier than normal twine, and wrapped it around that rock until it grew to be the size of a baseball. We tied it off and then we used some black tar tape and covered that ball with the tar tape. We wrapped that ball in all different directions. That was our baseball! Now we had a glove and a ball, and then we had to come up with a bat.

My family lived in downtown Goldsboro, but we went out into the woods and cut down a small tree about the size of a bat. The barrel of a bat was about the thickness we were looking for in a tree. We took an ax and cut the tree down and then we took this tool my father had and slimmed the handle down and we made our own baseball bat. It worked out well and we went out into the field and played baseball. This homemade equipment was all that we needed to be happy.

Eventually, we were given a catcher's glove as a present, so now we had two gloves. We had a fielder's/pitcher's glove, and now we also had a brand-new catcher's mitt. The homemade equipment is my earliest memory of playing baseball and one that I cherish because of all the excitement my brothers and I felt when we finished making our own equipment. We did it all ourselves. We didn't just stop there, however. We liked basketball and football as well. Playing all of these sports not only made us more athletic, because in any season we were always playing something, but these other sports made us more physically fit and kept us busy and off the street corners.

Coach Norris Jeffrey, the basketball coach at Goldsboro High School, gave us an old basketball that he couldn't use anymore in his practices because it had a little knot on it. When you would bounce the basketball, if it hit on that bulge, the ball would suddenly dart underneath the stands so you couldn't control it. We asked Coach Jeffrey if we could have the ball and he was more than willing to give it to us. We now had a basketball, but what we needed now was a goal. Certainly we couldn't afford to buy a basket and goalpost, and they didn't even have nice ones like you see today. So, we took an old tricycle with the big front wheel and took wire clippers and clipped the spokes out of that big front wheel, and then filed the "rim" until it was smooth. We then took two big nails and nailed that thing to a tree. It wasn't the regulation 10 feet, but it was a good 8 feet high on that tree. Claude and I took a stick and marked off the foul lanes on the dirt, and that's the way we learned to play basketball in our backyard. There were three or four or even more kids playing each other. We would have games of two on two and it was great. It taught me that basketball was a contact sport even though it wasn't regarded as one.

We played baseball and basketball. These were our sports. However, we loved to throw the football. In the wintertime when it was too cold to play baseball, we'd play another little game with the football. Our house was a two-story house. My brother Claude would get on one side and I'd get on the other side, and Bill, who was our youngest brother, sort of tagged along with us (until he got a little older and then he played with us of course). Then, each of us would get on an opposite side of the house and we'd throw a football over the house. We'd see how many times we could catch it without dropping it. So, we were playing something all the time, and we were throwing different sized and weighted objects at different angles. It really helped our arms gain strength without hurting us.

The most memorable times with a football are associated with tall pecan trees. That's right, pecan trees! An older lady lived behind us, and she had a couple of big, tall pecan trees in her backyard. She wasn't able to get the pecans down from the top of the tree, so she asked my brother and me to help her. My brother and I would take our football and throw it up in those trees and it would knock down the pecans. They would come down in droves. If you were to pass by her house, you would think that it was raining pecans! We'd pick them up and take them over to this lady, and she would give us half of them. She would actually share them with us. Half of what we picked up we got, and that's the way we were able to get pecans, otherwise we would not have been able to enjoy them. Brother Bill helped out once the pecans were on the ground.

By trying to throw that football up in the tops of those pecan trees, which were tall ones, I really helped strengthen my throwing shoulder and my forearm during my childhood. It's a lot different throwing a football straight up in the air than it is throwing it straight out like a quarterback. It takes more strength to launch the football almost like a projectile than it does just throwing it on a level plane. I firmly believe that this specific type of throwing motion strengthened my shoulder, and when I got to the big leagues I realized very quickly that pitchers need strong shoulders and that my shoulders were strong from childhood. We didn't lift weights back then and so my strength just came from normal play activity. This certainly helped me out during my playing days with the Brooklyn Dodgers.

One of the best times of life is when you're young; time doesn't really mean what it does when you're an adult. Your judgment of time is different. You just want to go out and play. You're not thinking of anything else but playing. Your only care is whether it's sunny or raining that day and whether or not your pals will come out and play. I've often said that this is where parents come in and family life becomes important. My mother and father were there for me, and this was the reason I was successful in sports. I had my family behind me. My mom and dad took care of me and were fully supportive of me.

My mother was a great Christian lady. She gave us lots of love, encouragement, and help when we needed it. She always had a hot meal ready for us when we came in. She was mother, nurse when we got hurt, and family doctor. My dad, as the man of the household back then, had to work six days a week to support us. In order to feed and clothe all of us he had to work very hard. He couldn't go to many of our games, but it was because he had to work. When he could go to our games, he was there rooting for us. Today, there are kids who play alone because the father would rather be playing golf, the mother would rather be playing bridge—the parents just aren't around. And we surely appreciated it. I know my interest in sports, my appreciation of school, and my positive outlook on life were because of the loving environment in which I grew up.

During my first three years at William Street School we'd play all the time during recess. There was a half-hour break during the day and whatever type of ball was around was what we used. There wasn't enough time for a game, but we had fun playing dodge ball. On Saturdays we met at the William Street School to play tag football. Although this game was called "tag," it ended up being tackle football without any equipment, and I don't know how I didn't get killed. There were 15 or 20 of us that met on Saturdays and this was when I was about 12 or 13 years old.

I can remember playing with my brother on a particular day some years later. The date was December 7, 1941, and my brother and I were down by the old train station playing on an empty lot. We had been playing football. We played almost till dark, and then we came home. This old train station was about 8 or 10 blocks from where we lived and when we arrived at our house, my mother met us at the door and said, "Boys, we're at war!"

Another day stands out in my mind for a different reason. There was a lady who helped my mother a lot on Sundays, and sometimes she would just come over and visit with us. Her name was Betty, but we called her Aunt Betty. Sometimes she'd stay with us after dark, and my brother Claude and I would walk her home. It was maybe 10 or 11 blocks from our house, so we would always walk her home to make sure that she got there safely. This one time after I had walked her home and had seen her safely to her door, I was walking back and I heard a cry. I wasn't sure what it was at first, until I investigated and found a little baby. The baby was lying in a hedge, and I brought the baby back to Aunt Betty. She knew immediately where the baby came from and she took the baby. She later told us she saw to it that the baby was safely returned to the baby's mother, although all she said at the time was that she "took care of it." We were a bit suspicious because she had a daughter, and some of the members of my family thought that the baby might have been the daughter's. I remember when I gave her the baby she knew right away what to do. She didn't say "goodness, I wonder who it belongs to" or anything like that. We never did learn the true story, but I'm glad I found the little baby and brought it back safely.

My father carried insurance and the insurance agent came out every week and collected the premium. He was a friend of the family; and one day when he was leaving our house, I was outside on the swing on the front porch. When he got in his car he dropped some money. The money had a rubber band wrapped around it. He didn't realize that he had dropped it, and so he drove away. The moment I saw it, I took it to my mother. She asked me where I found it and she immediately knew that the insurance agent had dropped it. She had seen him take out that wad of money with the rubber band wrapped around it and add my father's payment to it. My father paid one dollar a week for insurance. When I returned the money, the insurance man gave me a reward. He gave me a quarter. It wasn't a whole lot of money in comparison to the money I found, but to me it was a lot of money. It would have been a disaster for him if the money had not been returned.

My mother had a large black pot that sat on cement blocks. I remember my brother Norwood would start the fire before he went off to work and then she would pour buckets of water into that big, four-legged pot. It had to be high enough off the ground so that the fire would not go out. She would put our clothes in that big pot with its scalding water and stir with a hickory stick. She had another pot in which she placed the clothes in order to squeeze them out. Then the clothes would be hung on a clothesline strung between two trees in our backyard. Things were simpler back then, even laundry.

Perfect Practice Makes Perfect

Pat Crawford was my first coach. He was the coordinator for all of the Goldsboro city schools, making out the schedules for us and planning games for us during recess. He did this for both the boys and the girls. He was a former infielder for the old Gashouse Gang in St. Louis, when the Cardinals were World Series Champions in the 1930s. At that time Pepper Martin and Dizzy Dean were heroes to many midwesterners. Pat Crawford had a profound influence on my early life because of what he taught me. I was in the fifth grade when I met him. I was attending William Street School, which housed grades four through seven in three separate buildings. I guess he saw early on that I had some coordination and some athletic ability, being a former professional athlete himself, and he took an interest in me. He took me under his wing and taught me a lot of things. But the thing he taught me most of all was how to practice. I know that you've heard it said in modern days that practice makes perfect, but Pat Crawford was the first person I ever heard who put it in a different light.

Pat Crawford would say, "Perfect practice makes perfect," and he told me, "Clyde, you'll play in a game like you play in practice. If you goof off in practice, the chances are you'll goof off in the game too." After hearing this world champion say that, I always tried hard to do my very best in practice. It was because of what Pat Crawford told me as a kid that I became the kind of coachable player that I was later on in life. It helped me take instruction from Brooklyn Dodgers president Branch Rickey—whom I always called Mr. Rickey—and it helped me take instruction from great players. Even to this day that has stood me in good stead as a coach and instructor. Today, when I instruct major league players, I make sure that they practice properly, and if I see someone slouching off in practice or losing his interest I'll say, "That's all for today, we'll go again tomorrow." I just will not tolerate practice that is not disciplined and dedicated and serious. This type of dedication in practice has helped me in my life, both on and off the field. Hard work and giving it your best effort is what sports or anything you love is all about. You can practice something over and over again, but if it's incorrect it doesn't help you.

Pat Crawford taught me how to bend down and catch a ground ball. I used to bend at the waist when trying to field a ground ball hit to me, and a lot of times the ball would go under my glove because I wasn't low enough to the ground. If the ball would take a bounce up, I had no problem fielding it. However, if the ball stayed close to the ground, I had trouble with it. Pat taught me to bend my knees and get my bottom closer to the ground. He said, "You can't expect to reach just with your arms when you're half bent over to catch a ground ball that stays close to the ground." I played shortstop and center field also in my early years and this helped me a great deal.

Later on in high school, my friend and teammate Bob Warren and I would alternate playing shortstop and pitcher. We played twice a week on Tuesdays and Fridays. On Tuesday I would pitch and Bob would play shortstop, and on Friday we would switch positions. Bob was a better hitter than I was, and I was a better pitcher than he was. When I was pitching he really helped me win a lot of ball games with his hitting, but I can't say I helped him much when he was pitching with my hitting. He was also a good fielding shortstop and helped me get out of many a tough spot with his excellent defensive ability and with his strong throwing arm. Pat Crawford allowed me at only 15 years of age to play better ball because of his advice, and I was even able to play with grown-ups because of his lessons.

Harvey Pittman Literally Stole Second Base

There's one experience, however, that not even Pat Crawford could prepare me for, and it changed my thinking. While I was in high school, I was playing with a team in Goldsboro called the Borden Mills team. They were a bunch of grown men and, again, because of Pat Crawford's instruction I could hold my own with them and do fairly well. One game in particular stands out. We played a game in a little town nearby called Kenly. In those days on Saturday and Sunday afternoons there was baseball all over North Carolina. We used to have the most professional players and teams in baseball; every little town had a baseball team. On Saturday afternoons, especially, everyone would come out to the ballpark. We had about 1,000 people in attendance. I was pitching, and I hit my first over-the-fence home run. I had hit some home runs before, but those balls went over the outfielders' heads and into the cornfields, and I'd circle the bases before they could find it. This homer was the first home run I hit that went over the fence. It was in the sixth inning with a man on, and it scored two runs and we were going into the bottom of the ninth leading 2–1. We were playing on the road. The home team came up in the bottom of the ninth, and I got the first two hitters out.

Then came Harvey Pittman. He was a former minor league outfielder and was now playing first base at age 42, and I had gotten him out twice in the game already. He came up for what would be the last out. At that time we had one umpire, and he stood behind the pitcher and looked around the pitcher to call balls and strikes. That's the only umpire we had in those days. Harvey came up and I made a pitch to him. He hit a little bloop down the left-field line between the third-base bag and the outfield wall. The umpire had to leave his position behind the pitcher to run over to the line to see if it was going to hit fair or foul, and as he ran over to look at that ball I heard the pounding of footsteps. I was standing on the mound and Harvey Pittman came straight from home plate right through the mound to second base. He knew that umpire had to leave to go watch that ball and couldn't watch him, so he came right through the mound and into second base. Even his own home fans were yelling that he didn't touch first base. The umpire said to the manager of our team, "Well, I'm sorry I didn't see it. I had to watch the ball to see if it was fair or foul." So Harvey Pittman was now on second base. Fortunately, I got the next guy out and we won. The thing that impressed me, however, was that here was a guy who, though he was past his prime, used his mind to outsmart us. It made me think of how I could use my mind as well as my body to win, but I wanted to do that within the rules. I'll never forget Harvey's steal of second. Pittman's team ought to be called the "Kenly Thieves" because he literally stole second base.

The King Is a Mathematician!

Janie Ipock was my high school math teacher. She always encouraged her students. Math was my best subject then, and Miss Janie was the main reason for that, because of her personality. She took such an interest in all of her students that everyone went into her class happy to be there. Her class was the first class of the day for me, and she'd have us put our heads down on our desks and sing "Danny Boy." It is an old Irish song and it's still my favorite.

One day after class she said, "I know you're having some problems in a couple of subjects, and if you want to come by after school, I'll tutor you in those subjects." Janie Ipock was a big sports fan, and when we would walk into class the day after a game, she would tell the athletes in her class that she thought we did a good job and that she was proud of the way we conducted ourselves on the field or on the court. She just did a great job of encouraging us. In addition to teaching us, she taught us how to get along in life. If someone fouled me especially hard in a basketball game the previous night, she would tell me that she was impressed that I handled it in a calm manner and didn't fight back. Today they'd call that type of foul in basketball a flagrant foul. Things like that taught me a lot. I don't know how she found out that I was having trouble in a couple of subjects. She must have spoken with some of my other teachers. Well, she told me, "If you'll come by every Monday and Wednesday I'll tutor you." The amazing thing was that she picked Monday and Wednesday because, being a huge basketball fan and sports fan, she knew I played games on Tuesdays and Fridays. And I did just that for maybe six or seven weeks. In those days even if you failed one subject you could continue to play sports in high school. If you failed two subjects, however, well, that was it for you—you couldn't play sports. I was on the way to failing two subjects and she saved me. I went on to be a good student all because of Janie Ipock's help. She took the time to be there for me. She could have been at home enjoying the afternoons with her friends, but she chose to help me in my studies. This enabled me to get the practice and the training that I needed to go on to college. I would never have gone to college if it hadn't have been for my high school algebra teacher Janie Ipock, who was truly a saint.

Principal C. W. Twiford

Principal Twiford played a significant role in my life during high school. I can best describe him as a compassionate gentleman. He was very soft-spoken and very bright. He was a diplomat. He knew how to get the best out of a kid without jumping all over him. He was stern enough to issue discipline when called for, and he often disciplined his students. He took an active role in our school, and we appreciated that effort. I can remember one day in particular. We were taking a test and my best friend Bo Wynn, who was also a second baseman on the baseball team, sat behind me in class. I tell everybody Bo was smarter than I was because he always finished the test before I did. Well, he was sitting behind me and he had finished the test and was kicking my desk. I hadn't finished yet. He was really disturbing me. I couldn't concentrate, and I asked him two or three times to stop, but he didn't stop. After a couple of times I turned around and popped him in the face. The teacher saw me and took me down to the principal's office.

Principal Twiford told my teacher to go back to the classroom and that he would handle the matter. He told me he wanted me to take a walk with him. We went out of the high school, out the front door, walked around the tennis courts, and around Herman Park and did this for about 15 or 20 minutes, talking while we walked. He told me that he knew I wasn't a bad kid and because this was the first time this ever happened, he wasn't going to suspend me. Since it was the first time he wouldn't even tell my parents. He'd give me a second chance if I behaved myself, and he told me to go back to my room and be the kind of kid he thought I was, and that really helped. He didn't send me home or embarrass me.

Principal Twiford was also a great sports fan, above and beyond the call of duty. One time a group of us—not a team organized event but just a group of us kids—went to play basketball over at Pikeville. We were going to play outside because we couldn't get into the gym. I remember Mr. Twiford came with us, took a tobacco stick, and marked the out-of-bounds lines. Here's a principal of a high school who is taking time to go with a group of kids and help them. This wasn't even a team event. We were on the basketball team at Goldsboro High, but this was just an after-school fun game among friends. This just shows you how much he cared about us. He really was a big sports fan.

2

Childhood Mishaps and Games

WHEN YOU'RE A KID, YOU LIKE TO PLAY AND SOMETIMES YOU GET hurt. Well, like most kids, I loved to play and I had my share of bruises, childhood accidents, and brother-brother mishaps early on in my life. My brothers and I were always a team. We loved each other. We watched out for each other and were a very tight-knit family. However, when brothers play together, things can get a little rough. The most terrifying childhood event that happened to me, however, did not involve my brothers.

Being Bitten by a Dog and Partially Losing My Eyesight

It was the same time that Pat Crawford had given me some instruction and had taken me under his wing. I was in the fourth grade at William Street School and I was on my way home from school carrying my books, when I came to a wooden fence. This fence was the type that was built with heavy wooden boards that were so close together that it was impossible to see between the boards. It was a real old-fashioned solid, heavy wooden fence. Suddenly, out of nowhere, I heard a dog barking and chickens clucking and flapping their wings. Being a nine-year-old, I was curious, and I stood on my tiptoes to see what was causing the disturbance. When I did so, the dog jumped up and bit me in the face. His top teeth suddenly became embedded in the left side of my forehead and his bottom teeth became embedded just above my right eye. He was locked on to me, and I was shaking my head trying to shake him loose. He was a small dog, about the size of a rabbit. The more I shook, the more damage was done. Finally, he let go. My forehead was torn so badly that the skin had dropped down almost covering my left eye. At that point, our grocery boy was riding by on his bicycle and saw me kneeling on the ground bleeding. He picked me up, placed me in the big basket between the handle bars, and pedaled as fast as he could. (Some of you may wonder how a nine-year-old boy could fit in a basket, but during the 1930s delivery boys had big, deep baskets mounted on their bicycles so that they could make large deliveries.) My house was only four blocks away. For weeks you could see the blood trail on the sidewalk and on the street. You can just imagine how I felt each day when I took that same route to and from school and saw my own blood still on the sidewalk and in the street.

My mom called Dr. Deleon Best right away (he was our family doctor and he always made house calls). He came immediately and sewed me up. Doctors to this day, whenever I have a physical exam, always say "You've got a big scar. Who did the surgery on your forehead and eye?" My answer is always "Our family doctor." Then I'll hear "If the surgery was done today, there wouldn't be any scar."

Our doctor was not a skilled surgeon, and I have no ill feelings because I know that the medicine and surgical techniques were not then what they are today. He was a great family friend and was always very concerned about the health of each member of our family. Often he wouldn't even charge us for his services. After this accident I had vision problems, partially losing the sight in my right eye, because it was the one where the dog's teeth were embedded and nerves were damaged. That's the reason I didn't get in the service. My left eye is fine, however.

If I had had better vision in my right eye, I probably would have been a better hitter. I could hit pretty good in high school—but when I got to college I didn't hit as well. I was a switch-hitter, but I hit mostly left-handed, and when you do that you have to use your right eye, and that was my bad eye. I didn't wear glasses until after high school, when Dr. Eddie Bizzell, a friend of the family, drove up by the curb of my house and gave me a pair of glasses so that I would be able to see when I went off to college. My friend and I were playing catch. Dr. Bizzell stopped his car, and I went over to him and he handed me a pair of glasses. I still have them in the case in which they came. The lenses were tiny and I remember getting adjusted to wearing glasses. He never even gave me an eye exam. He just handed me that pair of glasses, and those were the ones I took with me to Chapel Hill. Although during ball games I didn't wear them, I wore them in class and on campus. I didn't know if they were over-corrected or under-corrected, I just wore them. However, because of Pat Crawford I instinctively knew how to play the game, and I could make an effort to overcome the near blindness in my right eye.

My brothers and I always enjoyed playing games, and one such game involved a fence in our neighborhood. We enjoyed seeing who could walk along the fence the farthest without falling off. I remember one time I really felt like I was the most balanced person in the world. I was walking along that fence and then, suddenly, I lost my balance! Even more unbelievable, when I lost my balance and fell off I landed on a nail! The nail went right through my right foot! I said before that things in this era were simpler, and it was so true when it came to medicine and homemade remedies. I remember my mother using a piece of velvet and burning it, thus allowing the smoke and the chemicals in the smoke to act as an antibiotic and kill the bacteria from the nail. Today, you would get a tetanus shot from a doctor. My mom's remedy must have worked because my foot did not become infected. I spoke before about my brothers and me acting as a team. When the nail went through my foot, my brothers raced home and told my mom what had happened. Even then, my brothers were concerned about me.

Another childhood mishap took place at about the time my brothers and I made our own baseball equipment. It was none-too-soon afterward when we were playing our little game that another unfortunate event occurred, only this time my brother Bill was the one bleeding. Bill was catching and my brother Claude was pitching. I was at the plate hitting with our homemade hickory-wood bat, and Claude threw me a pitch that was a bit too high to hit at first glance. However, I quickly realized that if I backed up I could reach that pitch. I backed up, swung mightily, and hit my brother Bill on the forehead, cutting his head open. Up until the day he died in 1997 you could see that scar from our jagged homemade baseball bat. My mom was hysterical. I remember her calling Dr. Best, and he came over immediately. When he heard the news, he rushed right over and tended to Bill. After being sewn up, Bill was out playing ball again within days.

I'll never forget the time that I cut my fingers with a butcher's knife. We used to enjoy watermelons in the summertime, and we liked to cut them ourselves and our mother usually let us. One time I told my brother Claude that I wanted to cut the watermelon. He said that it was his turn, but I was adamant that it was my turn. I took the knife and began to cut the watermelon when he suddenly snatched the knife, jerking it out of my hand with a mighty tug, and pulling it right through my hand and cutting three fingers on my right hand in the second joints. I still to this day have a crooked fourth finger on my right hand from that cut. Although my finger wasn't severed, my finger bled a lot and the tendons were cut so that to this day my finger won't straighten out. I didn't have any stitches at the time, and the bleeding stopped after a while. We were kids and I guess kids will be kids.

Then there were my school-yard boxing days. In my day, children were allowed to box during recess. The school provided gloves, and we went at it. We'd eat our lunch and then go and fight. It's actually amazing how long my winning streak went on at the William Street School. The streak went on from year to year, that is until Erskine Presley came along and beat me. You could say that he dethroned the King! We also had running competitions, and my record in our sprints competition stood until Russell Singleton beat me.

There was the time that I was hit by a taxicab on my way home from playing ball. My brothers and I had a bicycle which we put together ourselves. It was an old bicycle, and we had taken the fender off because it rattled around too much when we rode it. Needless to say, once that fender came off, our clothes had mud streaks up and down our backs on rainy days. Sports to me was everything in those days, and I just had to stay out until dark playing. I loved to play and I played behind our grammar school buildings with my brothers. They would go home in time for dinner. We had chores to do at home, and those chores included bringing in wood and coal for our stove in the wintertime and feeding chickens and collecting eggs in the summer. My brothers always came home at the right time and were able to finish doing their chores and eat dinner. Not me, however! I'd stay out late until I couldn't see the ball anymore.

One night I was out really late, riding home on my bicycle. I was crossing the railroad tracks when suddenly a taxicab appeared and hit me. There weren't any lights in the area, and the cab driver didn't see me. My bike went one way and I went the other way. I was bruised and bloodied, but I still managed to carry that bike home with me on my back. My house was about three blocks away, and when I arrived home my mom was standing there waiting for me. She asked me what had happened. I answered her like any other kid—I didn't tell her the truth. I told her that the bicycle had fallen down the steps. I knew she didn't believe me because the bicycle could not have gotten in that condition from falling down even several hundred flights of steps. We never fixed that bicycle, and it was at least a year before we got a replacement. We missed our bike because it was a fun means of transportation for us kids.

The year passed rather quickly and another bike was born. It wasn't a new bike, but it was in great condition. We bought it at Cogdell's bicycle shop in Goldsboro, and we loved that bicycle. This bicycle had two fenders and they didn't rattle. We rode that thing for a long time and loved every minute of it.

Wintertime was a fun time for us King children, especially for my brothers and me. We couldn't play baseball or basketball, or even football, because of the cold weather and the snow. We had our fun by being creative with the outdoors. Just as we had built our own baseball equipment, we managed to design our own wintertime pastimes. For instance, we had a homemade trap.

Now this trap was a real contraption. We built a trap that looked like an upside-down box. We made the trap from thin pieces of wood with our tools and then placed the trap outside in the snow and put crumbs underneath it so that a squirrel or bird would be attracted to the trap. I can remember just waiting with wide-open eyes from inside our house. It was too cold to stay outside and hide behind anything, so we stayed inside holding a long string in our hands. The string was attached to a little stick that held up the trap. It was strung from that trap across the yard and underneath a window in our house. This way, we could stay inside, and when a squirrel came to eat the crumbs, we could catch him. The birds would come to eat, and we'd pull the string and catch them. Let me say that we never hurt any animal. All we would do is keep the birds in our old canary cage, which my mom had saved, and we would feed them. Eventually, we'd let them fly away.

We had our famous metal slide to play with outside in the wintertime as well, and this made for some more excitement. This was at my home on Brownrigg Street. We had taken a heavy metal cable, which we got from Brown's Junkyard, and we climbed up a tall tree and attached the cable about 50 feet off the ground. We were able to take the metal cable and secure it around one of the large tree limbs. Then, we stretched the cable down at an angle to the ground and placed an iron stake in the ground to hold it firmly in place. Before this was done, however, we had taken a metal pipe which was about six to eight inches long and we threaded the cable line through the pipe. The pipe had to be long enough so that both hands could fit firmly around it. We then took apart a wire coat hanger and placed the end of the coat hanger inside the metal pipe and slung it up that cable line where one of my brothers was waiting to catch the pipe. After one of us caught it, we'd slide down on that pipe. I can remember the feeling of holding onto that metal pipe and sliding down from that tall tree. It was a thrilling experience. We slid down that contraption so much that pretty soon there was a hole in the ground right by that stake, where our feet had made deep imprints. I remember all of the neighborhood kids wanting to come over and try it out. We couldn't let the little kids try it because it could be dangerous. Even we had to cover the pipe with an old ragged towel when we slid down that cable line because of the burning friction that was created by our acceleration.

We played a game which we dubbed "rubber guns," because the game involved rubber bands. First, we used a smooth wooden board and we cut out the form of a gun. Then, we took a clothespin and placed it on the back of the handle so that we could stretch a large rubber band from the clothespin to the end of the gun. We'd mash the end of that clothespin and it would release the rubber band, enabling us to shoot each other with the rubber bands. We had some great rubber-gun fights. You could make that barrel long enough to stretch the rubber band so much that when it was released, it flew across the room. The trick was finding the thickest and longest rubber bands around the house. No one ever got hurt, but you could feel the sting when they hit you.

I remember our games of marbles as well. In the wintertime a friend let us use his house because he had a circular rug, and we'd play marbles on that rug instead of having to make the circle outside. We had a great time doing that as well. We had fun as kids, and we always thought that we had the best childhood anyone could pray for because our parents were so loving and so giving. We stayed at home, did our homework, went to church, and enjoyed each other.

I remember the time that I smoked rabbit tobacco, which was a type of tobacco grown at that time. I don't know if it still exists today or why kids back then wanted to smoke it, but I tried it and it was not very bright on my part. Kids would take some tissue and roll out the tobacco, like the cowboys did in the old movies. I got so sick from smoking it that when I got home, my mother knew I had done something wrong. She asked me if I had been smoking rabbit tobacco, and I said that I had. She warned me never to do it again and I never did. I felt so sick that, believe me, I would never try it ever again.

Walking along the railroad tracks was another fun game. The railroad tracks were located within three blocks of our house. My brother Claude and I used to get on the tracks near Brown's Junkyard and walk to the area where Applebee's and the Holiday Inn

Express were later built. We'd start at one end of the tracks and walk to the other and see who could walk the farthest without falling off. We learned that by placing our ears to the track, we could hear the train from far, far away. We always knew when the train was coming long before we could ever see it in the distance. It wasn't dangerous back then because the vibrations from the tracks indicated that the train was coming. I remember that when it came to walking along the track, Claude and I were even. This exercise actually helped me with my balance and coordination. We were young then and just trying to have some fun with the things near our house.

Another fun thing about Goldsboro was the curb market. I remember cleaning up for Mr. Liles on Saturday afternoons at the community building, and that was a lot of fun. Back then, and still to this day, on Fridays they had a curb market. All of the local farmer's wives would bring their food on Saturday mornings and arrange their wares on the tables and sell them to the general public. They had tomatoes, chicken salad, potato salad, freshly picked corn, homemade biscuits, and all kinds of great stuff. The ladies would bring their freshly cooked pies and cakes, not to mention their famous chicken pastry and fried chicken. It was wonderful. Just the smell of all of that food made me hungry. We used to wait, and as soon as the curb market was over in the afternoon, we would help Mr. Liles clean up. Now this market was a big affair for Goldsboro. The tables, when lined up, more than equaled the length of a full-size regulation basketball court. If Mr. Liles had to clean up by himself, it would have taken him two-and-a-half to three hours. We wanted to play basketball, and we were also very hungry. We'd show up at the end of the market and those nice country ladies would give us cupcakes, chicken salad sandwiches, and other leftovers. It was a real treat eating all of those leftovers. After we'd eaten, we would help Mr. Liles clean up and sweep up so that we could play and he wouldn't have the strenuous task of doing it all himself. He always enjoyed having us around, and he would even stay and watch us play. He was the custodian of the building and a great gentleman.

It's amazing to think back and recall so many diverse experiences that I've had in my life; let me say that my brothers and sisters really made being young wonderful. We played together. We got hurt together. We took care of each other. We went to school together, and we all dreamed together and tried to help each other out whenever and wherever possible. I think that my strong family background and my experiences in school really prepared me well for the biggest step in my life—college.

3

My College Days at UNC,
Being Saved by Al Mathes,
and the USO Tour

IT WAS 1942 AND I WAS 18 YEARS OLD. I HAD THE CHANCE TO GO TO the University of North Carolina at Chapel Hill, and I was so excited. I couldn't wait to go to college. This opportunity meant a lot to me and my family. There were seven of us children, and I was the only one to go to college. The day came for me to depart, and when I left Goldsboro to go to Chapel Hill I took my belongings in a little duffel bag and said goodbye to my parents. We didn't have a suitcase for me to use because we never traveled when I was a youngster. So off I went to UNC at Chapel Hill to stay in Steele Dormitory. But the first night didn't go exactly like clockwork. All students who were not on scholarships and who had to work their way through college were going to be housed in Steele Dormitory in the basement. The university was going to put bunk beds in the basement, and everything was supposed to be ready on move-in day. Well, those metal bunk beds had not yet been installed when I arrived, and so I slept on a bench in front of Steele Dormitory with my little bag, containing the few clothes I owned, sitting right beside me. Sleeping outside wasn't so bad because back in those days you didn't have to worry about anybody stealing from you or harming you. The following day they installed the beds and all of us moved in.

My daily college routine was as follows. My first year at college, I'd get up bright and early because I had a job that started at 5:30 A.M. This was during World War II. There was a preflight school based at Chapel Hill, and I would serve the preflight cadets meals at Lenoir Hall. I then would dash off to my eight o'clock morning class and begin my full load of credits. At the end of the day, I'd practice baseball, and in the early evening, when baseball practice had ended, I would practice basketball. After basketball practice I went back to

Lenoir Hall to serve dinner to the cadets. After that, I'd go back to my room and study and then sleep, and, before I knew it, it was time to get up and start the whole routine again.

Being Saved by Al Mathes

This routine continued for about four to four and a half weeks and I was losing weight—I was skinny to start with, so I couldn't afford to lose weight. I had gotten depressed and discouraged, and I put my things in a little duffel bag, the kind that hangs over your shoulder, and walked down to Woollen Gym. That's where we played basketball in those days. (Since then, the university added Carmichael Auditorium and then Dean Smith Center.) I was going to bum a ride home. In those days you could bum a ride, and people were happy to give a college kid a ride. You'd make your little sign that said "Raleigh" or "Goldsboro," and they'd come by and pick you up.

What you did was bum a ride from Chapel Hill to Raleigh, which was about 25 miles, and then from Raleigh to Goldsboro. They'd come by and say "I'm just going to Raleigh, do you want a ride?" You'd say "sure," and you'd go as far as they went and then on to Goldsboro. There was no fear of anybody kidnapping you or murdering you. So I was standing out in front of Woollen Gym, where basketball star George Glamack played when he was at Carolina. Now the first five or six cars passed me up and I was beginning to think I wasn't going to get a ride, when suddenly a car pulled up at the curb and stopped. I looked into the car, and there was my freshman basketball coach, Al Mathes. He said, "Clyde, where are you going?" I said, "Coach, I'm going home." He said, "Well, don't you know the basketball team has a rule that you can't go home for the first six weeks?" I said, "Yes, sir, I know that, but I'm not coming back." "Well," he said, "Why don't you get in the car and we'll take a ride."

I threw my little bag in the backseat and got into his car, and I can still remember the streets that we drove down in Chapel Hill. He talked to me for about 45 minutes, and he told me that I had ability on the basketball court and was a great competitor. He told me I just couldn't quit and give up, that's the worst thing I could ever do. He heard that I had some baseball ability and said that if I went home all that would go down the drain, and what I wanted to accomplish when I came here five weeks ago would be all for naught. Well, he did a great job talking to me, and I got out of the car, went back to Steele Dormitory, and of course went on to play both basketball and baseball at the university.

Soon afterward, I got some scholarship help and was able to quit my jobs and spend more time studying and being a normal college student. I could also concentrate on baseball and basketball. Al Mathes came along in my life at a time when I really needed some direction, and he took the time to give it to me. I later learned that he was on his way that Saturday morning to play golf, and yet he stopped and took time with me and helped me get my priorities in order.

If he hadn't come along, there's no telling what my life would have been like. What if one of those first five or six cars had stopped for me? I would have gone back to Goldsboro and that would have been it. My parents would not have talked me into going back to UNC. They would have treated me like the Prodigal Son and would have welcomed me home with open arms. If Coach Mathes hadn't come along I wouldn't have met my wife, who was in school at UNC when I was; I wouldn't have been able to go around the world. I would not have met several presidents nor been involved in several World Series, and I wouldn't have had the family that I have now. Al Mathes came along when I needed him.

Sometime in the mid-1990s, however, Norma and I were sitting watching *Wheel of Fortune* and *Jeopardy*, waiting for the Carolina–Duke basketball game to come on television. The phone rang and I picked it up, and a voice said "Is this Clyde King?" in a raspy manner.

I said, "Yes, this is Clyde King."

He said, "This is Coach Al Mathes." I asked him where he was, and he said he was in Tampa, Florida. At that point his wife picked up the phone and said, "Mr. King, Al has had a rough time. He's had several heart bypass operations, and he wasn't doing well at all. He would sit in his chair and he wasn't doing his exercises and was just giving up."

I had recently been on Dr. Bill Friday's television program at that time. It was a show hosted by the former president of the university called *North Carolina People*. I told the story of how Al encouraged me at UNC. Al's wife said one of the cameramen on the show was a nephew of Al's and when he heard me tell the story about his uncle, he sent Al a tape of it. She said to me, "He's watched that tape about four or five times and he's a changed man. He gets up and does his exercises now and eats properly because of the nice things that you said about him."

Fifty years ago when we were face-to-face, he changed my life, and 50 years later, without even knowing it, I helped him through his rough times. He could have gone and played golf that day in 1942. He had a lot of other young prospects. But he stayed with me and missed that golf game and really did change my entire life. I'm happy that he knows how much I appreciate it. He and his wife, Ann, had dinner with Norma and me during spring training in 1998 at Damon's Restaurant, and what a happy, emotional reunion it was! Thanks, Coach!

There are other coaches out there in sports who I hope will exercise their discretion to do something like Al did for me. We don't get to where we are in our lives, to be 75 years old as I am in 1999, and not have had someone who had a profound influence on our lives and pointed us in the right direction and got our priorities in order. Pat Crawford and Al Mathes did that for me, as did my math teacher Janie Ipock, Coach Norris Jeffrey, and Principal C. W. Twiford in high school.

When I was in school, the University of North Carolina had only about five thousand students, and we knew most of the people on campus. We had an open area called the "Y" where we could go and meet our fellow classmates. They had the best milk shakes there, and we could talk to our buddies. We always met there and talked about the game that we played the day or night before. There was another place down the street where we used to go at night to get milk shakes because the "Y" was only open during the day during classes. Milk shakes in those days were like beers are today; everyone on campus drank them.

The campus itself was unique. There was a big open area in the center of the campus in front of South Building and Steele Dormitory. On Sunday afternoons a group of us would get together and play tag football. We drew a big audience. There would be maybe one hundred people watching us play. Back then most college kids didn't have cars, and so there wasn't much to do on a Sunday afternoon. The girls would come and watch and sit on the ground and picnic. It was great. As time went on though, the games got a little bit too rough for me. My buddies and I eased off on playing because guys started to slap each other harder and harder with both hands, and sometimes they'd tackle so hard that people were injured. So, we decided to give up this Sunday ritual, but it was fun while it lasted. In place of the football game, we would sit on the long stone wall along Franklin Street and watch the pretty coeds walking by.

The campus back then was less crowded than it is today. The buildings were old and elegant, and we loved strolling around and looking at the architecture. There was also much more space in between the buildings. I also loved the fact that you could walk all over campus. You didn't need a car. Everything was in walking distance.

I remember my classes well. I took all of the regular subjects—history, English, math, physical education, and science. But I had one favorite professor. The nice coincidence about this professor was that his name was King. He was one of my professors as well as my advisor. I enjoyed his lectures and my talks with him. If I hadn't been asked to play professional baseball, I probably would have majored in mathematics and would have made teaching and coaching my career.

When I was growing up I had always wanted to be an FBI agent. My faulty vision didn't allow that, so I decided that I better choose another career. Since I had always liked sports and wanted to go to college, I thought I might become a high school coach. I also thought that I might be a math teacher. Again, when I went to Chapel Hill I had no idea that I would end up being asked to play professional baseball. When my opportunity came to become involved with sports, I switched my major in college from mathematics to physical education. But I liked Professor King. He took an interest in me individually and he was much like Janie Ipock in high school. He was a sports fan, and later on after I made it in the majors he always asked me, as well as my roommate and fellow Dodger Claude Crocker, how we were doing. He was the type of professor that when we walked into the classroom, he was always there waiting for us, as he arrived to class well before the students.

After that first-year routine, life was extremely different. I was more relaxed and had a lot more fun. I was more involved in school activities, and I had met a girlfriend there and made a lot of new friends. Doc Blanchard was one of my friends early on at Chapel Hill. He later left UNC and went into the U.S. Military Academy at West Point and became an All-American football player. I made new friends quickly, and we shared good times together. In fact, right after my first year things began to change quickly. I came back home to Goldsboro for summer vacation, and I worked at A. T. Griffin's Manufacturing Company to help me get through college. The second year came and I had some financial aid which made things much more enjoyable. I now felt like a student. In fact, I took notice of the campus, and some of the things I was exposed to were a far cry from my life in Goldsboro.

I saw a lot of things that second year that I had never seen before. One of the things that I had never seen at home was girls smoking. This was the first time I had ever seen a girl smoke. My mother didn't smoke and my sisters didn't either, so to see girls smoking just seemed strange to me. Also, I saw beer drinking. That was also strange to me because back home we had never gone to a bar, and I had never seen anyone drink. Now in college I was seeing people getting drunk and doing other crazy things. Most of the time I was with a crowd that didn't do those things. Believe it or not, I was not exposed to much profanity. I know that's hard to believe today, but back then things were different with regard to the language that students were allowed to use in public. Today you walk on a college campus and it's nothing to hear four-letter words from students.

My UNC days were great because I had the privilege of playing basketball with a great bunch of guys and for a great coach. The basketball players back then were nowhere near as tall as they are now. I think our tallest player was 6'3" and he was our star, John "Hook" Dillon. He was a hook-shot artist and I was a guard. My job was to get the ball in to John and let him hook; he could hook with either hand. We had speed on that team as well; we could really drive to the basket. From a speed standpoint the game hasn't changed, just from a hype and marketing standpoint and the dunking part. We didn't know what dunking was back then. We thought it involved a donut. I was playing regularly, and back then you could play both pro ball and college basketball, and I had made the team when this rule was in effect. As underclassmen, our first coach was Al Mathes, and then came Ben Carnivale, who was our varsity coach. I saw him in the late 1990s, in fact, when I went to Willamsburg, where he was living.

The thing about Coach Carnivale that was great for all of us was that he was a stickler for hard practicing, something that I had been taught by Pat Crawford, and now Coach Carnivale was telling us the same thing, just as Dean Smith did and his successor, Bill Guthridge. They wanted you to practice very hard and be very physical. The latter was new to me. Back in high school we just went out and ran our plays, but Coach Carnivale wanted some contact in our practices so that we would be used to it when the game started. We played in the old Woollen Gym that seated about 3,500 fans, compared to the Dean Dome where today's players compete and which seats 21,000. We had an old building across the way called "The Tin Can." It was there, during the war years, when Tommy Dorsey and Benny Goodman came and their bands would play and have dances for all of the college students. We'd go over there and work out sometimes, and we'd go to those dances and it was great.

In the summer of 1944 I was signed to play baseball by the Brooklyn Dodgers and immediately played in the majors. So after I had played that first year in the big leagues and had come back I was sort of a celebrity. I had my $5,000 bonus that Mr. Rickey gave me for signing with the Dodgers, and I used it to pay off the debts that my folks owed, such as the house rent and grocery bills. I took $1,500 out of my $5,000 and went down to Augusta, Georgia, to visit a friend there. While I was visiting there I saw a car, a 1941 red Buick convertible, and I fell in love with it. I never had a car before. It cost only $1,500, and I bought it. I drove it back to UNC and I stayed at the Phi Kappa Sigma house on the corner right across the street from the Carolina Inn. They brought me in even though I wasn't a member of the fraternity. They asked me to come live there and I stayed and roomed with Claude Crocker. I parked my red convertible on the street corner, and it was the only car in sight on the entire block. Guys would always come over and ride with me, and when I met Norma we took rides. It was a great time. That first year was tough, but after that life was sheer pleasure.

The school administration also thought it was unique that one of their students was playing pro ball for the Brooklyn Dodgers and going to school at the same time. There was one professor who was from New York and he once saw me pitch, and when he returned from summer vacation he told the whole class about it. I was sitting there in the classroom, embarrassed as he talked about me. However, I never will forget one Sunday when we were practicing in Woollen Gym. Coach Carnivale had to leave practice to go to Duke for a meeting. I didn't know it at the time, but during that meeting they reestablished the old rule that you couldn't play in college while playing pro ball. He came back from his meeting, and we were still on the floor practicing. He called me over and told me about the rule change. It was a sad time because I knew that we had a pretty good team, and they went on to play at Madison Square Garden in the NIT Tournament. Manny Alvarez took my place, and he went on to make the All-Southern Conference team. Coach Carnivale had a hard time telling me about the change, and it was hard for me to believe. I wasn't allowed to work out with the team and my playing days were over.

Thus, I formed my own team. I called it the Carolina All-Stars, and we had a lot of fun. Randy Brown, whose uncle, Ed Brown, owned an ice plant in Goldsboro, was on that team, and he was quite good. He was 6'10" and we thought he was Goliath. I took him and Claude Crocker, who was also now ineligible because of the rule change. We even had Don Anderson. Don was on the UNC basketball team, but he played with us under another name. We'd all get in my convertible and go around different campuses and play. We had no uniforms. We went down to Woollen Gym and checked out WG uniforms, our generic gym outfits, and used them. We hand-stenciled the numbers on the back. I remember we would go in my car with six players jammed in it. One time we were on the road playing Lenoir Ryne College, and I'll never forget what happened there. We got out of the car and walked into the gym and took our practice dribbles and the ball had a knot on it that we didn't know about until the ball bounced and suddenly darted underneath the stands. (This reminded me of the ball that Coach Jeffrey had given us many years earlier.) Here we were with our WG uniforms and hand-written numbers and the fans started booing. Well, we scored 15 points against that team before their players scored a point. We won something like 75–40.

The USO Tour

Going to school and playing professional baseball was rare in those days. It was the fall of 1945 and I never will forget my only chance to do something for the war effort. I was ready to take my college exams and the United States government called me. They asked me if I would be willing to go on a USO tour that was being put together to tour the South Pacific. They wanted me to play baseball overseas and help entertain the troops. They put together what they called a National League All-Star Team, and there was some great talent on that team. I had been declared 4-F by the War Board and was not allowed to be drafted. It bothered me because I felt that I should be there doing something for our country. This would be my only chance to do something. So I went to my professors and told them about the opportunity and they thought it was a good idea to go on this USO tour. I told them that I would take my exams when I returned, and they said that was fine.

The tour lasted about six or seven weeks. Ralph Branca, my best friend on the Dodgers, was also on that team. We played in Hawaii for three weeks, then on to Guam, Kwajalein, and Manila and the Philippines. We went all over. When we arrived on the island of Kwajalein, where they had one of the major battles in the South Pacific, there was not a baseball field in sight. The Seabees, however, in just five hours leveled the place and made a baseball diamond for us, and five hours later we were playing baseball. I can still remember that when we arrived on that sandy island we all looked around and said to each other "where are we going to play?" The officer whom we called "The Colonel," and who was in charge of our group, said, "Don't worry, we'll have it ready and you'll be playing at three o'clock this afternoon." Sure enough we played there at three o'clock that afternoon. I'll never forget those days on the USO tour. It felt really good to entertain the troops.

4

Howie Haak
My Big Break!

IT WAS THE SPRING OF 1944. WORLD WAR II REPORTS FILLED THE airwaves, and swing music filled the dance halls. The home front was a unique situation. I'll never forget it, as gasoline rationing played a key role in my getting scouted. Everyone did their part to help out in any way they could for our boys overseas. I was declared 4-F after numerous attempts to enlist. I even tried to memorize the eye chart, but the sergeant caught on because he asked me to read the chart just once more—backward! Needless to say, I failed that test. I couldn't help but think back to that little dog with its fierce teeth. I felt deprived of the opportunity to help my country. I'm glad I was able to contribute something by touring with the USO. The year 1944 is a year I'll never forget because I literally went from the University of North Carolina to Ebbets Field. Howie Haak would change my life, and I have him to thank for putting me on that train to New York and Ebbets Field in Brooklyn.

During World War II, preflight schools were prevalent on college campuses all over the country and particularly in the South. From 1942–44 the military had a preflight cadet school that was located on the UNC grounds. Now this was physical training. They weren't training the cadets in airplanes, rather they were getting them physically fit to go into flight training. There was a lieutenant commander there named Howie Haak. He had been a professional baseball player in the St. Louis Cardinals organization, and he was now in the physical therapy subdivision of this preflight school as a full-fledged lieutenant commander. He was also what we called a "bird dog" scout for the Brooklyn Dodgers. He would even umpire some of our games. We had what we called a "Ration League" during those days. It got its name because gasoline was being rationed due to the war. We couldn't do a lot of traveling, so we'd play other local college teams. The "Ration League" was comprised of Duke, Wake Forest, North Carolina State, UNC, and the preflight team. Believe it or not, those five teams were within a radius of 25 or 30 miles of each other so we didn't have far to travel, exactly the point of the "Ration League." During rationing, you couldn't obtain the gasoline necessary to travel out of the state.

Howie was instrumental in that preflight team, as both coach and umpire, but there was something curious about his umpiring routine. I noticed that every time I pitched, Howie Haak would umpire the game. The season progressed, and about three-fourths of the way through the season he called me over to the sidelines after I had beaten Duke and asked me if I would like to be a professional baseball player. After that game was over, Howie said to me, "If you'd like to play, I would like to give you an opportunity." I had to think about it because he was a stranger, and I was 19 years old at the time. I had never been any farther west than Charlotte and had hardly been out of the state at that point in time. So, when he said I could have a chance to play pro baseball, that excited me. I told him that he could drop by my dorm room any time, and we could talk about it. Mr. Rickey (part owner and general manager of the Brooklyn Dodgers) had asked him if he had seen any prospects, and he informed him of me, and Mr. Rickey told Howie to approach me.

One night Howie came by my room in Steele Dormitory, knocked on my door, and once again spoke to me about playing baseball professionally. I had no idea he was coming over that particular night. He also brought along a fellow by the name of Dusty Cook, who was playing on that preflight team, but who had formerly been a player in the big leagues. He was the only player to hit a home run so deep into right field that it landed on top of Lenoir Hall! I think Howie thought that by bringing a former big-leaguer he would impress me. It did to some extent, but it didn't sway me even though they came by my room and showed an interest in me. It was what Howie said that gave me an inkling that he was genuine.

At about the same time the UNC baseball coach, Bunn Hearn, offered me an opportunity to turn pro as well. He must have heard that Howie Haak had spoken with me and, being a scout for the Red Sox, he offered me a contract to go to Lynchburg, Virginia. Lynchburg was where the Red Sox farm club was located, and I could have gone there to play when our season was over. The signing bonus? $3,500! I had never even seen a fifty-dollar bill at that time and here

Bunn Hearn was offering me a $3,500 bonus to go play pro ball for the Red Sox farm club. It seemed too good to be true.

Howie came back to me about seven or eight days after Bunn Hearn had offered me that $3,500 signing bonus, and he once again said to me, "We'd like you to try out with the Dodgers." He was very persuasive. He said, "Clyde, I understand about your offer from the Red Sox and that's a good offer, and I couldn't blame you at all if you took it because of your coach, Bunn Hearn. But all I'm asking you to do is go to Brooklyn and work out, and if you don't like it, come back and sign with the Red Sox." This is what really made me place my trust in Howie Haak. He didn't try to demean my coach or tell me that Bunn Hearn's offer was too low. He was very positive and fair. He was a true gentleman and diplomat. All he really wanted was for me to go to Brooklyn and see if I liked what I saw there at Ebbets Field. Not having been out of the state to speak of, I thought it'd be great to do just that—go to Brooklyn and work out with the Dodgers and see for myself.

Howie drove me over to Raleigh from Chapel Hill and put me on the train headed for New York. I didn't even have the chance to go home and give my parents a real goodbye. I borrowed one of my friend's suitcases, since I myself didn't own one, and off I went to New York.

The suitcase was interesting in and of itself because this was not a normal, everyday suitcase. That suitcase got me in the papers, for a different reason. It was a homemade suitcase made out of heavy cardboard with a rope handle. We had played Duke the weekend before. Now understand we had a fierce rivalry with Duke University. My roommate, Claude Crocker, was the one who gave me the suitcase. Another friend of Claude's had written on that suitcase "Beat Duke," spelling it out with adhesive tape. Only he spelled it wrong, purposely. He wrote "Beat Dook." This was our way of putting down Duke. Well, I took that handmade suitcase with me to New York City, and it was a rather funny sight, watching me carry that thing. Later on, after I had signed with the Dodgers, the newspapers had some fun with me, and a big cartoon was drawn in the papers showing this big, homemade suitcase with "Beat Dook" written on it. They also wrote that the Dodgers had signed a college kid who didn't know how to spell.

Here I was on the train, and Howie's instructions were that I should get off at Pennsylvania Station and hail a cab and ask the cab driver to take me to the Dodgers offices in Brooklyn at 215 Montague Street. He wrote all this down for me, and I sat on that train waiting for my tryout in Brooklyn. I thought about what was happening to me and how quickly my life was changing. I also could not stop thinking about my parents and siblings back home in Goldsboro. I wanted so much to make them proud, and I really missed them. The New York City stop finally came and I got off, hailed a yellow cab, got in, and told the driver to take me to 215 Montague Street in Brooklyn.

The driver said, "Brooklyn?" I said, "Yes, Brooklyn," and then he asked me why I was going to Brooklyn. I told him that I was going to workout with the Dodgers, but I couldn't finish saying the word "Dodgers" because he suddenly jumped up in his seat and said, "Dodgers, that's my favorite team!" I said to him, "I'm not a professional, I'm just a college kid." He was still all excited to drive me over to the Dodgers offices. I asked him why wasn't he a Giants fan since he was working in New York City. He quickly interrupted and made it quite clear, as only a Dodgers fan could, that he was a die-hard Brooklyn fan and so was his entire family, and that he had been a Brooklyn fan his whole life! We talked baseball all the way to Brooklyn. He filled me in on the Dodgers players and how they were doing. It was quite an enjoyable cab ride and an introduction to New York that I'll never forget. Then, when we reached the offices, I couldn't believe what he did for me. He left his cab parked on the street and took my bag and carried it all the way to the Dodgers offices. He made me feel like someone special. I was a nobody, and here was this driver carrying my bag. I already felt like a "king" when he did that—no pun intended. I thanked him for a wonderful ride and his great welcome to New York and went inside.

The Dodgers offices were on the second floor, and I walked up the steps and set my bag down in the lobby. I saw the secretary and told her who I was and was told to go into Mr. Rickey's office and meet with him.

I went into his office, sat down, and there I was, face-to-face with Branch Rickey. Mr. Rickey put me through a "quiz" he put all his rookies through. He asked me a whole bunch of personal questions. He wanted to know if I had a girlfriend, whether I went to church, whether or not I believed in God, and whether I planned to get married and have a family. Mr. Rickey made it clear that the Dodgers organization was very family-oriented. I was immediately in awe of Mr. Rickey, particularly with his voice. His command of the English language was something to marvel at, and he had big bushy eyebrows and a cigar that he kept in his mouth and never lit. He just liked to chew on it. He also asked me if playing with black

baseball players would have an effect on me. I said, "Absolutely not."
He seemed quite happy with me and then he said, "Let's get a cab."
Now this was June of 1944, and Jackie Robinson didn't come into
the big leagues until 1947, which makes me think that he was already
planning for a black player to break the color line. I can't prove that,
but looking back on the situation it makes me think he was looking
ahead. Before we left the office to get in that cab, Mr. Rickey had his
secretary call Dodgers manager Leo Durocher, and the bullpen
coach, Clyde Sukeforth, and they met us at Ebbets Field.

Now here I was at Ebbets Field, but I didn't have a uniform or any
baseball equipment with me. I went on the field in what I was wearing
that day, my street clothes. I had dressed to see Mr. Rickey, not to play
ball, so I didn't have a uniform—and back then they didn't just give
you a uniform. Clyde Sukeforth got me a glove and a pair of baseball
shoes. He was my catcher. They put me through a 45–50 pitch workout, and then Mr. Rickey gave me an aptitude test. This wasn't just a
normal aptitude test, but a baseball aptitude test. They had me hold
the ball between my fingers and try many grips, and then they told me
to throw the ball low and outside, then low and inside, and basically
tested for pitch location. Mr. Rickey then told me to come back to the
office with him. Clyde Sukeforth patted me on the back and said,
"Good workout." Leo Durocher seemed pleased as well.

Mr. Rickey and I went back to 215 Montague Street and sat
down in his office once again. I must have passed their tests because
now he said to me, "Would you like to play pro baseball?" And I said
I would if I was good enough.

"Well, you're good enough. I can tell you that now. I'll give you
an opportunity to play if you want to play," he said.

"I do want to play," I replied. All was fine. Then, all of a sudden,
came the tough question; the one a rookie dreaded.

"What kind of bonus are you thinking about?" he asked me.

I was sitting in Branch Rickey's office, whose walls were adorned
with photos of him and all my favorite ballplayers, and I had just
worked out with Leo Durocher and Clyde Sukeforth at Ebbets
Field. He asked me if I would be nervous about appearing in front
of thousands of fans. I didn't realize at the time what he was asking.
We had a long conversation, and then he asked me about what kind
of signing bonus I had in mind. Awestruck as I was, I quickly
remembered that Bunn Hearn had offered me $3,500 to play for the
Sox, and I said to Mr. Rickey, "Five thousand dollars." He didn't
even hesitate. He quickly yelled, "Jane Ann, bring in a contract for
Clyde King for five thousand dollars!"

So his secretary, Jane Ann Jones, brought in the contract. I signed it, and Mr. Rickey made out a check for $5,000. He said to me, "Now, you're a professional baseball player." He then asked me if I would like to play in the big leagues and whether or not I could handle it. I said I could handle it, but in my mind I was thinking that he would send me down to Newport News or one of the Brooklyn minor league teams. Then he said, "Tonight." I said, "What do you mean?" He said, "You'll be in a Dodgers uniform tonight."

We walked out of the office, went downstairs, and walked over to the bank a block away. Mr. Rickey went with me, took my check, helped me deposit it in the bank, and taught me how to write a check, and now I had $5,000. He then told Harold Parrot, our traveling secretary, "Get Clyde a uniform for *tonight*." He said, "You're going to play right here in Brooklyn." Right *here* in Brooklyn! I couldn't believe it.

I didn't even have to go the minors. I had arrived and I was so thankful. I called my mother and told her what had happened, and that I wouldn't be coming back home. She wished me well, and now here I was in New York on my own and alone. I stayed right there in Brooklyn. Mr. Rickey took me down to the St. George Hotel and checked me in. I walked through that hotel via the back lobby, and I thought it was a castle. I mean it had a great big lobby with people all over the place. It was beautiful. On the way to my room the bellman said, "I want to show you the pool in case you want to go swimming." He took me over to it. Well, it was the largest indoor pool in America at the time, and it looked more like the Atlantic Ocean. Here I was staying in a hotel for the first time, with a heated swimming pool as big as my backyard at home, and taking a cab out to Ebbets Field. It was a lot to behold.

The first few days I took the subway to Ebbets Field. Having never rode a subway before, it was an experience. The cars were packed like sardine cans, and you would be bumped and shoved, but in those days you didn't have to worry about pickpockets. I'd ride the BMT subway to Ebbets Field and then walk over to the ballpark from the station. The crowds were large, and people would be yelling and calling your name, and you'd talk with the folks. I was made to feel at home.

As for the game, it was June 20, 1944. I was to relieve Ralph Branca. The call came to the bullpen to get me warmed up. I can remember warming up in the bullpen and thinking about my family back home and how proud they would be if they could see me now. I wasn't physically nervous. I wasn't all over the place with my pitches. I was excited. Here I was. I had just turned 20 years old. My birthday was on May 23rd, and here I was on June 20, less than a month after my birthday warming up in the bullpen. Leo Durocher walked to the mound, gave the signal to the bullpen, and in I came, and suddenly there I was on the mound. Mickey Owen, our catcher at the time, came to the mound and said, "Hey son, don't pay any attention to the fingers I put down. Just throw all fastballs." Thinking about his comments later on, I figured he said this because he thought I was some young college kid who threw hard and was wild. Well, bases were loaded and Mickey wanted me to throw all fastballs. So I did. All fastballs. Twelve straight fastballs. In that string of 12 pitches I got the first two guys out. The next guy up? Mel Ott! The first pitch to Ott? A ball. I was behind the great home-run hitter. Then came a strike right down the middle. The count now was 1–1. The next pitch? Another fastball and he swung and missed. Now I had a ball and two strikes on Ott. The next pitch? He hit a ball off the scoreboard in right center field in Ebbets Field scoring three runs. The next guy up after Ott I got out, but I had given up three runs in my first professional game. I went into the clubhouse and felt sad. I had given up three runs in my first professional game, and they were charged to my friend Ralph Branca. I felt badly about that. Eddie Basinski was one of the few who came up to me and said, "Hang in there." Nobody else said anything to me. I knew that Ott, being a great hitter, knew I was going to throw a fastball again. He saw I didn't mix any pitches to the hitter in front of him, and I had thrown him all straight fastballs. It didn't take a genius to know a fastball was coming. I went back to the hotel after the game and that night I just absolutely could not sleep. I was excited that I had pitched in the big leagues, and yet I also knew I didn't fare well in my first game.

I awoke the following morning, came downstairs from my hotel room, and found a note in my mailbox from Mr. Rickey. The note said that he wanted me to come by his office at ten o'clock. I immediately went to his office but with great trepidation. The box score in the newspapers all had the same recantation of what had taken place on the field yesterday: "Closing with seven runs in ninth against two collegians, Ralph Branca of NYU and Clyde King of North Carolina, Giants overpowered Dodgers 11–2."

I was now in Mr. Rickey's office once again, but today it felt awkward. I had a feeling that this meeting would not be like our first encounter. Mr. Rickey asked me how I felt about my first performance. I told him I felt disappointed giving up three runs. He asked me if I knew why I gave up three runs, and I said, "No, sir. I don't."

He said, "Well, what kind of pitcher are you? What pitches do you throw?" I told him I threw a fastball and a curveball. The curve was my best pitch. He asked me how many curves I threw that previous night, and my response was none. He asked me how many total pitches I threw, and I said 12. (To this day I can remember pitches I made 50 years ago.) Mr. Rickey asked me how many of those were curves—to be sure to make the point to me. I said none. He said, "Why?" I told him what Mickey Owen told me when I walked on the mound, and he said something to me I'll never forget: "This is your first lesson, young man. You're in charge. You're the pitcher. Nothing can happen until you throw the ball, and you throw the pitch you want to throw. If the catcher wants you to throw something you don't want to throw, you call time and go in and talk to him." I told him that to me this was the great Mickey Owen from the '41 World Series. He told me that it didn't matter. I was in control because it's the pitcher who takes the responsibility for the loss, not the catcher. They're not going to blame the catcher after the game because everyone knows that the pitcher is in control. They'll just place the blame on the pitcher for having a bad day. This was my first lesson in baseball, and because of the way Mr. Rickey instructed me, he became very close to me, like a second father, and we stayed in very close touch all through the years. When I was in the minor leagues he had me come to the big league training camp and instruct younger players.

Mr. Rickey is also the one who got me interested in reading the Bible. He asked me in that preliminary interview if I read the Bible, and I had to tell him I didn't because at that time I didn't. He said, "You know, the greatest instruction you can get is from the Bible." He told me that I should start in the book of John, and that's where I started. That was my first introduction to the Bible. I realized that he was a Christian, but he was also a lay preacher and an orator. He was one of the greatest orators that I ever heard. He could have you crying one minute and laughing the next. He could give you something in every speech he made that would make you think and reexamine yourself. I think he could have been president because he was so intelligent and had so much common sense. He could relate to anyone, whether it was a famous politician or a man on the street or a baseball executive. I can't begin to say what Mr. Rickey meant to me, and even to this day I know that he had much to do with my desire to become involved in public speaking. I have some heroes in my life—Abraham Lincoln, Branch Rickey, Winston Churchill, and at the top of the list is God. Mr. Rickey was certainly one of my true heroes. I valued the time I spent with him. I remember going into his home later on in Pittsburgh. We talked about life and religion and how important being a Christian was.

I remember one time in 1944 I got an invitation to try out for the Knicks basketball team. I got the invitation from Coach Lapchick and I was invited for a workout in New York. I went up to work out with the Knicks and it got in the newspapers, and Mr. Rickey read about it. He asked me if I had read my contract. I told him that I hadn't. He said that there was a clause in my contract that said I couldn't play two professional sports. He told me I'd have to choose between baseball and basketball, and of course my answer was baseball. I don't know if I could have played pro basketball or not because I never had the chance, but that was another influence he had on me. These are the memories that stick with me to this day. Mr. Rickey is also the reason my baseball career didn't end in 1955. It was because of Mr. Rickey that I had the chance to be associated with baseball from 1955 until the present. Many players finish their career as a pro player and that's the end for them. I was lucky enough to embark on a managerial career that was another exciting phase of my baseball life.

5

Ralph Branca

My Best Friend in Baseball

RALPH BRANCA IS MY BEST FRIEND. WE MET IN JUNE OF 1944. HE WAS out of NYU, and we hit it off from the start. Both of us being college kids helped, I'm sure. He was an outstanding pitcher. Ralph was a much better pitcher than me because he was big and strong. He had a great curveball, an above-average fastball, and a change-up that he really didn't have to use much because of his skill in throwing his other two pitches. He was extremely tough on the mound as well. I can even say that he was mean at times. If you looked at him the wrong way, he would throw a ball right under your chin, and he wasn't afraid to do it again if you didn't like it. I learned early on from Ralph, with his competitiveness, that I had to do something other than just try to throw the ball past hitters. I tried to learn the little things that I could use in games to baffle the hitters.

I think one of the first things that I remember about our relationship was when he invited me to his home in Mount Vernon, New York. Ralph, at that time, was unmarried and living with his family, and his mother cooked us an old-fashioned Italian dinner. I will never forget that night. I never had a dinner like that before in my life. First, she brought out chicken and spaghetti and Italian bread and salad, and I ate that, and I thought that the dinner was over. I enjoyed my dinner and figured that we might have dessert. So there I was waiting for dessert. His mom came out from the kitchen with more food, but it wasn't dessert. It was more main course. She brought out meatballs, and then she brought out some pork. It was like a six-course dinner, and I thought that the first course was it. I had eaten enough of that first course to last me for a week, and his mom kept bringing out more food. I never will forget how funny it was, and Ralph and I have laughed about it in retrospect. When I think of Italian dinners, I think of that night at his house. The older Italian folks, like Ralph's parents, who came over from the old country, really liked to entertain their guests, and this they did. I think the thing that brought Ralph and me together was that we each came from a big family. Ralph had a much bigger family than mine. We had 7 kids in my immediate family, and Ralph had about 11 or 12 brothers and sisters. We were both family-oriented. Ralph was a down-to-earth guy. He didn't smoke or drink. We were both pitchers and always talked about how to get hitters out. We talked baseball and hit it off immediately. It was divine that we were brought together, and I didn't even realize it.

When you hear the name Ralph Branca, you think of Dodgers baseball. However, what about the name Mulvey? Mulvey is his wife's maiden name and her family name is a storied one. Ann Mulvey, Ralph's wife, was quite familiar with Brooklyn baseball. Her mother owned a portion of the Brooklyn Dodgers. The Mulveys were also a coast-to-coast family. Ann's father, Jim Mulvey, was the president of the Samuel Goldwyn Motion Picture Company, giving them the best of everything, baseball and the movies. Jim Mulvey was gone a lot because he worked at the studio in California. Bud, her brother, was in school at Notre Dame, and Chickie, her sister, was at home.

I remember the first time I met Ann. It was down in Daytona Beach during spring training. We were standing out on a corner under a lamppost talking, and Ann came out and joined us. She was 13 then and we talked and became friends. One Sunday afternoon at Ebbets Field, her mother invited me over for dinner. I guess she saw that I was a young guy from North Carolina with no attachments in New York. They lived at 39 Maple Street in Brooklyn, and I never will forget those dinners. We always had roast beef, baked potato, salad, and then cheesecake for dessert. This was the menu every Sunday when I came over for dinner. It certainly was a lot of fun. Then, after dinner, we'd go out back and shoot baskets at a hoop on their garage. Afterward, they'd walk me back to the subway and I'd go back to my Hotel. Ralph and Ann got introduced to each other later on and dated for a while and then got married. Ann gave birth to two beautiful daughters, Mary and Patti. Mary married New York Mets manager Bobby Valentine, and Patti married Billy Barnes.

Ralph and I had some great times on our USO tour in the fall of 1945, but one story I'll never forget. Some of the American soldiers in Manila wanted to challenge us in a basketball game. We also played a Philippine team, and all of a sudden Ralph calls time-out.

We were winning and he calls time-out. I said to him, "What are you doing?" He said, "There's six players on the court." I said, "Ralph, there's only five." He said, "Yes, there are." What had happened was that the smaller Philipino players were so fast that you looked over your shoulder and turned around and the same player had changed positions quicker than you could imagine. So when Ralph looked around he thought there were six men. It was a little embarrassing.

Ralph was on that National League All-Star Team with me, and we of course roomed together on the tour. Norma was teaching swimming and dance at the YWCA in Syracuse, New York, at the time. Ralph, knowing how much I missed Norma, decided he would do something about that. So he took a quarter and traced it with his pen on an envelope. He put "Syracuse, N.Y." inside the circle and addressed the envelope to me and put Norma's return address up at the top. He also wrote me a letter as if Norma was writing me. We alternated in picking up the mail. One day he'd pick up the mail and the next day I'd pick up the mail. Well, it was his day to pick up the mail and he came back and said, "You got a letter from Norma— here!" He handed it to me and I didn't even take the time to look at what was on the envelope. I just tore it open and started reading it. I had only read three or four sentences when I realized that Ralph had written it. It very well could have been from Norma, however, because Ralph did a good job. Then I looked at the envelope and saw his homemade post office cancellation that he did with his pen and a quarter. It was really something. That's something I'll never forget, and I told that story in a roast I did for Chase Manhattan Bank in October 1997.

We came back to San Francisco from the Far East and everyone went their separate ways. Some players were at home because they lived in the San Francisco area. Those of us who lived back East got on a train and went to Chicago. From Chicago we went in all directions. It so happened that the train we were on was going on to New York City. I was going to get off in Chicago and take the train from there to Raleigh. Ralph was going to continue on to New York.

On the way I kept saying how much I missed Norma and he said, "Well, why don't you stay on this train. It's going to New York and right through Syracuse."

I said, "But I don't have a ticket or berth or anything."

He said, "When we get to Chicago we'll have an hour-and-a-half- or two-hour layover, and you can get out and get your ticket."

I thought that this was a great idea. So we got off and went to the ticket counter, and there was not a space available. Not even a chair that you could sit up in all night. Well, I was really disappointed. Ralph said, "Why don't you sleep in the same berth as me." I said, "Are you sure?" He said, "Yeah. Come on. We can sleep in the same berth."

Ralph had an upper berth and for those of you who have never been on a Pullman car, the bottom bunks are pretty wide but the upper berths are narrow. I had no idea that Ralph had an upper berth, and he didn't tell me because he was afraid if he told me that I wouldn't want to go. So when it came time for the porter to come by and make up the berth, Ralph pulled down the top berth. I said, "Ralph, which one is yours?" He said nothing and sheepishly pointed toward the upper berth. I said, "Oh, gosh." I couldn't imagine sleeping in an upper berth with Ralph as big as he was. He was at least 6'3" and weighed about 220 pounds. When the time came we went to bed. Whenever one of us wanted to turn over, we had to do it in unison. I would say "one, two, three turn." I eventually made it to Syracuse and visited Norma. We were married in November, but the time we spent in Syracuse was special. It really solidified our relationship. There again was Ralph trying to help me out, and he did. That time I spent with Norma was special, and I have Ralph to thank for that weekend.

The story that I always think of when I think of Ralph and myself happened when we were back in Brooklyn after the USO tour. The Dodgers were in Pittsburgh. Ralph at that time was rooming with Eddie Stanky, and we stayed at the old Scheneley Hotel. It was a big old hotel with a front porch with chairs on it. I was in one room and Ralph and Eddie were in the adjoining room. There was a big door that connected the rooms. Now Eddie didn't care too much for college players. I think deep down he respected them, but he was always kidding them. In that first game I pitched in at Ebbets Field, for instance, when I came in to relieve Ralph with the bases loaded and was on the mound, Eddie Stanky came over to me and took the ball and slammed it into my glove. He said, "Now, you're a smart college guy, let's see you get out of this situation!" That was my first introduction to major league baseball. It was really an "encouraging" one, and I hope some day Stanky will read this and remember it.

We were there at the Scheneley Hotel, Ralph opened his adjoining door and came into my room. It was the afternoon before that night's game and we were both sitting around in our shorts just relaxing because there was no air conditioning. We had to open the windows to get some air. Ralph and I were talking in my room about the game coming up, and while Ralph was in my room, Eddie Stanky closed the adjoining door to Ralph's room and locked it. Ralph was in his shorts banging on the door and Stanky wouldn't open it. Stanky, in fact, went out and just left the room and the hotel. Here was Ralph, without a key and in his shorts, and no way to get in his room. We finally got a bellman to open his door. That was the kind of thing that veteran players did to younger players back then and nobody really got mad about those types of pranks. It was all in fun.

We always had Mondays off, and back then we played a 154-game schedule. We'd play a Sunday afternoon game in Brooklyn and get on a train to go to St. Louis to open up on Tuesday night. That meant that we had Monday off and traveled on the train all day. It was a long trip. In those days the teams traveled by train, and some of the players felt like the trains had square wheels because they couldn't sleep too well on them. I always enjoyed the train rides. The rhythm of the train shaking and rattling always put me to sleep. I still love trains. I would love to take another long trip on a train because I learned to love it so much. We had our berths. We had our own Pullman cars. There was a dining car in the back. We'd go aboard hungry after a game and rush immediately to the dining car. The porters and the waiters knew us well because we had taken this trip many times. If we wanted two steaks they'd let us have two. Once in a while they'd even make homemade ice cream. It was so much fun and we were in no hurry.

In those days the teams didn't transport the players to the trains. You had to get to and from the trains and the ballparks on your own. Three or four of us would split the cab fare. It was not like it is today with team buses taking players to and from the team hotels.

One time, on our way to St. Louis, the train stopped to put water in the steam engine, as the trains customarily did back then. Hugh Casey knew somebody in that area, and when the train stopped his friend brought on barbecue ribs and coleslaw and corn bread. There we were at four o'clock in the morning eating that stuff. We knew it was coming and it was so much fun. This was on Sunday night, and we didn't have to worry about eating at four o'clock in the morning because we knew we had Mondays off.

Another train ride I remember was not so pleasant. We were going from Chicago to St. Louis. There was an area that was near the men's room where there were seats to sit around and talk. We were sitting around and talking about how to get hitters out. We got to Joliet, Illinois, and it was in the middle of the night. In those days the servicemen occupied the Pullman cars. It was 1944 and we were in the chair cars. We were glad that the soldiers got the better accommodations. It was three o'clock in the morning when the train hit a truck loaded with gasoline and it exploded. By the time the train stopped, there was such a fire that the flames set a yard on fire across the way and melted the glass windows in our cars. We had a player by the name of Luis Olmo on our team. When that train hit the tanker and everybody saw the flames, we dropped down on the floor, Luis got up and panicked. He ran from one end of the car to the other, stepping on us as he ran, and hollering and yelling. Finally, the car came to a stop, and we all got up and realized that we weren't burned or injured. We got out of the car and went down toward the engine, and when we got there the engineer had nothing left on him but his belt and his shoes. That was all that was not burned off of him. His head started to crack. He had no hair left on his head. His eyebrows were gone. The brakeman was there on the floor with his arm bent in an awkward angle, and we all assumed that that's when he reached to get the brake to try to stop the train and that's the way his arm was. The engineer was not dead. They put a sheet on him and I remember when they put the sheet on him how he screamed from the pain when it touched him. When we were in St. Louis we read a few days later in the newspaper that he died, and that was a tough thing. I can't even really remember how we eventually made it to St. Louis. I think they disconnected that car with the melted windows and we went on.

Ralph and I are still great friends. I've often said that baseball friendships are so strong because of the bonds made between the players. Ralph and I went through so many situations together that we were just drawn into a close friendship. Ralph sang at each of our daughters' weddings.

6

The Brooklyn Dodgers Family

I'VE OFTEN HEARD PEOPLE TALK ABOUT THE CLOSENESS OF THE Dodgers, and I know the reason why we were so close. We all shared similar values and we lived in Brooklyn, the greatest place in the world to play baseball. To know Brooklyn is to love it. Just imagine that you've got an old-fashioned New York milk shake in your hand, munching on a Coney Island hot dog, while sitting behind the third-base dugout in Ebbets Field. Now that is like heaven.

Life in Brooklyn

Norma and I were married in November of 1946 and spent the next year as newlyweds in Brooklyn, New York. I had loved Brooklyn and its environment ever since my first taxicab ride to 215 Montague Street, but now I had a wife and was hoping to start a family. We couldn't have landed in a better place. Brooklyn was great to us, and the other Dodger players and wives were great to us as well. I'll never forget that first year of marriage. It was wonderful. Playing in Brooklyn was such a pleasure that I'd wake up in the morning and be anxious just to get to the ballpark. It was, for me, like being at home in Goldsboro. I often tell people that being in Brooklyn back then was like being in your own hometown. If people were to fly over Brooklyn in an airplane and be dropped out in a parachute and not know where they were, they would think that they were back in their own hometown. The streets were tree-lined and beautiful, and the homes housed the same families for years. We lived in various areas, but when we lived in our large home in Bay Ridge, Rube Walker and his wife Millie lived upstairs, and next door to us lived Duke and Bev Snider. Down the street and around the corner lived Pee Wee and Dottie Reese, and Carl and Betty Erskine lived just down the block from us as well. Preacher Roe, Andy Pafko, and Joe Hatten all lived by us in Bay Ridge.

We'd ride together to the ballpark, and when we went to play the Giants over at the Polo Grounds we'd ride through upper Manhattan together, and it was such a wonderful ride. We always talked baseball all the way to the ballpark. We didn't talk stock market, but rather baseball and what was happening around the league. In those days, even when we rode in the trains on road trips, we would play bridge and hearts and gin. I introduced bridge to the Dodgers. I loved to play bridge and many of the players liked the game as well. We would read *The Sporting News,* and during those eight months of playing baseball we just lived and breathed the game. We didn't think about golf, except in the off-season. I just couldn't wait to get to beautiful Ebbets Field. The fans were great and we were appreciated back then.

I can remember a pharmacy–soda fountain on 94th Street. The owner was a man by the name of Herb Schwartz. He was terrific. I loved that shop. One day he stopped me and gave me a quart of hand-packed ice cream, which was the best dessert anybody could have given me—and still is to this day. He knew that I loved ice cream, and I had played in the game that day and had pitched well. So he was ready when I came walking down the street; he wouldn't let me pay for it. Whenever I played in a game he'd stop me and give me a quart. I loved his ice cream so much. His place was typical of the '40s- and '50s-style pharmacies that had the soda fountains and the stools at the counter where you could sit and get a nice milk shake or some fresh ice cream. Years ago when they'd make a soda, they'd mix the syrup and the carbonated water and it would all be made right before your very eyes. I would tell Mr. Schwartz that I wanted to pay and he'd always tell me, "You're a Dodger. This is free." It was people like Mr. Schwartz who made Brooklyn so special. Often Norma and I would walk down to the water and watch the ships that were coming into the Brooklyn Navy Yard. The community in Brooklyn really embraced us. That's why those years that I spent playing in Brooklyn were some of the best years of my life.

My First Big League Win

I earned my first major league win on September 27, 1944, in Brooklyn, a game against the Cardinals. That game against the Cardinals was telling for several reasons. Not only did I pitch a complete game for the victory, but the opposing pitcher, Bud Byerly, pitched a complete game as well. This is a rarity in baseball—both pitchers in a single game getting complete game decisions.

Whitey Kurowski, the Cardinals third baseman, hit a solo home run off of me. Danny Litwhiler, the left fielder, was up next, and I hit him in the ribs with the very next pitch. Danny is a great guy and went on to coach at Michigan. I'll never forget his reaction. He trotted to first base and yelled out, "Hey Clyde! Why did you hit me? Whitey hit the home run off you!" I was that type of pitcher. A pitcher needs to send a message to the opposing hitters that they can't hit home runs without consequences. I didn't hesitate to knock a hitter back.

I also helped my own cause out in that game, as I bunted Tommy Brown to second base and also beat out a bunt to score our first run of the game. Pitchers back then took pride in their hitting, and they had to at least be able to bunt a man into scoring position, but I was not a good hitter.

Lastly, I'll always remember the length of that game: 1 hour and 43 minutes! That was it! Can you believe I tossed a seven-hitter in only 1 hour and 43 minutes! It could never happen today! Players now adjust their batting gloves and go into their routines, applying pine tar, and so on. That was my first win, and it felt great to be a starter. It felt even better, however, to be a reliever, and I'm so glad that Leo Durocher made me a reliever. I loved coming into games that were on the line. I liked the pressure. I always enjoy scouting young, good "closers" even today for that very reason. The closer is an integral part of the team.

The box score for this game follows.

Brooklyn 3, St. Louis 2

St. Louis	AB	R	H	RBI	Brooklyn	AB	R	H	RBI
Hopp cf	3	0	2	0	Bordagaray 3b	4	1	2	0
Sanders 1b	4	0	1	0	Aderholt lf	3	0	1	1
Musial rf	4	0	0	1	Galan cf	4	0	1	1
W. Cooper c	4	0	0	0	Walker rf	3	0	0	0
Kurowski 3b	4	1	3	1	Shultz 1b	4	0	0	1
Litwhiler lf	3	0	1	0	Bragan c	4	0	1	0
Fallon ss	2	0	0	0	Stanky 2b	3	0	0	0
Garms ph	1	0	0	0	Brown ss	3	1	0	0
Verban 2b	2	0	0	0	King p	2	1	1	0
O'Dea ph	1	0	0	0					
Antonelli 2b	0	0	0	0					
Byerly p	3	1	0	0					
Totals	**31**	**2**	**7**	**2**		**30**	**3**	**6**	**3**

E—Kurowsi 2, Fallon, Verban, Bordagaray. 2B—Aderholt. HR—Kurowski. Sac—Fallon, King. DP—Brooklyn 3, St. Louis 2. Left on base—St. Louis 5, Brooklyn 6. Bases on balls-off—Byerly 2, King 1. Struck out—by Byerly 1, King 4. Hit by pitch—by King (Litwhiler). Time of game—1:43. Attendance—5,514.

Pee Wee Reese: Our Captain

When I think of the late 1940s, I think of Brooklyn and the great players I played with. Brooklyn had it all. It had the fans, the ball-park, and the Dodgers family. Pee Wee Reese was legendary in Brooklyn. I remember when Norma gave birth to our first daughter. Dottie Reese came to help out, as the Reeses were family to us. To me, Pee Wee was both friend and teammate. Most baseball fans, when they think of the shortstop position, think of Reese and Rizzuto. The age-old debate of who was better still goes on today. When they are compared, you can't help but marvel at how great the position of shortstop was in those days. It is even better today with Jeter, Rodriguez, and Garciaparra—each an outstanding shortstop.

Pee Wee Reese and Phil Rizzuto—two baseball greats. Well, you can't fault either one of them. You're in a no-lose situation if you have to choose between Reese and Rizzuto. You can't lose. They're both great players. It took Rizzuto a lot longer to get into the Hall of Fame than it should have, and I don't know the reason why. Rizzuto was great, and if I had a vote I would have voted him in long ago.

Pee Wee, because he was my teammate and a close friend, will always be special to me. He was a leader, and he led by example. He didn't need to yell or scream or have to pop-off to be a leader. He showed you on the field his great talent. Pee Wee Reese would steal 20 bases out of 21 tries. He stole a base when we needed it. Pee Wee Reese was an unselfish player who would do whatever it took to win the game. He could bunt or sacrifice to score a run or to get that run-ner into scoring position. If it took a hit and run to do the job, he would do it. If there was a runner on third and less than two outs, Pee Wee would get that runner in somehow. Once in a while he would hit a home run. Most of the time, though, he was the leadoff man. He was such a team man that his example rubbed off on every-one. He would beat the opposing team in so many different ways. He always did the little things, which turned out to be the big things, that won the games. He'd go in the hole and backhand a ground ball and get the force at second base to either end the inning or to get the lead runner. Pee Wee always had such good coordina-tion and balance. He was seldom off balance and he'd always make the play. As a runner, he was graceful. His wasn't a case where every time he ran the base paths you'd hear the pounding of his feet. He ran the bases gracefully. Pee Wee certainly could do it all.

For the kids of today who don't know Pee Wee as a player, but rather as a star who their parents and grandparents talk about, I can

tell you that he was a good man. He was a good and faithful husband, a good father, and great with kids. He didn't run away, as players sometimes do today, when fans asked for autographs. He was always willing to sign, and one year the *Happy Felton's Knothole Gang* television show had him on so often as the star of the game, that the story about Pee Wee was that he never had to cash his Dodgers paycheck because he appeared on that program so often that he made enough money to live on all summer. The pay was $25, so I'm sure he didn't get rich.

I can remember so well coming back from the Polo Grounds one time when Pee Wee was driving. We were all going to my house that night for dinner. Now as soon as the game was over the girls left the ballpark to go home and get dinner ready. We were in a hurry to get home and Pee Wee was going—zoom—really fast and a cop pulled him over for speeding. The cop came over, looked at him, and said, "Captain Pee Wee," and Pee Wee smiled. The cop said, "Listen, take it a little easy. The Dodgers need you guys. Don't be driving so fast!" He didn't give him a ticket. We went home and all was great. Two days later the same thing happened. Only this time Duke Snider is driving and he's the one pulled over for speeding. The cop looked at him and said, "Where are you guys going?" He didn't recognize us. Duke said, "Hi, I'm Duke Snider, the center fielder for the Dodgers." The officer looked at him and quickly said, "I don't like baseball," and wrote him a ticket. We never let Duke forget that Pee Wee didn't get a ticket but that he did.

Another time Pee Wee and I were riding together, and I was driving. Now when I drove I always told Pee Wee that we were going to leave at a certain time in order to get to the ballpark early. Then when the game was over I wanted to leave quickly. I didn't want to hang around. I didn't smoke. I didn't drink beer. They'd sit around and smoke a cigarette and drink a beer.

I once said to him, "Pee Wee, we've got to go."

He asked me, "Clyde, why do you always want to get to the park so early and leave so quickly after the game?"

"Well," I told him, "I'm not a star like you are. If I don't get there early I'm afraid somebody will get my uniform."

He thought about it and asked me, "Why do you want to leave so quickly?"

I said, "I'm afraid Durocher will call me into the office and send me to Montreal."

He said, "OK." He understood. That was not the real reason. I really wanted to get home to my family and couldn't wait to get there. To play at Ebbets Field was such a pleasure, I would have played for nothing if I could have afforded it. When the game was over, however, I was anxious to get home to my family.

I've got many memories of Pee Wee on the field, but the only time I ever saw him get mad on the field stands out in my mind because it was uncharacteristic. We were playing in Philadelphia. I was pitching and Richie Ashburn was on second base. Pee Wee came over to me and said, "Clyde, Richie is taking a big lead and if we don't hold him close, he'll steal third base on us." I said, "OK, Pee Wee. You give me the sign and we'll try to pick him off."

Well, I made a pitch to home plate, and Ashburn took a big lead off second base but didn't make a run for third. I looked over after Campy threw the ball back to me, and Pee Wee gave me the pick-off sign. I came to the set position on the mound, turned and quickly threw the ball right on target, where Pee Wee had his glove. Ashburn slid right into Pee Wee's glove and the umpire called him safe! Safe! Pee Wee went crazy. I went crazy. Jackie Robinson pushed me aside because he didn't want me getting thrown out of the game. This was the only time I ever saw Pee Wee mad.

Pee Wee was a good base stealer. He stole 18 to 20 bases a year at a time when we really needed runs. He could have easily stolen more if he was solely concerned about his statistics, but he wasn't. The Dodger players back then were more concerned with the game, not their individual statistics. He had a great percentage of steals per attempts.

Defensively, Pee Wee was the best; he could make the play from the hole and could make the hard plays look easy. His grace at shortstop paralleled DiMaggio's grace in the outfield. He could adjust to every situation in a game. If we had a man on second base, nobody out in the ninth inning, and the score was tied or we were down by a run, Pee Wee would make sure to get that runner to third base by hitting the ball to the right side of the infield. If the third baseman backed up, and we needed a runner, Pee Wee would bunt his way on base. He took advantage of every single opportunity that the opposition gave him. Usually, he did it well. He was the most level-headed player on our team. He taught by example. He was a true captain.

Pete Reiser: The Other Gold Dust Twin

Pete Reiser was to the Brooklyn Dodgers what Ernie Banks was to the Cubs. Ernie was "Mr. Enthusiasm" and still is today and so was Pete. He was always ready to go out and play and was always encouraging people in the clubhouse. He hustled all the time to the point where he ended his career prematurely. I remember that I used to love to shag fly balls during batting practice; it's a good way to stay in shape. I had played outfield in high school and on that USO tour, and I liked to shag fly balls.

One time Pete Reiser was in left field shagging fly balls and even back then some outfielders didn't shag fly balls during batting practice. Pete Reiser always did because he just loved to play the game. The outfield was crowded with players as is customary during batting practice, and Pete was in left field. I was in center field, and I was rather aggressive. Players often kidded me about my aggressiveness. I would try to catch every ball hit in the air.

"Get out of the way, here comes Clyde!" I would hear the players yell.

Well, that day I was being myself and trying to catch every fly ball hit in the vicinity, and I took off after one and ran right into Pete and knocked him out! My head, I guess, was harder than his, and they took him off the field. I was devastated. I felt terribly for Pete and then felt scared that Durocher would send me right to Montreal for knocking out one of his prized "Gold Dust Twins." Pete recovered and played in the game that night.

Another thing about Pete was his ability to steal home. Next to Jackie Robinson, he was the most exciting base runner I've ever seen. I remember him stealing home to win a game for us, as Jackie often did. Pete was so aggressive in a game that he often ran into the outfield walls. The reason for padding today on outfield fences is because of the traumatic injuries that Reiser suffered and that led to his premature retirement.

On one occasion, Pete ran into the center-field wall, and you could hear the impact in the dugout. I mean you could hear the thud of his head hitting the wall. I took off from the right field bullpen and ran to center field. Dixie Walker had a head start on me from right field, and he got there just before I did. Pete was lying on his side facing the outfield wall. His glove was lying on the ground face-up. The ball was lying about six or eight inches from the glove. Dixie picked the ball up and put it in Pete's glove. The umpire came out, saw the ball in Reiser's glove, and called the runner "out." Dr. Harold Wendler, the Dodgers' trainer, came out with the stretcher and carried Pete off the field.

Pete was a great player, great teammate, and the only player I've ever seen who needed to be told not to play so hard. He played the game with so much enthusiasm! I cringe every time I think of him running into those outfield walls. Many believe he was surely destined for the Hall of Fame if it were not for his injury-plagued career. I agree with them. He was something else!

Developing as a Pitcher

I did not have an off-speed pitch when I first arrived in Brooklyn back in 1944, but I learned to throw one during my rookie year in Brooklyn. I made it my business to go over and ask hitters on different teams which pitch, they thought, was the toughest pitch to hit. Mel Ott told me that a straight change-up was the toughest pitch to hit, as did Ernie Lombardi. And don't you know that 9 out of 10 hitters that I asked all said that the straight change-up was the toughest to hit. Only Dixie Walker said that the slow curve was tougher to hit than the straight change-up. Now that I had an answer I wanted to know why this was the case. Why was the straight change-up the toughest pitch to hit? I didn't just take it as their answer, I wanted to know why. Almost all of them said the reason why it was so difficult to hit was because a straight change-up was like a white cue ball, a billiard ball, because you could not see the seams on the ball as it arrived at the plate. I had my answer! I was more determined than ever to develop this pitch, and I did just that. I developed a rather good straight change-up and used it effectively in the majors for years, but it wasn't as good as Carl Erskine's.

I also learned other invaluable lessons in my early days: that you didn't have to throw the ball 95 mph and that you didn't have to be 6'6" to be a winner. That is, you didn't have to be big and strong to be a winner. My teammate, Carl Erskine, at 5'10" and 160 pounds, threw hard and won ball games. So did another Dodger, Preacher Roe; he was 6'2" tall, but he only weighed 170 pounds. Carl not only won games, but he pitched two no-hitters in his career. If you could locate the ball and if you had the courage and weren't afraid to challenge the hitter, then you would be successful, I was told. All you needed to do was pitch quickly, throw strikes, and change speeds. And I still say to this day that the successful pitcher has got to be able to throw strikes and change speeds. If you can do these things, then you can be a big success even if you are not big and strong. I firmly believe that watching guys like Carl Erskine and Preacher Roe was invaluable to a young player like myself. Greg Maddux and Tom Glavine are two current pitchers who are not power pitchers like Roger Clemens or Randy Johnson, but they locate well, change speeds, and challenge hitters. Everyone knows they're winners.

My Montreal Days

Being a father started for me in June 1948. Norma was pregnant and I was worried about being farmed out to Montreal to play for the Royals, the Dodgers AAA farm team. I had an infected finger, and I just could not pitch. June 17, 1948, was the day that Mr. Rickey called me into his office to tell me that the best thing for me would be to go to Montreal. While I was in his office the phone rang and it was for me. For me? In Mr. Rickey's office? Yep. It was the hospital calling to tell me that my daughter Norma was born.

I remember that when the phone rang in Mr. Rickey's office he had just finished telling me that they didn't want me to "waste a season." Mr. Rickey told me, "You go down to Montreal, and that way you don't take up a spot on our big league roster. You can get that injury squared away and be back up here pitching."

Well, the phone call changed everything in Mr. Rickey's mind. When Mr. Rickey heard that I had just become a father, he quickly told me in an excited voice, "You won't go anywhere. You'll stay right here in Brooklyn to be with your wife and little girl."

I told him that I needed to go to Montreal and that I would go in a couple of days. This was the end of our conversation. I got in a cab and went right to Methodist Hospital. I stayed there one day and one night, and then I went to Montreal. This impressed Mr. Rickey. After all, he had given me permission to stay in Brooklyn as long as was necessary.

Pee Wee and Dottie took Norma into their home after she came home from the hospital so that I could go to Montreal. The Reeses couldn't have treated Norma any better. I know Norma felt blessed by their graciousness. But Pee Wee was the same guy that put his arm around Jackie on the field that day in Cincinnati. The Reeses had a daughter of their own, Barbara, and they still took care of Norma and our daughter Norma. Little Norma would cry in the middle of the night, and Pee Wee never complained. In fact, we named our second daughter, Barbara Prince King, after Barbara Reese, their daughter.

Getting back to Montreal, that doctor there got ahold of me and fixed my finger. It turned out that there was an "airhead" in my finger causing the finger to puff up. I couldn't even get the finger in my glove, it was so swollen. One Saturday morning the doctor lanced it and suddenly my finger started to ooze like a tube of toothpaste being squeezed. Finally, the swelling went down. For weeks my finger was tender, but I could pitch again. I stayed on in Montreal during my rehab, and I won 17 games there in 1950 and came back to the Dodgers in 1951, when I had my best year. I won 14 games, lost only 7 games, and had 6 saves. I attribute my success in Montreal to that doctor who lanced my finger and to the fact that I realized I needed to learn another pitch. I decided to learn the slider. It helped me a great deal when I came back up to the Dodgers. We didn't have a pitching coach in Brooklyn like teams do today. Clyde Sukeforth was our bullpen coach, and he helped, but he was not a pitching coach. I sort of coached myself through my early years. I'll never forget one interesting event that happened while I was with Montreal. It involved Hall of Famer Monte Irvin.

The Montreal club was playing the Jersey City Giants in Jersey City. Monte Irvin was playing for Jersey City that year, and I was on the mound pitching to Monte. Chuck Connors—who later won fame as star of the television series *The Rifleman*—was our first baseman and he was holding a runner on first. There were runners on first and third and two outs. It was the bottom of the ninth, and we were ahead by two runs. Monte was at bat and he was some hitter. I threw a pitch and he hit it over the right field fence for a home run. That should have been the game winner since he was playing for the home team and it was the bottom of the ninth. Game over, right? Unfortunately for Monte that was not the end of the story. The umpire had called "time" because he said that I balked. Back in those days an umpire could call a balk regardless of the action taking place, and the game was considered to be stopped at that point. Monte was called back to the plate to hit again, and I made a pitch. Only this time he popped it up, and we won the game. The next year they talked about changing the rule, and two years later the rule was changed so that if a balk call is made after the hitter makes contact with the pitch, the hitter can choose whether to take the hit or get another at bat, in case he made out. Boy, was I lucky.

Roy Campanella: My Partner in Pitching

When I returned in 1951 to the Dodgers from my rehabilitation in Montreal, Campy and I developed our best trick yet. We were ready to try it out on our opposition. We called it the "Bubblegum Trick." I came on in relief one night when the Dodgers were playing the Giants. It was the top of the ninth inning with runners on first and third with two outs. We were leading the Giants 4–3, and all I had to do was to get this one batter out and the victory was ours. Whitey Lockman, the Giants first baseman, was up at the plate, and he was a real nemesis to me. Campy came out to the mound to talk to me.

"Professor," he said. "Let's try that bubblegum trick of yours. This guy Whitey Lockman hits you pretty well, so why don't you go ahead and try that bubblegum trick." I said, "OK, Campy, but if we're fortunate enough to get this guy out, you head for the clubhouse before he asks the umpire to check the ball. I'll be running right off the mound and into the clubhouse also."

We were in agreement. We had a full house at Ebbets Field that night, and the fans were on their feet yelling for me to strike Lockman out. The Dodgers–Giants rivalry in those days was fierce. I mean it was unbelievable. Those two teams still have a fierce rivalry to this day. I always chewed two pieces of bubblegum. The gum was about the size of a golf ball. I turned my back to home plate and cupped my glove at my side, if you can imagine, and I just let that big piece of bubble gum fall right out of my mouth and into my glove. Now I had this big wad of gum in my glove. I knew what to do with that gum! I positioned the ball in my glove so as to mash the gum onto the ball. I threw that ball like I would throw any other change-up. I could see Whitey grinning as the ball approached the plate. He was ready to crunch that ball right out of the park, and just as he started his swing, that ball broke straight down and Campy had to dive to catch it right off the top of the ground. It was strike three, and the game was over. Campy and I took off for the clubhouse. When the umpire yelled "strike three" I was out of there.

Whitey yelled, "The Tar Heel threw me a spitter!"

The umpire asked, "What did you do to that ball?"

I told him that it must have been a gust of wind or something, and he didn't press the issue.

The game was over. We had won. The players were now in the clubhouse. Campy was standing inside the clubhouse door waiting for me with a big grin on his face, and we were just laughing and having a great time together. All of the Dodgers came over and asked me what I did to that ball. I told them the same thing that I told the umpire. I asked Campy for the ball, and he said I could have it if I could get it out of his glove! The ball had stuck to his glove but good. We got that ball out of his glove, and I kept the ball for years. Eventually, the bubble gum got really hard and just fell off, leaving only a mark where the gum had been. Campy and I sure had some fun together.

People always ask me what made Roy Campanella such a great catcher. To me, what made him a great catcher was that he could make you think that you were Walter Johnson or Sandy Koufax or Bob Gibson, or any of the other great pitchers. For someone like me, who wasn't a top pitcher at all, Campy did wonders for my pysche. He would come out to the mound, and when he knew that I couldn't get someone out he'd improvise, as he did with our famous quick-pitch on Willie Mays. He would say things like, "Hey, we've got two strikes on this guy, and I've seen you make great two-strike pitches. Let's see you make one here." Campy was the ultimate confidence builder. He could make you think that you could get anybody out. Campy was also a good hitter, and a dangerous one, as he had such a quick bat. He had such a strong arm behind the plate as well. He had a quick release to go along with his strong arm, and he could nail any runner. He caught me when I had my best year in 1951, and I know that I had such a great year because of his confidence in me. He was a three-time MVP. Most people forget that, and I'd like to remind them right now. I feel privileged to have been able to play with this Hall of Famer.

A Concert Violinist in Our Clubhouse

Eddie Basinski was another player in the Dodgers family who made the games interesting. Agile on the field, he was an adept musician off the field. He played the violin in the Buffalo Symphony. He was a good second baseman with good range. He could turn the double-play well. I'll never forget, though, what took place in our clubhouse one day after the game. We had played a game at Ebbets Field, and Frenchy Bordagaray was at the end of his career. He was a pinch-hitter and a utility infielder. He pinch hit that day for us in the seventh inning and then went into the clubhouse, took his shower, and got dressed waiting for the game to be over. The game ended and as we came in, Frenchy had gotten Eddie's violin, or Eddie's fiddle as Frenchy called it, out of its case. Now we had won the game in the bottom of the ninth inning so we were all happy coming into that clubhouse. Frenchy was standing there playing "Turkey in the Straw" on Eddie's violin. Eddie saw him playing and became upset. He said, "You don't play 'Turkey in the Straw' on my violin." He said, "That's a sophisticated instrument and you don't play songs on it like that." Frenchy was just doing it to aggravate him because he was the clubhouse prankster.

One Big Happy Family

Happy Felton and his TV show, *Happy Felton's Knothole Gang*, was a tradition in Brooklyn. The players loved him. The fans loved him. Oh, I can remember him as if it were yesterday. What a great guy

Happy Felton was. He had a quiet, easy way about interviewing you. He knew you, and he knew your record and what you did that day during the game. His television program was so important to the kids. He had a regular following among all of the schoolchildren. It was so easy to be an interviewee on his show. He meant a lot to all of the Dodgers because of his demeanor. If a regular player, like Pee Wee, was the star of the game, as he was very often, Happy would invite another player on the show so that the player could get his $25 check and appear on television. This player might not even have gotten in the game, but Happy had him on so that he would be noticed.

The Brooklyn Dodgers Sym-Phony Band was something else. I've got a picture of them and myself on a calendar, and it reminds me of their antics. The Sym-Phony Band was so loyal to the Dodgers players. They knew the players, respected them, and knew how to get them to have fun. The band was funny and their music was not always on key, to say the least. But no one cared. They entertained the entire crowd. Let me make it clear that it was not the "Symphony," but rather the "Sym-Phony." They were phony. They weren't accomplished musicians, rather they were great fans who played their instruments and had fun. Their music applauded us and ridiculed the opposition. They were an integral part of the Dodgers family at Ebbets Field, much like Hilda Chester.

Gladys Gooding was the organist at Ebbets Field, and she was also Dodger family. She played at Madison Square Garden for other sporting events—the Knicks and the Rangers. Whenever one of the Dodgers ran onto the field during pregame workouts she always knew his home state's song and she played it. When Pee Wee walked out on the field before the game she played "My Old Kentucky Home" because she knew he was from Kentucky. He'd turn around, look up to the press level, where the organist booth was, and he'd salute her. When I came out on the field, she played "Carolina in the Morning," and I would look up and give her a big wave. One time, I remember, Eddie Miksis and two or three other players came out together and locked their arms to see what Gladys would do. She played three tunes at once! We knew her as a friend behind the organ making Ebbets Field come to life.

Hilda Chester rang her cowbell. She had lungs of steel. You could hear her from the upper deck. I'll never forget the day Hilda gave me a real surprise. Surprises are great, especially when you can eat them. One day before a game Hilda came over to me and said that she had something for me. Now it was my 21st birthday, but I certainly did not expect a present. I came out of the clubhouse and

walked on the field and she was there and presented me with this little box. It was a pastry box so I was happy already. Inside was a real
surprise. It was a small cake with my birthday number written on
it—a little "21" on the cake just for me. It had a chocolate base with
white icing on it. I couldn't believe that anybody would bake me a
cake. She did! That was Hilda Chester. She was a real fan. She knew
everyone by his name and age. You could hear her all the way inside
the dugout underneath the roof. She was a loyal Dodgers fan, and
she made Ebbets Field an exciting place to watch a game.

There was an Italian barbershop near where we lived. The barber's name was Cosmos. All of the children got their haircuts there,
and I remember Carl Erskine was a frequent customer of Cosmos.
Then there was Joe Rossi, the butcher. Joe had the best meat anywhere as Carl will tell you. Carl Erskine was so fond of Joe's service
that whenever he came to Brooklyn, he would call Joe in advance
and have 10 pounds of veal cutlet ready and waiting for him at the
airport. When Joe retired and passed the business down to his son
Freddie, Carl did the same thing. You see, back then the store owners would have the players over for family dinners. Brooklyn was
really one big happy family back then, and it was so much fun for
Norma and me to be there because of the festive atmosphere.

Nicknames were prevalent back then in baseball. It seemed as
though everybody had one. Well, I had mine. One of the names the
players called me was "Professor." I guess it was because I was a college guy and wore glasses. It wasn't because I was so smart. The
other nickname was "Comet." I got that nickname when I pitched at
Richmond in 1944. I struck out 12 men in a game one day and threw
mostly fastballs. One of the writers nicknamed me "Comet." I
remember Furman Bisher always embellished that name and helped
keep it alive. Furman, a sports editor of the *Atlanta Constitution and
Journal*, has been a good friend of ours for years. It was my pleasure
to give the speech at his induction into the North Carolina Sports
Hall of Fame.

An Autograph

Back then a player seldom refused a fan an autograph. Not us
Dodgers anyway. I had dinner one New Year's Eve with the Duke
football coach Fred Goldsmith. He told me that when he was five
years old his grandfather took him to a game at Ebbets Field, and he
came down to the bullpen where I was, down the right field line. His
grandfather asked him if he'd like to have a ball, and he said he

would. So his grandfather called me over to the rail, as Fred told me, and introduced himself. He asked me for a ball and I signed it for him. I did not remember this taking place at all. Fred obviously did remember this event as if it were yesterday. Forty-eight years later he and his wife, Pam, came to have dinner with us at our home, and I gave him a Brooklyn cap. I had performed a chapel service for him before the Duke–Georgia Tech football game and he gave me a Duke jacket. I had asked him what I could do for him, and he told me he'd like to have a Brooklyn cap. I didn't know if I had one—the old one with the "B" on the front. I asked Norma to search the house, and she finally found one up in our attic. When he came over for dinner I presented it to him, and now it was complete. I had given him his first baseball and 48 years later his first Brooklyn cap.

Ebbets Field was such an intimate ballpark, like Fenway Park. The stands at Ebbets Field were close to the playing field. You could almost stand in the first-base coaching box and reach way over and touch somebody in the stands, it was that close. It was a great atmosphere.

My Camel Ad

Not being a star player, I was flattered when asked to do an advertisement. The product? Cigarettes. I didn't smoke. Nobody in my family smoked. At that time nobody knew that smoking was bad for your health, and I was approached by John Cameron Swayze of Camel cigarettes. The company asked me to do a Camel TV commercial. I told them that I did not smoke. They told me that I would only have to smoke while shooting the commercial. We went down to a mansion on the water in Miami Beach. They had arranged to use this beautiful house to shoot the commercial. I had my little speech all memorized that they had given me, and I had the cigarette in my hand. I had never held a cigarette before in my life, and I placed it in my hand and put it to my lips and blew the smoke out. Suddenly the director yelled, "Cut!" I knew that I had said my lines correctly because I had rehearsed them, and I said, "What's the problem?" He said, "Look at your cigarette." Apparently, I had wet the cigarette about an inch down the outside. If you know how to smoke a cigarette you don't wet it like that. My cigarette was all wet, and the director said that we'd have to shoot it again because we couldn't have that showing in the commercial. They all laughed at me. All the cameramen thought it was so funny. It was friendly laughter all in good humor.

I received two cartons of cigarettes a week from Camel for two years as part of the deal. I would receive those cartons on Wednesdays, and all my friends that smoked would just happen to drop by my house. One of them was Jack Lee who was a sports editor of the Goldsboro *News Argus* paper, and he smoked. I gave him a lot of those cigarettes. If I had any idea that cigarettes were harmful to your health I would not have done the commercial, even though I received $1,500. I also had a chance to do a liquor commercial, but I told them that I could not do that because I did not drink and I did not want to encourage drinking. I've got a picture of me and my cigarette from that commercial, I had it in the corner of my office, tucked away. I didn't even want to put it up at all, but my daughters insisted that I hang it on the wall to remind me that there was something in my past that I wasn't proud of, because we all have something that we regret doing.

The 1951 Season

As I mentioned earlier, I spent the 1950 season in Montreal on our AAA team in the International League. It was there that I developed a slider, and by the time I returned to Brooklyn in 1951 I had complete confidence in my new pitch. Without a doubt this was the reason I won 14 games and lost 7, with 6 saves.

Something unique happened to me that season. I appeared in both games of a doubleheader on two occasions. One of those doubleheaders turned out well for me because we were playing the St. Louis Cardinals and I came on in relief in both games and ended up being the winning pitcher. It was August 22, 1951, and I will never forget it. I worked three innings of relief in game one and one inning of relief in game two. Jackie Robinson went two for five in the afternoon game and five for six in the night game. The other doubleheader in which I appeared in both games was against Cincinnati, and I remember that day only because of Ewell Blackwell. "The Whip," as he was called, was something else. He had great stuff, and he pitched a complete game and struck out nine batters in nine innings. He also went one for three at the plate, his hit being a home run! The Reds won that first game by a score of 5–2.

The season could have been even better if I had not developed arm trouble. I did not pitch effectively during the final weeks because of soreness in my right shoulder. In those days we did not know about rotator cuff injuries, and I'm sure that was my problem. At one time I could not even raise my arm to comb my hair. My condition worsened with three weeks to go in the season. On the very last day I pitched and I knew that this would be my curtain call. I had the helpless feeling of sitting on the bench, watching that famous playoff between the Giants and Dodgers. The teams split the first two games, and the third game would decide everything. One team would be in the World Series against the Yankees. I wanted to pitch. I wanted to be in that game. As Ralph Branca's friend I knew he had been overused. Starting pitcher Don Newcombe was so strong in that game. He had a fantastic performance, and he was still strong at the end, but manager Charlie Dressen called for Branca to relieve with a two-run lead and Bobby Thomson due to bat with the tying runs on base. When I saw that ball Thomson hit leave the Polo Grounds, my heart sank. I felt as if I should have been the one to stare down the mighty jaws of disaster. I knew if I had not been hurt I would have had the task of trying to get Thomson out. Ralph was a fantastic young pitcher who was used, and used, and used for too many days. During the off-season, Dressen said, "If Clyde King had been able to pitch like he did during the first half of the season we would have won the pennant." I deeply regret not being able to contribute more positively.

7

Jackie Robinson

A Tribute

I DON'T KNOW OF ANY PLAYER IN MY ENTIRE CAREER IN BASEBALL who had a more difficult time than Jackie had back in 1947. Jackie's arrival into professional baseball started in Montreal, at Brooklyn's AAA farm club. When Mr. Rickey sent Clyde Sukeforth out looking for a star black athlete, Jackie Robinson was the only choice when it came down to a final decision.

Clyde Sukeforth was the one who told Mr. Rickey what a fine young man Jackie was and what a great ballplayer he was. When I think back to 1947, I remember what a great help he was to young Jackie Robinson. He was a great help to all the young guys coming into baseball, and on a personal note, he was a great help to me as well. We didn't have a pitching coach in Brooklyn, but Clyde was the bullpen coach and he really encouraged his pitchers. He was always there to help in any way he could. He was also the bullpen catcher. He was a confidant to Manager Durocher and a friend of Mr. Rickey. Mr. Rickey made so many great decisions. There were several possible players who could have been chosen to break the color barrier. He could have picked Don Newcombe, Dan Bankhead, Larry Doby, Jim Pendleton, or several others. Clyde Sukeforth, though, said that Robinson was the best player and that he would be better suited to handle the things the first black player would be subjected to.

In addition to playing ability, Rickey wanted someone who would be willing for the first year or so to take all of the abuse that would go along with breaking those racial barriers. Mr. Rickey knew what Jackie would be subjected to when the Dodgers played in cities like Philadelphia, St. Louis, and Cincinnati. Racial slurs, bean balls, and other cruel treatment would be directed toward Jackie when he played in those cities, and Mr. Rickey told Jackie that the hardest part would be *not* fighting back. He told Jackie that he had to "put on the cloak of humility," which he did. Mr. Rickey also told Robinson that "if we fail in this endeavor it won't be tried again for 20 years at the earliest." Jackie knew that Mr. Rickey wanted him to succeed and, knowing this, it put an awful lot of pressure on him. Mr. Rickey wanted to place as much verbal pressure on him in his office in order to see if he could handle it. Jackie did! Clyde Sukeforth did his job by scouting Jackie, and Mr. Rickey did his part by getting Jackie to be able to handle all of the nightmares that were about to take place.

Jackie had earned the opportunity to play in the major leagues by having an outstanding year at Montreal in 1946. He led the International League in batting with a .346 average, led in stolen bases with 40, and led the league with a .985 fielding average. He led his team, the Royals, to the International League Championship, and then on to the Little World Series Championship by beating the Louisville Colonels.

It was a great year for Jackie, but the pressures were so tremendous that he almost had a nervous breakdown. Without his loving and caring wife, Rachel, he would not have made it. With Rachel's help, his promotion to the Dodgers was virtually assured.

It's easy to talk about Rachel Robinson because she was a lady. There are a lot of women, but there aren't a lot of ladies. She was the "Rock of Gibraltar" to Jackie, and he said many times that he would not have made it through that first year in Montreal, the year before he came to Brooklyn, if it had not been for Rachel. Rachel was always there for him, whether it was to pat him on the back or tell him that things would work out. Rachel was a strong person, and she was there to encourage him and to make him believe in himself. She kept telling him that he'd make it in the big leagues and go on to stardom, and he did. The two of them together made it. Jackie and Rachel were a team the way a husband and wife should be, and they were great to be around. She came to the Dodgers in Brooklyn, and I remember that Gabby Hayes, the old character actor in the cowboy movies, was with them as well. I guess he made them feel relaxed. I know the wives admired Rachel. She wore designer clothes, and they looked great on her. She was a pretty lady. She was educated and had class. All the wives that I knew loved her, and I mean all!

Jackie went to spring training in 1947 as a member of the Montreal club. Here he was converted into a first baseman, the third position he had played in three years. Eddie Stanky was the established second baseman and Pee Wee Reese the shortstop, so in order for him to break into the Dodgers lineup, he had to be willing to play first base—and this he did! He batted .627 in a seven-game exhibition series against the parent Dodgers, thereby proving to everyone he was ready.

I can remember coming north in the spring of 1947, stopping in Atlanta to play an exhibition game at old Ponce de Leon Park. That day every inch of space was occupied. Some came to see the Dodgers, but most came to see Jackie Robinson. There was a very high embankment beyond the right-field fence, and it was covered with fans. There was a large tree in center field, and it was loaded down with fans. There were fans in a roped-off area inside the outfield fences. They were on top of the dugouts. They were sitting in the aisles. It was the largest crowd ever in that old ballpark, estimated to be over 20,000 people.

Jackie Robinson's first game in the major leagues was on April 15, 1947, against the Boston Braves in Ebbets Field. He went hitless but made two good plays at first base. The next day, April 16th, he got his first hit—a bunt. I can still see it to this very moment, an exciting play that really brought the fans to life!

We went to Philadelphia soon after Jackie made his major league debut, and it was terrible. Those fans threw black cats on the field. After having to endure that on the field, off the field he couldn't even stay in the hotel with us. One time in Chicago, he asked me how I thought he was doing, and I said, "Jackie, you're doing great. I couldn't do it, and I don't think anybody else in the entire world could do it."

When Jackie came up, I was a young player. In 1947 I was 22 years old. The other players weren't interested in what I thought. I never saw a petition, but I knew that some of the older players objected to Jackie. Bobby Bragan was one of those players. In fact, Bragan later became a close friend of Jackie's and even went to his funeral. Bragan became a close friend of Jackie's after he realized that he had been wrong and admitted it. I do remember Durocher came into the clubhouse and said, "This guy's a part of our team. If you want to play with him, fine. If not, let me know and we'll do something about getting you on another club." Jackie was staying. If anyone objected, Durocher made it clear that player would be the one going, not Jackie.

I'll never forget our first series in Cincinnati that season. Pee Wee Reese went over to Jackie and put his arm around him, and all the fans in the stands who were booing him saw that gesture and eased off on the booing. That broke the ice a little bit, but only for that moment. Then came the death threats. Jackie got some death

threats that said if he walked out on the field that Sunday in Cincinnati he was going to be killed. Several of us walked out with him,
not as a shield especially, but you might call it that. It wasn't organized. We just did it. We were saying to Jackie, without verbalizing
it, "If you're going to get shot at, we're here with you and we'll get
shot at, too." Jackie didn't know that we were doing that on purpose because nobody told him. We weren't about to let him walk
out on that field by himself.

One day, in a game I was pitching, someone threw at Jackie. I
told him that I'd take care of it, and he said that I didn't need to do
that, but I did anyway. In those days, the pitchers had to bat. Well,
when that pitcher came to the plate I knew what pitch I was going to
throw. He got set in his stance, and I went into my windup and
threw a ball inside under his chin. His bat went one way. His helmet
went the other way. He hit the ground. I took care of things for my
friend and teammate.

By June 15th, Jackie proved himself as a major leaguer. He hit
safely in 21 consecutive games and was steadily improving as a first
baseman. That year Jackie hit .297 and led the league in stolen bases;
he was named Rookie of the Year by *The Sporting News*, and he led
his team to the National League pennant.

Jackie was such an exciting player that he got the attention of
every person in the ballpark when he came to bat or when he was on
base. His own teammates, the opposing players (including pitchers
warming up in the bullpen), the ushers, the vendors—*everyone*
stopped to watch Jackie. Now, that's an exciting player!

Picture, if you will, Jackie on third base with the thought that he
might steal home—and he did 17 times! I can see him now—
bluffing, bluffing, with the pitcher getting more nervous each time
he runs up the line. Then, after four or five bluffs, here he comes,
thundering down the line on his way to pay dirt; a slide, a tag by the
catcher, but too late! The umpire signals *safe*; the fans jumping to
their feet screaming approval as Jackie jogs to his dugout to be welcomed by the entire Dodgers team. What an exciting spectacle!

Jackie was the best base runner I've ever seen. I do not mean the
best base stealer, although he could do that, too. I mean the base
runner with the greatest instinct. It was a thrill to watch him run the
bases. One of his favorite tricks occurred when he was on first base
and there was a hit to left field. He would round second base with a
big turn, and the left fielder would see that he was far off the bag and
throw the ball behind him to second base. Jackie would then trot
into third base! What a play!

Jackie came along at just the right time to give baseball a real lift. It was right after World War II, when our game was struggling to regain the stature it enjoyed before the war.

I have many memories of Jackie that stand out. One time, I was sitting in the lobby of the Knickerbocker Hotel in Chicago reading *The Sporting News* when Jackie came in, saw me, and came over to ask if he could look at the paper with me. I was checking the box scores of our Montreal team in the AAA listings. He proceeded to give me a rundown of the Montreal players—telling me that this pitcher has a good arm and will be here with us as soon as he improves his control; and this hitter will make it if he can learn to lay off of a curve ball in the dirt. On and on he went. He knew each player and his capabilities, which showed his keen sense of observation. For this reason, I believe he would have been an outstanding manager.

In a night game in Ebbets Field, I came in to relieve with runners on first and third, two outs, in the ninth inning, Dodgers leading by one run—a very tight situation. Jackie came to the mound and said, "Clyde, I think we can pick off this runner. Do you want to try it?" "Sure," I said. I made a couple of pitches to the batter, then Jackie gave me the sign to throw over. I did, we picked off the runner, the game was over, and the Dodgers won! Jackie was responsible for that victory, because he encouraged me, a young pitcher, to try something. He was thinking of how to win the game. He could beat the opposition with his bat, with his legs, with his glove, and with his head! He was one of the greatest competitors I've ever known or been associated with. His ability to rattle a pitcher was unbelievable. He used every ounce of his athletic ability and savvy to try to get the upper hand on the opponent, and he *usually* did!

I will always remember a Sunday afternoon in Philadelphia, the last game of the 1951 season. We had to win or the season would be over for us, and we would be on our way home. It was a must win! Jackie was the catalyst in that game also. It was the bottom of the twelfth inning, score tied, bases loaded against us, two outs, and Eddie Waitkus hit a ball through the box and on its way into center field. But our second baseman, Robinson, moved quickly to his right, dove at the ball, and caught it to end the inning. When Jackie hit the ground while diving for that ball, we could hear the wind being knocked out of him, but he recovered quickly. The game went on until the top of the fourteenth inning, score still tied, when Jackie came to bat. I can still see it now—a curveball low and over the plate. Jackie reached out and hit it into the left field seats of old Shibe Park for a home run, which put us ahead. We got 'em out in the bottom of the fourteenth and won the game to tie the Giants. Jackie had risen to the occasion and provided the spark that we needed to win!

In spring training during an intrasquad game, I was pitching against Jackie when my catcher Roy Campanella came out and said, "Let's try your quick pitch on Jackie." Of course I said, "OK." I had worked on this trick pitch during batting practice. I had told Campy about it but forgot about it until he came out and reminded me. The play was with runners on first, or on first and third, and with two strikes on the batter. I would come to the set position and as soon as the batter looked away or reached out to tap the plate with his bat, I would fire the pitch quickly over the plate for an out. On this occasion, I had worked the count to one ball and two strikes. I came to the set position, and as Jackie tapped the plate with his bat, boom, I pitched a strike and the umpire screamed, "Strike Three!" Jackie never saw the pitch. He stood there dumbfounded, not knowing what had happened except that he struck out. He reached up and pulled on his uniform shirt to show me his Dodgers emblem and said, "Hey, Clyde, we're on the same team!" Behind the plate, Roy Campanella was laughing his head off.

During the regular season we were playing the New York Giants in a night game at Ebbets Field. I was pitching, and we were ahead by one run in the top of the ninth inning, with two outs, runners on first and third, and I had two strikes on Willie Mays. Jackie came in from his second base position and said, "Clyde, try your quick pitch on this guy." Roy Campanella had come out from behind the plate, and he said, "Great idea, Jackie. Let's do it, Clyde, 'cause this guy hits you mighty good." So I came set, just as I had done with Jackie in the spring; when Mays tapped the plate, I quick pitched and the umpire yelled "Strike Three!" Willie Mays was screaming to the umpire and saying, "I wasn't ready!"

The umpire said, "Sorry, Willie, but you were in the batter's box, and there was no time-out called, so the pitch is legal." I looked around and Jackie was bent over laughing his head off at Mays just as Campy had laughed at Jackie when we did this to him.

Later in the clubhouse, Jackie came up to me and said, "This tells me that you and I have something in common." "What is that?" I asked. He said, "We'll do anything to win a game, as long as it's legal and within the rules." Campanella heard this conversation and started laughing again. Duke Snider, our center fielder, came over to my locker and said, "Hey, Clyde, someone will have to give me a sign or something when you're going to use that quick pitch because I never saw that pitch. I was pleased that the game was over and that we had won, but I did not know what happened until Campy explained it to me." He said, "If Mays had hit that ball to center field, I would not have caught it because I never saw you make that pitch. I glanced at the ground, and when I looked up the game was over."

Early in the season in Jackie's first year in Brooklyn, my wife, Norma, sat with Rachel and their son, Jackie Jr., at a night game. When the game was over, they went down to the area where the Dodgers wives waited for their husbands. This was inside an enclosed area, by the Dodgers clubhouse, to protect them from the polite, but aggressive, Dodgers fans. Norma noticed that Rachel stayed outside and did not come inside with the other wives. She asked the guard to open the gate. When he did, she went out and invited Rachel to come inside—which she did. I can remember then how proud I was of my wife for doing this.

Jackie definitely had an impact on Dodgers baseball. In 1947, his first major league season, the Dodgers drew 1,807,526 fans into Ebbets Field—a National League record at that time. The Dodgers also drew 1,863,542 fans on the road, and many of those were black fans.

In Robinson's 10-year National League career, the Dodgers won six pennants, and he finished with a lifetime average of .311. In 1949 he led the National League in batting with a .349 average and was voted the league's most valuable player. In his first year of eligibility, 1962, he was elected to the National Baseball Hall of Fame in Cooperstown.

I made a speech about Jackie Robinson in 1995 at Frostburg University. I titled the speech "Jackie Robinson: A Remembrance; A Tribute." Many of the stories in this chapter come from that speech, which ended with these words:

> Jackie Robinson symbolized for so many Americans in the 1940s and 1950s the struggle for human rights and brotherhood in our country. Jackie believed that "a life is not important except in the impact it has on other lives." His accomplishment had a profound impact on millions of Americans, both black and white.
>
> On October 24, 1972, Jackie, who for many years suffered with diabetes, died of a heart attack in his home in Stamford, Connecticut. He was 53 years old.
>
> Jackie Robinson, even though a Dodger in the baseball world, was truly a giant in the world at large. He can never be replaced; we can only attempt to imitate him. My prayer is that what Jackie did for baseball, for his race, and for his country, will not have been done in vain.

8

I Called Them "Skipper"

I'VE HAD THE PRIVILEGE IN MY MANY YEARS IN BASEBALL OF playing for many managers. My first manager was Hall of Famer Leo Durocher, and the relationship between Leo and myself was a special one. I was also privileged to have played for Burt Shotton, Walter Alston, Chuck Dressen, Clay Hopper, Kerby Farrell, Birdie Tebbets, and Rogers Hornsby, my last manager in the big leagues. These were great men.

I'd Go Through a Brick Wall for Leo Durocher

The first time I saw Leo Durocher in person was that tryout I had in Ebbets Field back in June of 1944. At that first meeting I had virtually no contact with him because Mr. Rickey ran that show; he was even in charge of my workout. However, when the season started I quickly got a sense of what made up Leo Durocher. Remember, I signed in early summer, so there was no spring training for me.

During my first few games as a Dodger I can remember sitting on the bench near Leo and listening to him get on umpires and yell at other players and fire his team up. He was something. Here's one story that shows what kind of a man Durocher was to players who played hard for him. I had pitched in relief against the Cubs at Wrigley Field two days in a row, and we won those two games. Gil Hodges hit a home run to win one of those games. We were on the train going from Chicago to St. Louis and he came over to me and said, "Clyde, now during this series with St. Louis—three days we're going to be there—I don't want you to pick up a baseball. Just leave your glove in the clubhouse, and rest up and be ready for the series in New York against the Giants." So, I said that it was fine with me.

I ended up going into a game anyway and saving it for Preacher Roe, after Leo told me that I wasn't going to pitch. Well, we arrived home to New York after our weekend series in St. Louis and in those days we usually had Mondays off because there were only eight teams in the league. Most of the time we played doubleheaders on Sundays, which made Mondays our off day.

I can remember going to the ballpark on Tuesday and John Griffin coming over to me. Danny Comerford was the head club-house man, and John Griffin was his assistant. Johnny came over to me and said, "Leo wants to see you in his office." The first thing that came to my mind, even though I had pitched well recently, was that he was going to send me to Montreal. I thought a moment and told myself that this couldn't be the reason. I had pitched well of late so there must be another reason why he wants to see me. I entered his office and he said, "Clyde, take that coat hanging there in my locker and try it on and see if it fits you." It was a beautiful sports coat. It was of Carolina Tar Heel colors. It was a coat with a nice checkered design. I tried it on, and it fit perfectly. He said, "I ordered it, and it's too big for me and I want you to have it." I was so happy. I went outside and put it on. This all took place before that Tuesday night game, before we even took the field for batting practice.

Ben Dillon was the tailor at the time who came around and measured everyone for tailor-made suits and sports coats and overcoats, and he gave us a real good price on everything we bought. So Ben came up to me after the game and said, "How do you like that sports coat?" I said that it fit beautifully. I asked him why he was asking me because at this point I was puzzled. He said, "I just wanted to make sure it fit you." I said, "Leo gave it to me because you had made it for him, and you made it too big." He said, "What do you mean?" I then told him the whole story. Ben said, "Leo called me from Chicago and asked me if I had your size and I said that I did, and he told me 'I want you to make him a sports coat.'" I wore that sports coat for years and loved it. See, Leo didn't want to tell me that he did it especially for me. It was his way of doing something for me.

Another time, and this was early on in my career as well, we were playing with Howie Schultz as our first baseman. This was 1944. Howie, Ralph, and myself were the only three college guys on the team in 1944. We were playing the Giants at Ebbets Field, and the game was in extra innings. The bases were loaded with two outs in the bottom of the twelfth inning and Howie Schultz was coming to the plate. Durocher called Howie back and told him, "If you get this runner on third to score, either with a base hit or a base on balls or anything, I'll give you $100." Nowadays, you can't do that. It's against the rules. Howie went up there and hit the first pitch right back through the box. The game was over, and we had won. And I had pitched the last two and one-third innings in that game for the victory. Well, Durocher came over to Schultz and gave him $100 as promised. But then after everybody got dressed and we were sitting by our lockers waiting to go home, John Griffin came up to me and handed me an envelope. I asked him what it was and he told me that Babe Hamburger, the head of the ticket office, had told him that Leo wanted John to give it to me. I asked him what was in the envelope and John said he didn't know. I opened it up and there were ten brand new $10 dollar bills with that little wrapper around them. He gave me $100 too, and he hadn't even promised it to me. So you can see why I would have run through a brick wall for him!

Leo Durocher was two or three innings ahead of the game. He was always thinking down the road as to what he was going to do if a particular situation arose. He was something else to watch. He would fight for his players as well. On train rides I didn't get to talk to him much because he always played cards. He liked to gamble. He was a slick card player, and he won at that as well. I loved Durocher. He had class and being married to Laraine Day, the famous movie actress, made him even more interesting.

In 1948 the Dodgers trained in Santo Domingo, Dominican Republic, and this was one year after we had trained in Cuba and I had my pitching match against young Fidel Castro. The Dominican Republic was something else. We stayed at the Jaragua Hotel. There was nothing to do down there but play ball. I enjoyed it. One year ago I had been in Havana and now I was in the Dominican. At night Arky Vaughan, Hugh Casey, Curt Davis, and other players would sit outside and talk. Bill Hart was a great person. All of the older guys would talk about the game and life. Arky used to talk about hunting mountain lions in California. Just this quality time with these older players made me realize that baseball was a profession that I wanted to be involved with forever. Leo's wife, Laraine Day, joined the Dodgers down there to be with Leo, and she had movies shipped out from Hollywood. There was a room in the hotel equipped with a big screen and we'd watch those new movies for our entertainment. Leo was responsible for that as well.

The fieriest I ever saw Leo get was during a game between the Dodgers and the Cubs. Jocko Conlan was the umpire, and he and Leo had a great rapport off the field. However, there was a play at the plate and Jocko called our man out, and Leo went out to argue with him. In those days the umpires had those chest protectors that they held in front of them, and Leo was out there arguing and they were going at it and Leo kicked dirt at Jocko. Jocko then kicked Leo in the shin, and Leo kicked him back in the shin. Then Leo went back to the dugout and sat down. A couple of innings later as the two teams were changing sides, Jocko looked over into the dugout and Leo gave him a salute as if to say, "Everything is OK." They were friends off the field but in baseball things get tense between the lines. Jocko was a great umpire, and Leo was a great manager. I guess the reason Jacko didn't throw Leo out of the game was because he had kicked Leo in the shins—they were even.

In fact, one of my favorite pictures taken of me in a baseball setting is one where Leo Durocher, Gil Hodges, and myself were all together again years later in the late 1960s. Durocher was in his Cubs uniform because he was managing them at the time. Hodges was wearing his Mets uniform because he was their manager then, and I was there in my Brooklyn uniform as an old-time Dodger. I don't even have that picture. I saw it recently in a Mets book on their history. I love that picture because it shows me with my first manager, one of the greatest managers of all time, Leo Durocher, and with one of baseball's greatest first baseman, Gil Hodges. I've said it before and I'll say it again, it was exciting to play for Leo, and I learned a great deal from him about baseball in my early years.

Burt Shotton

Burt Shotton was a guy who came in at a difficult time for any manager. Leo Durocher had been suspended right before the 1947 season for talking to gamblers down in Havana, Cuba, where we were training in the spring of 1947. Burt came in after spring training and, just like Connie Mack, didn't get into uniform. He stayed in his street clothes all the time while he was managing in the dugout. He had his straw hat just like Connie Mack. Again, he was a good manager and considering the awkwardness of the situation, he was extremely good at getting his players to play hard. He adjusted quickly to the situation and to the Dodgers players from a personal standpoint, and he was like a father figure to the ball club. He was not too demanding and was a lot like Bob Lemon was for the Yankees in 1978. He let you take your bat, ball, and glove and play. We had Clyde Sukeforth, Jake Pitler, and Johnny Corriden. All three were good coaches. They helped Burt a lot. They told him about the National League and our players, and he did a good job. We made it to the World Series in 1947, which I thought was a tribute to Burt Shotton. We lost to the Yankees that year, but it was in a seven-game World Series and it was his first year with our ball club. I call what Burt Shotton did that year phenomenal in terms of success. He was a good player in his day, and in later years I often reflected on his success as a manager. You appreciate things like that as the years go by and you become interested in managing. It certainly was the case for me. I appreciated Burt Shotton more and more as my desire to manage seemed to be coming true. Once again, the choice of Burt Shotton was another perceptive decision of Mr. Rickey's.

Charles Dressen

Chuck Dressen was the manager of the Dodgers in 1951. He was an altogether different type of manager than Burt Shotton. He was a man of super confidence. He was cocky and aggressive, but likable. He was a good manager. He is the guy who made the statement that if his team could hold off the opposition for seven innings, he'd think of something. He was that type of person. A lot of people held that against him, but that was his style.

I think that Dressen did overuse and overwork his pitchers. I had my best year in 1951, but the last three weeks I couldn't pitch because I had a sore arm. I was a reliever back then and warmed up a lot without getting into the game, and this was hard on my arm. I can't blame Dressen completely, but I threw too much that year and didn't get into the games. I would have been in 60 or 65 games if I had not had a sore arm for the last three weeks of the season. In fact, I would have been the guy pitching to Bobby Thomson, who hit his famous home run to win the pennant against our 1951 Dodgers team, if I had been healthy because that was my job. My roommate and lifelong pal Ralph Branca was put in that situation because I wasn't available.

Speak Softly but Carry a Big Stick

I first became acquainted with Walter Alston while in Montreal, when he was the manager for the Dodgers' AAA ball club. Walter Alston was a physically strong man. He wasn't loud or obnoxious. He was a guy who when he said something you knew he meant it. You saw the expression in his eyes and you knew he meant business. You also knew not to cross him. If you did, he could pick you up by the back of your collar and lift you right up off the floor because he was so strong physically. He was an excellent billiards player, and he and Leo Durocher would have great billiards battles because they were both good. I would have to say that the games were a draw. They were fun to watch and fun for the players to chat about during train rides. Durocher was a fierce competitor, as was Alston, but Alston was a quiet competitor. In baseball he would walk slowly toward the mound. He was not the type of manager who would walk quickly toward the mound, as Durocher did, but he made his point when he had something to say. He spoke softly but carried a big stick. He only went to bat once in his entire career as a major league player, but his managerial career made its stamp on baseball. I played for this Hall of Fame manager in Montreal that one year, and I remember one time I was called for a balk. He reprimanded me for balking because I was trying to trick the runner on first base, who was a base stealer. I had picked him off the time before, but this time the umpire called a balk on me. I remember Walter getting after me because of that attempted pickoff, and he told me that I should forget about him. Walter said if he was going to steal, he'd steal anyway, and that I should just forget about him. This I could not accept.

I remember one of the few times that Mr. Rickey ever made a wrong prediction. It had to do with Walter Alston. In those days, in the late 1940s, the Dodgers had two AAA teams in the minor leagues. They had St. Paul in the American Association and Montreal in the International League. The Dodgers stocked both of those ball clubs with great young talent. To me, the very fact that an organization could carry two AAA clubs and have both of them loaded with talent showed how many good players there were back then and how shrewd the Dodgers were as an organization. In the late 1940s the Montreal team played St. Paul for the Little World Series. It was really exciting. Two organizational teams playing each other at the same level today would seem strange, but it happened. Clay Hopper was managing one team and Walter Alston was managing the other. One time Mr. Rickey told me that he was thinking of making a change in managers, and I advised him not to do that because I told him that our team in Montreal was a good team, but we had three injured key players. I said that as soon as they were available again, we would be fine. He said don't worry about this change hurting their managerial careers because neither one of them, Alston or Hopper, is going to ever manage in the big leagues. Of course, Walter Alston went on to manage 23 years with the Dodgers and was inducted into the Baseball Hall of Fame. He was truly a great manager. Mr. Rickey was wrong on that evaluation.

Clay Hopper

Clay Hopper was the manager for the Montreal Club in 1949. He was from Mississippi. He was really laid back—to the point of almost being lazy, but he had a good baseball mind. He's another guy who would let you play and seldom criticized you, almost to a fault. When he did correct a player, he did it in private. If a player, however, reacted on the bench or on the field in front of everybody, then he would handle that problem right then and there. I learned that from him as well. If the player didn't publicly react, then he'd give the player the benefit of the doubt and he would talk with the player in his office, which is admirable. He would never show a player up, unless the player asked for it. He taught me a lot about managing. If he reacts in public, like what happened with one of my players when I was managing the Yankees, then you handle it in public. If they keep their feelings to themselves and tell you how they feel in private, then you handle it in private behind closed doors.

The Great Rogers Hornsby

In 1953 during my last year in baseball as a player at the big league level, I had the privilege to play for the great Rogers Hornsby. He was the manager of the Cincinnati Reds at the time. As a player he had a hitting legacy that was unprecedented. He was a terrible manager, however. He didn't communicate with his players. He was almost always negative. He didn't say anything positive to me all year. I think he expected the players to be as good as he had been, and he couldn't accept the fact that they were not the player that he was back in his day. I don't think he knew when to take a pitcher out or when to leave a pitcher in the game. He never gave me any advice and held very few meetings. I wanted to talk to him because he was a great player, but you couldn't talk to him. From my personal experiences he did not do much instructing. We were in Tampa in spring training in 1953, and we had a catcher named Ed Bailey. He was in the batting cage taking batting practice during workouts, and Herm Wehmeier was a sinker-ball pitcher who was throwing batting practice to Bailey. Ed fouled off five pitches that didn't get out of the batting cage, and Hornsby, being the manager, was watching Ed. He said, "Wait a minute! Give me that bat. I'll show you how you're supposed to hit." Bailey gave him his bat, and Hornsby went into the cage. Hornsby didn't know what kind of bat it was, whether it had a thin handle or thick handle, whether it was 35 inches or 36 inches, or how much the bat weighed. He just took that bat and went right into the batting cage to show Ed how it was supposed to be done. Everybody in the ballpark knew that Herm was not fond of Hornsby and was going to throw him the best sinker that he had ever thrown in his life, and he did. He threw it down about his knees, and Hornsby took one swing and hit the ball off the center-field fence on one bounce. Everybody was standing with their mouths open. They couldn't believe that, at Hornsby's age, he could still hit like he did when he was winning batting crown after batting crown. It had been years since he was in a batter's box, and he did it like it was yesterday. He took that bat and handed it back to Bailey and said, "Now that's the way you're supposed to hit. Get in there and hit." Everybody was stunned. It made an impression on everyone. I was standing in center field and saw the ball bounce off the center-field fence and thought to myself, "Gosh, if he could just put that in so many words and help these young hitters."

He didn't believe in going to the movies. He'd sit in the hotel lobby with his palms between his knees bouncing his heels, and he always wore a blue suit and brown shoes. One time we came into the lobby of our hotel just before boarding the bus to go to the ball park. He asked us where we had been, and we told him that we had been to a movie. He said to us, "Oh, you shouldn't go to movies. It's bad for your eyes." Here I was a pitcher with bad vision anyway. Movies couldn't affect my eyes any more than the childhood accident had already. Who knows? It might be true. I tell you that if I had been a hitter I would have had to try it out to see if it worked, because it worked for him.

Joe Schultz

Joe Schultz was another aggressive manager. I think it was a shame that he didn't get enough of a chance to manage in the big leagues. He managed the Tulsa club, the Reds' AA club in 1954, when I was with them finishing my career. He was a player's manager. He encouraged players. He was constantly on umpires but in such a way that he never became belligerent and seldom got thrown out. He gave pitchers every chance to pitch out of trouble, and it increased their confidence. He worked hard and was a great fungo hitter during batting practice. He was always on the field early and was always willing to listen to you. He not only knew the game from A to Z, but he was willing to talk to you in the kind of language and terms that you could understand. A raw rookie could sit down and chat with

Joe Schultz about anything. I wish he had gotten a better chance to manage in the big leagues. I think he would have been a good big league manager.

Kerby Farrell

My playing days were at an end in 1954, and one of the great treats of the game—watching great young talent—came at the end for me. I got to know Rocky Colavito and Herb Score really well that year with Indianapolis. Kerby Farrell was the manager for the Indianapolis Indians, the AAA club for Cleveland. He was a hyper guy, but knew the game. I only played for him for a short time. Gabe Paul encouraged me not to give up. Here I was back at the AAA level. I pitched once in a while when games were out of reach, just to save the other pitchers' arms who were on our staff. This was the year I roomed with Herb Score and Rocky Colavito. That year Herb Score struck out 331 men, and we knew that he was destined for stardom. We were 13 or 14 games ahead, and Kerby Farrell was so excited that he dove in the dugout. I was in the bullpen, and we saw him actually dive into the dugout. He got a chance to manage in the big leagues and brought that excitable personality. He knew how to manage the game on the field. He was positive and really knew his players.

That year I was the veteran on the team. Herb and Rocky approached me and told me that they had rented a big house, and they offered to let me come and stay with them. This is how I became roommates with Herb and Rocky. I was delighted. They had bought an old jalopy for about $300. It was barely good enough to drive to the ballpark, and I remember we never knew whether we were going to get to and from the ballpark. It was a fun time in my career, even though I had a sore arm and couldn't pitch well.

Rocky Colavito had a great arm. He told me that one of these days he was going to prove to me he could throw the ball over the scoreboard in left center field. I said, "Rocky, don't do that. You'll ruin your arm, and you've got a chance to be in the big leagues for a long time. Don't do that just to show me that you can throw the ball a long way." Well, one day I was hitting fungos between home plate and third base to the right fielder. Colavito was in right field. The infield warm-ups were over, and he was running in from right field and I was heading back toward the dugout. I heard somebody say, "Hey, Professor, Professor!" I looked around, and it was Rocky. He was in foul territory between home and first base with the ball in his hand and he said, "Hey, watch this!" Before I could get to him in time to stop him he wound up and threw that ball with all of his might. I just cringed. He threw that ball right over the left center field scoreboard. What an arm he had. If he had grabbed his arm and pretended that he was hurt, I would have literally had a heart attack on the field. Thank God he wasn't hurt. I was very upset that he did that in the first place. He had one of the best arms that I've ever seen in baseball. He threw so hard that it was difficult for the third baseman to handle his throws from right field. As a person, Rocky was truly a great guy.

Herb Score had a great curveball that he could throw on a 3–2 count and expect it to be a strike. The velocity on his fastball was unbelievable. It was a pleasure to watch those two young guys play and perform. It was such a tragedy when Herb Score got hit in the face by a line drive off the bat of Gil McDougald. That injury ended his career. Herb was a gentleman and respectful of the game. I'm glad that he went on to such a long and storied broadcasting career. He is one of the game's treasures, and I'm glad that his run as broadcaster with Cleveland went on for such a long time. It saddened me that he retired after the 1997 season, but he obviously wanted a change of pace. Herb Score's early retirement as a player because of his injury was really a loss to baseball. He truly would have been one of the great pitchers of all time and, without a doubt, a Hall of Famer.

9

Mr. Rickey's Telegram
and My Chance to Manage

AFTER I HURT MY ARM AT THE END OF 1951, I TRIED TO DEVELOP A knuckleball during that winter. I knew that I was not going to be able to throw like I did before I had arm problems, and my wife Norma decided she was going to help her husband. So she played catcher. She actually would catch for me. I'd throw those knuckle-balls, and there she'd be with her glove playing the role of catcher. In the really cold weather I'd go into the gym and I'd practice throwing the ball from different distances. At 40 feet I could really throw a good one, and I soon developed a decent knuckleball. However, when the weather got warm and I went outside and moved out to 60 feet, 6 inches, regulation distance, the ball wouldn't knuckle. I had nobody to instruct me on how to throw a proper knuckleball, so I didn't really learn how to do it. Maybe one out of every four pitches that I threw that winter knuckled, and that's not enough to be a successful knuckleball pitcher in the big leagues.

Spring training came and in 1952 I pitched for the Dodgers. I finished that season for Brooklyn and at the end was told it was to be my last season playing for them. My days in Brooklyn had abruptly come to an end. In 1953 I finished my playing days on a major league team with the Reds. Gabe Paul was the general manager of the Reds who had traded for me in 1953. My last manager was, of course, Rogers Hornsby, the great hitter. What I remember about that final season was playing for this great hitter and being in awe of him because of his hitting legacy. In 1954 Gabe Paul had encouraged me not to give up and thought that the warm weather in Tulsa would do me some good, and it did.

True to his promise of trying to resurrect my arm, Gabe Paul brought me up to Indianapolis, the Reds' AAA club. My first game was good, but after that it was difficult for me. When I played for Tulsa in the Texas League I knew it was the warm weather that helped my arm. I had the velocity back and felt great. I also knew that going to a cooler climate would not be good for me. I went to Indianapolis of the American Association, and suddenly my arm trouble came back. I knew that this was the end of my pitching career. I finished playing baseball for the Atlanta Crackers of the Southern Association in 1955. I played in only nine games that year. However, a new career was just around the corner for me.

I came back home to Goldsboro. My arm was hurting and I was worried. My days as a player were over, and now I didn't know if I was going to be an insurance salesman, a car salesman, or work in some other profession. Norma and I were praying about what was to happen to me. I thought about going into life insurance. I had met Charles Corcoran, vice president of Equitable Life Insurance Company in New York. We met his family and I brought his little girl down to meet players, and I thought that this was what I might do if I was not offered a managerial job or a coaching job. In 1952 the Dodgers lost to the Yankees, but each Dodgers player received $4,200. This was a lot of money to us. We were thrilled, and it helped us to put a down payment on our first home. There was one nice thing that happened in spring training in 1953.

The Reds in 1953 trained in Tampa, Florida, and one Reds fan decided that he would see how his favorite team was doing—in person. Rocky Marciano donned a Reds uniform and played catch with us one day during camp. We trained at the old fairgrounds in Tampa, and he was wonderful. What I especially liked was that he told me about his different fights and how he prepared for them. I was a fight fan back in those days and remain so to a degree. It was wonderful to give him some pitching pointers and get some boxing pointers from him in return. We took a picture together, and it was a big thrill because he was such a boxing legend. I remember him being so down-to-earth and friendly, and yet in the boxing ring he was vicious. Spring training finished and this was to be my last season playing baseball at the major league level.

I had written Mr. Rickey in early November of 1954, and we corresponded back and forth. When 1955 arrived, I finally asked Mr. Rickey if he knew of any managerial jobs for which I could be considered. I knew that my playing days were over. A pitcher knows when he can't pitch anymore. Mr. Rickey sent a telegram to my home in Goldsboro. He told me the following:

I have just wired Earl Mann as follows: "I have just learned that Clyde King is applying for the job as manager of the Atlanta club. I do not know this chap at all as a manager. I do know him as a gentleman and as a student of the game. I believe he would get along with players and most surely he would be able to instruct. I have had him in mind for management for several years and if I had an opening, for example, at New Orleans, I would not hesitate to give Clyde King the job. I wish every good thing to you personally and your club, except when it meets New Orleans."

I got that job as manager of the Atlanta Crackers all because of Mr. Rickey. Once again, he gave me a big break in baseball. Earl Mann, the owner of the Atlanta Crackers, gave me the job, and I went down and started managing there July 23, replacing George McQuinn. We were in sixth place at the time but ended the season on a positive note. In 1956, the very next season, we won the pennant in the Southern Association and went on to play in the Dixie Series, which was like the World Series for the minor leagues. I received the Southern Association Manager of the Year Award that year. The Atlanta Crackers was an independent team. It was not affiliated with any major league team, but they had some real talent through the years. The Crackers sent up players like Eddie Mathews to the Braves, and he went on to be a Hall of Famer.

I think the job was God-sent. I had played for the Crackers the first half of the 1955 season. I got to know the players, and that really helped me in settling in as manager. I was concerned about whether they would accept me now as their manager after having been their teammate the same season. It went well. We finished strong that year and, in fact, in the last game of the season, which we played in old Ponce de Leon Park, our home park, we drew 12,000 people. I think that this impressed Earl Mann as well.

I remember the first time I had to discipline a player after taking over the ball club, just a few days after I came on as manager. We were playing in Atlanta in Ponce de Leon Park. There were runners on first and second, and a ball got by our catcher and went all the way to the backstop. He went back after the ball. Well, he didn't exactly go after the ball. It was either a fast walk or a slow trot. By the time he got back there, at that slow pace, the runners had advanced, and in fact the runner from second base came all the way around and scored. If he had hustled back for that ball, as he should have, the runner would not have scored at all. The runners would have stopped at second and third base. I knew that I had to do something right away. We had played for manager George McQuinn who was sort of passive, and he didn't pick up on things that the players did that should be corrected or at least pointed out to them. So I went right out to home plate, called time, and told our catcher, "You're out of the game."

He said, "What?" in disbelief.

I said, "Yes, you're out of the game."

He said, "For what?"

I said, "For loafing back after that passed ball."

He said, "Well, I don't think I loafed."

I said, "Well, do you think a guy could have scored from second base all the way around third to home if you had run back there, gotten that ball, and thrown it to the pitcher right away?"

He said, "Well, I don't know."

I said, "Well, you're out of the game."

"You're kidding!" he said to me.

I said, "No, you're out of the game." I took him by the arm and led him off the field. We did not have a second catcher at that time. Paul Rambone was our shortstop, and he volunteered to catch. I couldn't worry about that as a manager. Although I did not have a catcher, I knew I could not let that type of playing happen, because if I let that catcher get away with that kind of mistake, all of the players on the team would have said, "Well, we've got a manager who's not going to discipline us, and we can do anything we want and get by with it." Paul Rambone finished the game, and everyone admired him for it. A few days later that catcher was not on our team. I could not have a player who would do that and set that kind of example. We did have quite a few older players, but we had some very young pitchers. Bill Wilhelm, one of our young catchers who was hurt at the time, went on to be baseball coach at Clemson University. He would have been my catcher had he not been injured. That was my first test as a manager, and it had to be done. It made it easier for me to do it in later years when I managed in the big leagues. I had to suspend a player with the Yankees after I had sent him up to pinch-hit and he came back to the dugout, after not being successful, and threw his bat, mumbled something, and then said, "I don't want to be a pinch hitter!" I followed him up the runway, and I told him to take off the uniform. I suspended him until he apologized.

To receive the Southern Association Manager of the Year award, 1956, was special. I think that one of the best assets a manager can have is to be able to pick the best 25 men when spring training ends. Earl Weaver could always do that, and that's why he is a Hall of

Fame manager. Well, that year Mr. Mann, myself, and one of our coaches, all got together and picked the team we thought could be successful in the league. Winning the championship that year was great for me because it encouraged me to strive to make it to the big leagues as a manager. Earl Mann called me at home in Atlanta and told me that I had been selected as the manager of the year in the Southern Association. I remember how happy I was to receive this news. Two of our daughters were really young, and Janet was just a baby. The award made for some genuine family excitement.

Thanks to Mr. Rickey and my start in Atlanta, I was able to go to Hollywood in 1957, where I managed the Hollywood Stars in the Pacific Coast League. It was great because the Dodgers had not yet moved out to Los Angeles. They were playing their last year in Brooklyn. Meanwhile, out in California, the Hollywood Stars and the Los Angeles Angels, with whom Chuck Connors played, had a great rivalry and some exciting times. We finished third that year with 94 wins. The reason I left was because the Dodgers came out in 1958, and Triple A baseball was no longer needed in that area.

I was now off to manage Columbus in the International League. It was AAA level baseball and it was great to be in Ohio. The Columbus Jets, later known as the Clippers, was the Pittsburgh Pirates' AAA club in the International League. Ohio State University was nearby, and it was great to see the Ohio State basketball team play. The girls enjoyed our stay in Ohio and so did I, as the whole town and area were extremely nice to us. After this managerial job I went on to manage the Rochester Red Wings, another AAA team.

10

Hollywood, Here I Come!

THE SEASON THAT MY FAMILY AND I SPENT OUT IN HOLLYWOOD, I've often said, was one of the best years for my entire family. So many great things happened to us in that one year that I still can't believe we did so much in one baseball season. California was great to us, and it was because of the Hollywood Stars and their owner Bob Cobb that we got to do everything we did. One person that made our stay in Hollywood special was my Goldsboro pal Johnny Grant. He introduced us, as did Dr. Norman Vincent Peale, to so many great people. I never thought I would meet as many movie stars in my entire life as I did that spring in Hollywood. Another person who made being out in Hollywood special was my pal from my Montreal days, Chuck Connors, who was out there playing first base for the Los Angeles Angels, our rivals. The two of us had known each other since 1948 when we were in Montreal and he was my roommate.

The Montreal Days: Rooming with the Rifleman

The year was 1948 and I had a swollen finger, and couldn't pitch. In four weeks my finger healed and I was able to pitch again. But I stayed on in Montreal and didn't come back to New York. I learned a lot there and that's when I roomed with Chuck Connors. He was our first baseman and was a good player in the minor leagues.

If you want some insight into Chuck, there's one incident I'll never forget. We were playing a doubleheader in Syracuse, and in the first game of that doubleheader someone in the stands kept yelling at Chuck. And I mean really yelling at him. In that ballpark, the visiting dugout was on the third base side. The roof of the dugout was very low, as the dugout was partly beneath ground level. Well, that fan kept yelling at him. After the game, we had to exit the dugout and go back onto the field because our clubhouse was in right field. As Chuck and I were walking together back to the dugout he turned to me and said, "If that fan gets on me again, I'm going to go after him." I said, "Chuck, you can't do that. You'll be suspended and we need you. You just can't do that." Well, we came back onto the field for the second game of the doubleheader and we walked across first base and toward home plate. We got as far as the third base line and that fan stood up, came down to the front row, and stood right in front of the dugout. He started yelling at Chuck. He called him "a big long-legged gook" and all 6'6" of Chuck responded. He handed me his first baseman's glove and took off after the fan. He leaped on top of the dugout, which had a rounded, metal top, and as he leaped over the top of that dugout, that fan saw how powerful and angry he was, and the fan just took off and went back up the aisle and down the runway leading to the concession area. And Chuck went right after him, right through the stands. Chuck didn't catch him, however. I know one thing—if Chuck would have caught that fan, he would have killed him that day, he was so angry.

Chuck was also a prankster. He always played jokes on people. He didn't do it to be mean, he was just a practical joker. One time Larry Knapp, an umpire in our league, who later made it up to the big leagues and was a good major league umpire, was in the dugout in Montreal waiting to go onto the field. The umpires were about to go to home plate for the exchanging of the lineup cards. Chuck and Larry evidently grew up together, and Chuck wanted to play a prank on him. He went up to Larry and put his arm around him as if to strangle him. Well, he put his arm around Larry's neck in a headlock. Chuck had no idea he was squeezing Larry's neck hard enough to choke him. Pretty soon Larry just collapsed right there on the dugout floor. He literally just fell to the ground. Everybody was scared to death. They thought that Chuck had broken his neck, and Chuck was down on his knees slapping Larry's face to revive him. He kept saying, "Larry, come on!" Larry was all right in the end, but he didn't go back out until the second inning.

On other occasions Chuck would light matches and put them in his teammate's shoes when they weren't looking and give them a hotfoot. They'd be sitting on the bench. He'd light that match, and soon afterward they'd leap up from the bench and put out the fire by hopping around in the dugout. They knew right away that Chuck was the culprit.

Chuck had other talents besides baseball. He used to recite "Casey at the Bat" and that's what he did at nightclubs and entertainment spots. He could recite "Casey at the Bat" as good as anybody. I mean he really did it with feeling. I knew he'd be successful. When I went back to Brooklyn and finished my career years later as a player, he was out in Los Angeles. His career in Hollywood took off when he went out to Los Angeles to play with the Los Angeles Angels. They were in the same league as the Hollywood Stars, which I managed in 1957. Chuck was playing first base for the Angels and I was managing the Stars. Chuck performed "Casey at the Bat" at clubs and banquets, and he caught on quickly. People liked to hear him perform. He had a great personality. He was articulate and so was Johnny Crawford, who played his son in *The Rifleman*. The show was a real success. Then Chuck became involved in the movies. He played the role of a cop in *Pat and Mike*. He should have played the role of a baseball player in a movie, especially one who was a jokester. It would have been the perfect role because it would have been the real Chuck.

Chuck knew how to act around people. If you have that talent, you'll go far in life because people from all walks of life will like you. If there were ladies around he knew how to act. He'd be kind and considerate and polished. But if there weren't ladies around, he could act up with the best of them. I can remember one incident in Montreal so well that just thinking of it brings back all of the memories I've had of Chuck over the years.

We were playing Jersey City and Joe Becker was the Jersey City manager. It was Sunday afternoon in Montreal and when we played at home on Sunday in Montreal we filled the park. When we played the Toronto Maple Leafs, our rival in the International League, we'd have 20,000 to 21,000 fans, and Carl Erskine and I used to be the Sunday pitchers as we always played doubleheaders on Sunday. Late in a game that day, there were men on second and third and Chuck was the batter against a right-hand pitcher named Tomasic, who was pitching for Jersey City. We had men on second and third with two outs and first base open. Jersey City was leading, and Joe was telling his pitcher to walk Chuck intentionally.

I'll never forget that day as long as I live. The catcher gave the signal for the intentional walk, and the pitcher threw the first pitch and it was called a "ball." The second pitch, naturally, was called "ball two" by the umpire. As these pitches were being thrown, I could see Chuck moving up on the plate. He was batting left-handed, and he was gradually moving right up on that plate as if to swing. The third pitch was again thrown outside for a called "ball." The fourth pitch was also far outside, and Chuck swung at it. He obviously couldn't reach it, but he swung and missed. The count's now 3–1. The next pitch was also outside, and Chuck swung at it and once again missed. Now it's 3–2. Joe Becker called time and went onto the top steps of the dugout and yelled to the pitcher, "Pitch to him. If he wants to hit so badly, pitch to him." The pitcher did exactly as Joe told him, and he pitched to Chuck. The next pitch was strike three. He struck him out. Chuck had swung and missed for the final out of the game. Chuck was so mad—and remember he was as strong as an ox—that he took his bat and broke it over his knee. He then took the small end of the bat and brought it over near home plate, and used the larger broken piece of bat to drive the small piece into the ground, as if he was hammering a nail. The fans at this point were standing up and yelling and cheering like mad. They loved it. I mean he was on his hands and knees driving that small end into the ground. He drove it down so deep that the groundskeeper had to come out onto the field and pry it out of the ground.

Chuck was funny, and he made those Montreal days very enjoyable for me. We became good friends and always kept in touch. I'm so glad he had so much success in his acting career. It was great to turn on the television and see the show *The Rifleman* and know that Chuck had made it big in Tinseltown. Norma and I saw Chuck a few years ago, right before he died. We were in New Jersey and he was on his way up to Canada to make a movie, and he looked very tired. We really felt for him. He was a good friend of ours and a year later he passed away. It was so sad to see a man of that stature and rugged complexion look ill. We really miss Chuck, and whenever I think of him I'll always remember that he could play ball and then go out at night and charm an audience at a night spot. Hollywood really got a nice guy in Chuck Connors, and a good first baseman as well.

Disneyland

Thanks to Mr. Rickey and my start in Atlanta as manager of the Crackers, I was able to go to Hollywood and manage the Hollywood Stars in the Pacific Coast League and be reunited with Chuck Connors. Hollywood was special to me because Norma and the kids got to be there with me. It was special for our girls because this was the only time that Norma and I had ever taken our girls out of school. We entered them in school out there in California. I think that taking them out of school in Goldsboro probably was a mistake because schools out in California were so different from what the girls had experienced in North Carolina. We lived in Van Nuys and had a nice house with a lemon tree in the yard. What made everything so special was that we got to know a lot of the movie stars and went to a lot of the sets and watched many actors and actresses at work filming. Irv Kaze, the traveling secretary for the Hollywood Stars, made all of the arrangements. Norma and Princie were in school, and Janet was one year old. Janet celebrated her first birthday in Hollywood. We drove cross-country and that drive was a lot of fun. Irv did so much to make everything so wonderful that we would just like to say thanks once more for all of the great planning and arrangements that he did for us. He was, and still is, a good friend.

California reunited me with a fellow Goldsboro school pal by the name of Johnny Grant. Johnny and I had played high school baseball together, and he was now out in Hollywood as a disk jockey for Gene Autry's radio station, and he made it possible for us to go backstage and meet all of the actors and actresses. We roamed everywhere. Norma and the girls knew some of the stars because they spent time with them. You see, I'd leave home on a given morning after an early lunch and then I'd go to a set, watch the movie stars in action for a couple of hours, and then go to the ballpark for our night game. Norma and the girls would come later and have lunch with the crew and lots of fun. The Stars' home park was Gilmore Field, a beautiful ballpark that was located at 770 Beverly Boulevard, right across the street from Radio City and Farmers Market. Farmers Market was a great place for food. Every nation in the world was represented there, like a food United Nations. I'd eat there and then go to the ballpark. It was such a joy to be constantly around such good homemade food.

When I managed the Stars every beauty queen and pin-up girl passed through our camp. I remember that Miss Czechoslovakia and Miss Sweden visited us. However, no one beauty queen stands out more than Jayne Mansfield. We had celebrity bat girls at that time, and one year Jayne Mansfield was the bat girl for the Hollywood Stars. Well, our hitters were in a slump, and she sent me a card featuring her in a bathing suit. On the card were techniques for unlocking your hips as a method of curing the batting ailments of the hitters. After showing this card to my players they said, "Let's hire her as our hitting coach!" She was very much aware that people were looking at her and she was sort of on stage. She was a very, very pretty girl. There was always a beauty queen doing something or a charity organizing the players for an outing with a celebrity actress or actor. It seemed as if most of Hollywood took some time out of their busy day to see what our ball field looked like at night. Burt Lancaster used to bring his two sons out to the games on weekends. You could look up in the stands and see him sitting with them on a regular basis. Groucho Marx and Gene Autry were always there as well. In those days, before big league baseball came there, we were the big show for baseball. William Frawley, who played the character of Fred Mertz on the *I Love Lucy* show, was on the board of directors of the Hollywood Stars, and I've saved my stationery with his name on it to this day just because it reminds me of him and my days in Hollywood.

I'll never forget Bob Cobb, either. Bob was the owner of the Hollywood Stars and the Brown Derby restaurant. The Brown Derby is legendary to this day. It was a popular place that all of the stars frequented back then, and, if it wasn't for Bob, we wouldn't have met the celebrities we did at that restaurant. He would prearrange outings for us, and he really took great care of Norma and me.

To describe the beauty of the Brown Derby for the person who has only seen it on television, I would have to say that the first thing you would notice about the Brown Derby is its exterior. The top of the restaurant was shaped like a big, brown derby hat. It's just a friendly looking place. Inside the restaurant were caricatures of famous people. We'd go there a lot, and one time when Norma and I were there eating lunch, Hedda Hopper was there with her entourage. Mr. Cobb introduced us to Hedda and I never will forget she had on a big floppy hat. She was a famous gossip columnist in those days, and I enjoyed talking to her. Bob Cobb had in his office the original three Mickey Mouse drawings that Walt Disney had in his productions in Disneyland. They hung on his wall, and I remember how impressed I was to see those drawings. Another time there we met Frank Lovejoy. That was sort of by design, though—it was an arranged meeting. We met Doris Day and Robert Stack there as well. We met Pat Boone on the shooting set of the movie *April Love* and Shirley Jones as well. We met Clark Gable and Doris Day on the set of *Teacher's Pet*.

The Stars trained in Anaheim the first year that the Disneyland Hotel opened and we lived in that hotel. The girls would get out of school during spring training and go directly there, and we'd spend Friday night, Saturday, and Sunday in the Disneyland Hotel. Then they'd go back home to Van Nuys for school on Monday, and I'd stay on for our spring training practice. We got to ride all of the rides at Disneyland. We got passes to go because they'd take pictures of some of my players on the rides and send them back to their hometown papers.

One of our outfielders, Joe Duhem, saved a little girl. There was a pool at the Disneyland Hotel and a little girl fell in. Joe jumped in and saved her life. She was maybe four or five years old. We had a clubhouse guy by the name of Nobe Kawano who later was the clubhouse manager for the Dodgers at Chavez Ravine for many years. Our trainer, in his late sixties, died during the season. We didn't have a trainer so I asked Nobe if he would take over as trainer, and he said he would. He did a good job. We're still friends. His wife, Chessie, would come down on the weekends where we trained. She would bring food, and the guys would go out to the park with their girlfriends and wives and we would picnic there. These were the types of things that made living in Hollywood so enjoyable. I remember Esther Williams frequented the games a lot. Charles Coburn was there as well.

Joe DiMaggio was often seen at the Hollywood spots. He had a restaurant in San Francisco where he lived. Joe in his later years spent much of his time in Florida. It was through his annual baseball classic to benefit the Children's Hospital that I really got to know him. Joe DiMaggio's annual baseball classic is a great one. The event benefits Joe DiMaggio's Children's Hospital in Florida.

I first met Joe DiMaggio when I played with Brooklyn. The Dodgers and Yankees always played three exhibition games right before the season started. One year, two games in Ebbets Field and one game in Yankee Stadium, and the next year it was reversed. These exhibition games were a lot of fun and they were relaxed enough so that you could go over and say hello to opposing players that you admired. Since then I got to know him, and I had a good conversation with him in 1996. He was sitting in the dining room with his grandchildren and I was in there with Carl Hofheinz and his son. Well, the grandchildren left, and Carl and his son left after breakfast. I was about to leave and Joe asked me to sit with him. I had the nicest time talking with him. This made me realize that he really was a private person. I admired that about him. As I sat there I realized that it was an honor to be in his presence.

Gene Autry was another great baseball fan. He used to come out early to watch batting practice at Gilmore Field. Norma and I met Gene through Johnny Grant. Gene loved to watch batting practice. I think he loved it so much because he really knew the game so well. He knew everything about each of our players. He knew their batting averages and how we were doing in the standings. When I fell out of my tree house he sent me a big plant. I'll never forget that gesture as long as I live. I was so touched.

I was in the hospital and the deliveryman brought this big plant to my room. In fact, the deliveryman asked me whether this plant was from the "famous singing cowboy Gene Autry." I said that it was indeed from Mr. Autry.

"My goodness," he said, "I'm going to tell all my friends that I brought up a plant sent by the singing cowboy Gene Autry."

Gene's message on the plant was: "You are a winner! Hang in there!"

Gene Autry was a quiet, modest person. You would never know that he was the one who sang "Here Comes Santa Claus" and all of the other great songs that he recorded. When I would go to California to scout for Mr. Steinbrenner and Gene would hear that I was in the ballpark, he would always send for me and I'd go over to greet him either in the dining room or in his private box at Anaheim Stadium. I know that when Edison Field opened in April of 1998 he was there for the christening, and I think that was just wonderful. Norma and I planted that plant, and it grew to be about six feet tall. We've saved Gene's Christmas telegram that he sent to us a few years ago, and whenever I think back to 1957, I can't help but think of the singing cowboy himself. Gene Autry was just a wonderful person to be around. When he participated in the inaugural ceremony that opened Edison Field I knew that he really was "back in the saddle again."

Most of the wonderful things we were able to do in Hollywood were because of my hometown classmate, teammate, and friend Johnny Grant. Thanks, Johnny.

11

My Pitching Exploit
Against Fidel Castro

DURING SPRING TRAINING IN 1947 I HAD MY DATE WITH
political history and didn't even know it. I was playing for the
Brooklyn Dodgers, and we trained that spring in Havana, Cuba. I
think Mr. Rickey wanted us to train in Cuba because he was planning on Jackie Robinson making his debut that year in baseball early
on in the season. I'm not sure that this was the reason; I'm just spec-
ulating from what I've heard over the years. The Dodgers stayed at
the Nacional Hotel in Havana. There were no other major league
teams training there. It was just us Dodgers. One Sunday afternoon,
however, we split the squad. One squad went to the University of
Havana to play, and the other squad stayed in Havana and played
another local team. I went with the squad to the University of
Havana. Little did I know then the political consequences of that
split-squad decision. I was the starting pitcher in that game and we
beat them. The pitcher for the University of Havana was another
young college student like myself. The game was over and we went
back to our training facility. Soon after spring training was over and
the regular season began, Jackie Robinson made his big league
debut. Well, years went by and after my playing days were over I
once again found myself in Cuba.

In 1960 the Rochester club opened the season in Havana. It was
our first games of the regular season and it was being played in
Havana because the Havana Sugar Kings were in our International
League. So there I was 13 years later back in Cuba, only this time I was
the manager of the Rochester Red Wings AAA club. Before the game
started the Havana Club had a ceremony for the throwing out of the
first ball. At that time Frank Horton, a Congressman for 30-plus years
from Rochester, who was also the president of the Rochester Red

Wings, was with us in Havana. He and I were representing our club and the United States by throwing out ceremonial pitches. So we went out to the pitcher's mound to greet the dignitary of Cuba who was about to throw out the ceremonial first pitch. When we got up to the pitcher's mound there was Fidel Castro.

We shook hands and he said, "Mr. King. You remember me?"

I said, "Yes. You're Fidel Castro."

He said, "No. Do you remember that you pitched against the University of Havana?"

I said, "Yeah" in a happy voice.

He said, "Do you know who you pitched against?"

I said, "No," now a little puzzled.

He said, "Me!" pointing to himself.

"Really?" I said in amazement.

He said, "Yeah, I pitched against you."

I asked him, "Do you remember the score, Fidel?"

He shook his head and said, "No. No. I don't remember."

It was 16–1. He didn't want to remember. He gave me a Cuban flag and cigars and wanted me to be on television. That night we had 22,000 people in that stadium. At this time we didn't know anything about his politics. It was just baseball.

The very next night, when we came to the ballpark in Havana, we walked through the Stadium Club, into the runway, and into our dressing room. When we passed the Stadium Club, we saw that the television set was turned on, and we saw Castro on television. This was about 5:30 in the afternoon. We then played a 10-inning game, and Luke Easter won the game for us with a home run in the tenth. This was a 10-inning game, remember. After the game we got dressed, came back the same way as we entered the ballpark, went through the Stadium Club, and he was still on television. He was still talking. At the game that night we had only 2,000 people in attendance because everybody stayed home to watch Fidel Castro on television.

12

Red Wings to Red Birds

MANAGING THE ROCHESTER RED WINGS WAS CERTAINLY AN experience. I managed them for four years, from 1959 to 1962. During the first two years the Rochester club belonged to the St. Louis Cardinals organization. The next two years the team belonged to the Baltimore Orioles. I remember Boog Powell during my Rochester days before I joined the Cardinals as a trouble-shooter. Boog had tremendous power. He was some hitter. I had Luke Easter there as well, and he was something else. The minor league days were a lot of fun for me for the very reason that I was able to see so much great young talent developing right before my eyes.

In addition to my second meeting with Fidel Castro while I was with Rochester, I also had another unique experience. I was managing Rochester and we had played a night game in Havana. This was not the same trip as my meeting with Castro, but another trip later on that year. The Havana Sugar Kings were in our International League at the AAA level. We played a night game in Havana, and the game went past midnight into extra innings. After that game we boarded a plane and flew home to Rochester and immediately headed from Rochester to Toronto, Canada, for the All-Star game that afternoon. After that game I flew back to Rochester for a night game in New York. So, I was lucky enough to be in Cuba, Canada, and New York all in the same day. I'm probably the only person to ever have played baseball in three different countries all in the same day!

When I think back to my Red Wings days, the first thing that comes to mind was my friendship with Congressman Frank Horton and his wife Marge. Frank and his family went to a beautiful old Presbyterian church in Rochester which we attended with them. Our children loved that church. I know that Frank was one of the most important people in my daughter Princie's life. He ran for Congress in 1960, and he often took Princie campaigning with him. He invited her after church that summer to come home with him and then the two of them would go campaigning. Little Princie's campaigning experience was both an education for her and a lot of fun. She went to a lot of different ethnic gatherings, and I know that she liked the people. She also enjoyed the food. They had food that Princie had never tasted and it was a treat. From that point on, Princie loved history and government. The time spent with Frank those summers really instilled in her a love of politics that still fascinates her to this day. She majored in social studies, with a concentration in political science. She even wanted to go into government work. We always went to visit the Hortons when we went to Washington, D.C. We ate in the private dining room in the Capitol, and Frank took us on the floor of the House of Representatives. We really were treated like "Kings."

There was one player I'll never forget, and I was recently reminded of him. His name is Steve Dalkowski. He was in the Baltimore organization when I was managing Rochester and the Red Wings were affiliated with Baltimore. They were their AAA Club. This was in 1961 and 1962. Paul Richards came over to me and asked me to look at Steve. He told me all about him and then said something which shocked me.

"When he pitches batting practice, I'll guarantee you that of the first five pitches he throws, at least one will be out of the batting cage," Paul cautioned me.

I just looked at Paul. I then let Steve go to work, and sure enough the third pitch that he threw was over the batting cage. That was my first look at him. Then I had him in spring training and he just couldn't throw strikes. Well, I thought about how to solve his problem. It took me two days to get two guys who had enough guts to let me try out my plan. I worked with Dalkowski before this and found out that he was mechanically sound. Once I knew that he was mechanically fine, I knew it had to be mental. After I surmised that to be the case, I worked with him so that he could come to trust me and have confidence in me. Next, I had these two players stand in the batters box facing each other, with only their toes touching home plate. This left an opening which was just small enough to house that 17-inch plate! I told him to throw the ball between these two men. I didn't tell him to throw strikes. I told him to throw the ball between them. The first six pitches he threw were perfect strikes, right between the two players. They were all strikes. They had to be because he would have literally creamed these guys if he didn't throw strikes. Steve went on to strike out more men than he pitched innings, which is something power pitchers dream of doing. He certainly had the best fastball, without a doubt, that I have ever seen.

Boog Powell

Another player who made a lasting impression on me was Boog Powell. In spring training of 1961, Boog was sent by the Baltimore Orioles to Rochester, and our spring-training camp was in Daytona, Florida. He thought he was in pretty good shape, but I guess I ran a tough camp because he told me later that after my camp he found out he wasn't in such good shape after all. Boog had a hard time making an adjustment to the AAA-level pitching. When you go from A ball to AAA, or AA to AAA, the adjustment is not as easy as it may appear. It is a big jump, especially back in those days. I called him in my office and we talked about hitting. I told him I thought his main problem was hitting the breaking ball. I asked him if he wanted me to work with him. He said, "Yes."

We went to work and I started him off with a bag of 50 baseballs. "I'll help you learn to hit a curveball," I told him. I knew that if I just got him accustomed to seeing enough curves, he'd hit them. So, I threw him 50 curves every other day at four o'clock before the team began working out. After several of these sessions he had a sense of accomplishment because he was making much better contact. He told me later on that he was more concerned as to how I was feeling. I loved to throw so I felt fine. I desperately wanted to keep him on the roster to prevent the management from sending him down to Little Rock. Our exercise worked because he started hitting, and he caught fire like I could never have imagined. That year he came within one percentage point of winning the Triple Crown. He led the AAA league in home runs and RBIs, and finished second in batting average, hitting .324. I was so proud of Boog. He was successful because of his attitude. He loved learning and wanted to do everything in his power to excel. If a player of that caliber is willing to work at the little things that may not be going right, then he will be a consummate ballplayer and will be a success in the majors. Boog had a storied major league career, and I'm so proud of him.

Bing Devine

When I finished my tenure with the Rochester ball club, Bing Devine wanted me to come to St. Louis and be a scout and trouble-shooter with the Cardinals. He was very smart, not impulsive, very thoughtful, and usually made the right choices. Bing Devine was a super guy. I really enjoyed being around him. He was my kind of guy. He was low-key and he relied on his men to give him accurate reports. He made working for him fun. I enjoyed those two years. I saw him in 1997 in spring training in Dunedin, Florida, where the Toronto Blue Jays hold their spring training camp and I had a good visit with him. He told everyone in the press room there, "I almost went to work for Clyde one year." I had asked him, when I was general manager of the Yankees, to come back and be my assistant, and he thought about it for a couple of weeks and realized that he didn't want to come back to New York. I was with them when they beat the Yankees in the World Series in 1964. Johnny Keane was the manager. Spring training in 1998 once again gave me the chance to revisit my old boss Bing Devine on a scouting assignment for Mr. Steinbrenner. Bing is just a wonderful man and has contributed much to baseball.

I was a trouble-shooter and I went through the St. Louis organization and worked with all of the Cardinals' different minor league players. I'd go for a week or 10 days and spend time with different players. I really enjoyed that because I got to work with young players. I worked with Steve Carlton and Tim McCarver. Tim McCarver had played for me at Rochester, and I remember his first at-bat. We were playing Montreal and he hit a ground ball to Bobby Morgan, the second baseman, and Bobby threw the ball routinely to first base. The umpire yelled, "Safe!" Here was a catcher who had beaten the throw to first base cleanly, and catchers were not supposed to be that fast. Both benches were impressed. Nobody expected this young catcher to run that fast.

Stan Musial

Stan "The Man" Musial was something else. He is one of my all-time favorite players. I remember pitching against him in Brooklyn. His demeanor on the field and off always impressed me. Every player would like to have been a ballplayer like Stan Musial. He had the best work habits and the most natural ability. One year at Ebbets Field he hit .500. We played 11 games at home and 11 on the road. On one occasion he hit five home runs in a doubleheader at the Polo Grounds. He hit me so well that when he knew I was going to pitch he'd send a cab out to my house to make sure that I got to the ballpark. The thing about Stan Musial that was really scary was that he had no weaknesses. He hit the ball to all fields. The scouting report on Stan was the following—throw the pitch and pray; throw the pitch and duck. He started out his professional baseball career as a left-handed pitcher and he hurt his arm. Stan could do it all. He was the complete ballplayer. He plays a mean harmonica and he played a mean tune with his bat, especially when I pitched.

Bob Gibson

Bob Gibson was another fierce competitor and really a wonderful man. As a player, he was an overpowering pitcher. He was intimidating. He was mean. He had great stuff. Bob had a hard, live fastball that he could ride up in the top of the zone. He had a fastball that he could throw in on you. He had a pitch, and to this day I don't know whether he called it a curve or slider, that was a real bat breaker. It had such a quick, sharp break on it that when the pitch rode in on your hands, it just shattered the bat. He would knock you on your back. He would throw one under your chin, or behind your head. He would take a few steps off the mound and stare at you as if to say "if you don't like it, I'll do it again." Batters generally did not take him up on his offer. Bob was a great fielding pitcher as well. When he put on his game face, you just stayed out of his way until the game was over. Bob Gibson was a great competitor and a great pitcher, and it's fun to see him and reminisce. He is a gentleman off the field.

Red Schoendienst

Red Schoendienst was another great Cardinal. He was a switch hitter and a good hitter from both sides of the plate. I think he had a little bit more power from the right side of the plate. If you saw the home run he hit in an All-Star game batting right-handed in the tenth inning to end the game, you would never forget it. It went a mile. Red did everything well. He knew how to play the game. He had great range at second base. He turned the double play well. He could go a long way to catch a pop fly. He and Julian Javier could go the longest distance to catch a pop fly that I've ever seen. Red could catch a ball with his back to the infield running toward the outfield and make it look so easy. He was a good hitter and a smart base runner. He loved to talk baseball and knew every phase of the game. I'm sure that when he was managing the Cardinals, all of those youngsters sat around and listened to him. I would have if I was there. Red Schoendienst is a credit to baseball, on and off the field, and he is an example for all of us. He's been in the game a long, long time.

Joe Morgan

There's one scouting assignment that is memorable only because the player went on to be a Hall of Famer. It was August 22 and 23 in 1964. Lou Fitzgerald was the manager of San Antonio in the Texas League. This San Antonio team was part of the Houston organization. It was the Astros' farm club. Well, those days saw many talented hitters. As a scout I had a sheet that detailed everything a manager or general manager would want to know about a hitter or pitcher. I had to determine whether or not a player had good fielding range, soft hands, batting power, speed, and what type of position player he was as well. I even had a printed column on my scouting sheet for hustle. Well, I saw a young man who had the best of everything. On my scouting form, which I signed and attested, like a golf scorecard, was my comment that this young man was "the best prospect in the Texas League." I wrote down further comments on the back of the sheet, and these were looked at as well by the Cardinals management. For this player I wrote the following: "In my opinion he is the best prospect I've seen in the Texas League this year. He has all the tools: speed, arm, range, hands, power (42 doubles — .316 BA), 45 stolen bases. I like him very much and he will be a star some day." I look back at that scouting form, which I managed to photocopy, and smile to this day. The player I scouted back then really did have all of the right tools. He would go on to be a regular in their ball club in 1965, a Hall of Fame second baseman playing for the Cincinnati Reds, and a TV announcer for major league games. His name is Joe Morgan.

My days with the Cardinals came to a close for me at the end of 1964. However, a new major league experience gave me the chance to be back at the big league level. I was asked to become a coach for the Pittsburgh Pirates before the start of the 1965 season.

13

The Pittsburgh Pirates

I'M VERY PROUD AND THANKFUL TO HAVE BEEN A COACH WITH the Pirates. It was my first coaching job at the big league level. Teams back then didn't employ the number of coaches that they do today. In those days teams had only four coaches. The Yankees had more coaches than any other team and they had six. It was tough to break into coaching. I really enjoyed teaching, especially the young kids who had potential and didn't know how to throw a curveball or hold the ball to make it break in certain ways. I got a lot of pleasure out of telling a young player how to do something and then seeing him do it in a game. It made me feel as if I were throwing the ball myself.

I like old parks. I like Fenway Park and Tiger Stadium, Wrigley Field and Ebbets Field, and the old Polo Grounds. Forbes Field was different, however, from the other ballparks. Although we didn't have the big crowds like we had at Ebbets Field, the vendors were friendly and they all took care of our daughters at the concession stands. The city of Pittsburgh itself was a great city. We lived in suburban Homestead. Joe L. Brown was the general manager of Pittsburgh and he was just a perfect guy for the job. He knew baseball and knew how to handle people to get the most out of them.

Joe L. Brown was the general manager throughout the '50s and '60s and the son of Joe E. Brown, the famous comedian and movie star. Joe L. Brown was the epitome of what a general manager should be in baseball. He was intelligent. He was articulate. He was understanding. You could go to him with a problem about a player and he always had time for you. I can remember one time when the Pirates were having a golf tournament and I had the flu. I couldn't play in the tournament and it was an off-day. The golf tournament was in Fort Myers, Florida, and everyone else was playing in the tournament but me. He said to me, "Let's go down to Naples." He took me in his car and drove me down to Naples, where we had dinner together. This was the type of person he was—always trying to do something nice for someone. He knew that I couldn't play in the tournament so he decided that we'd spend time together eating dinner out and taking a drive. He was a smart baseball man and very good to me and to my family. He gave me a chance to be a coach and really encouraged me. I enjoyed my three years with Joe and I feel badly that in later years we weren't able to spend more time together. His dad was an avid baseball fan. He loved baseball so much that when he signed his contract with Warner Brothers, he made them insert into his contract a clause that stated that they would field a Joe E. Brown's All-Star team so that he could continue to pursue his childhood love, baseball.

Pittsburgh was special to me because it was my first coaching job. Norma and I, when we did eat out, ate in those restaurants out in Squirrel Hill and they were great. We ate at home mostly, however, because Norma is a great cook. We lived in Danny Murtaugh's house one year, who was the manager of the Pirates for several years. I enjoyed dining with Hal Smith, Alex Grammas, and Johnny Pesky, but remember I was a coach so it was not quite the same as it was in Brooklyn when I was a player. I remember reflecting on how life had changed for me from a camaraderie standpoint. The Pirate days were great for me for another reason—our wonderful players. We had great players who were fun to coach and fun to watch.

Vernon Law

We had some good pitchers on our staff. Vernon Law, who won the Cy Young Award during my tenure there, was both a great pitcher and a great person. Vernon and his family lived in a little town, Murrysville, outside of Pittsburgh, and we'd go out there as a family almost every Saturday when we played at home. The Laws had five children, and all their kids' names started with a "V," as did his wife's name. His wife, Va Nita, would cook for us, and we had the best time in the world. Vernon Law was special. I can remember 1965 and his 17 wins, but even more astonishing that year was his 2.15 ERA. He made the job of being a pitching coach a lot of fun because of his skill on the mound. There was one particular game that I'll never forget and it was against the Giants.

We were going into the bottom of the ninth inning at Candlestick. We were ahead in the game, and I desperately wanted Vernon to finish that game because he was having such a good year. Well, the first player reached on an error. Gene Alley, our shortstop, made an uncharacteristic error, and I say uncharacteristic because he was a great shortstop. The next batter hit a little bloop just out of reach of Bill Mazeroski, our second baseman, into shallow right field. At this point there were two men on and nobody out, with the go-ahead runs on base. I was in the dugout debating whether I should suggest to our manager, Harry Walker, to take Vernon out of the game. Al McBean was our relief pitcher and he was having an effective year. However, I knew McBean didn't especially like to pitch in San Francisco because of the cold weather. I also felt that Vernon could finish the game. So, I said to Walker, "Let's give Vernon one more hitter." But the next guy got on base. Now the bases were loaded and our lead was threatened. Harry asked me to go out and talk to Vernon. Ninety-nine times out of 100 whenever I went to the mound, I knew I was either going to take the pitcher out or leave him in before I even said a word. This time as I walked toward the mound I didn't know what I was going to do. It was a long walk for me. I don't know why I didn't know, but I just didn't.

"Vernon," I said, "I really want you to finish this game. I've got more confidence in you than any other pitcher on this staff, and I really want you to finish the game."

I couldn't even finish the last few words of the sentence because he quickly took me by the arm and said, "Clyde, if you let me stay in, I can do it. I won't disappoint you."

I said, "Vernon, that's all I wanted to hear."

He struck the next batter out. The batter after him hit a ball to Alley at shortstop. Alley then threw to Bill Mazeroski at second, who threw to Donn Clendenon at first to complete the 6–4–3 double play. The game was over. Now if Vernon would have said "Clyde, I'm a little tired," or something to that effect, that would have been my answer and I would have taken him out and brought on McBean. Vernon, though, wanted that ball. He wanted to stay in the game, and he gave me the answer I was hoping to hear. The result was that he ended up winning the game and notched another complete game for himself in the process. Vernon Law really made being a coach a pleasure. He was not only an outstanding pitcher, but a wonderful husband and father, and a dedicated man of God.

Bob Prince

My good friend in Pittsburgh, Hall-of-Fame announcer Bob Prince, was a great storyteller and we shared many wonderful memories at restaurants. The one thing I'll always remember about Bob is that he was always nice to us on road trips. Once a year he would take all the coaches to the Drake Hotel in Chicago for dinner. Alex Grammas, Johnny Pesky, Hal Smith, myself, and Bob would go for dinner there. It was wonderful, but the amazing part wasn't the food as much as the service. Bob knew everybody, it seemed like, in Chicago. We would get off the team bus in the early morning hours, and Bob could open up a closed restaurant like nobody else could. He'd have that place serving everyone food. Everyone at the Drake knew him, and everyone loved him. He was just as thoughtful at home. I can still see my daughters learning how to swim in the swimming pool at his home. He'd have them doing the "alleycat" dance.

Bob also had a half-hour television show. I certainly got my point across on that show, and I set my girls' dating lives back 100 years, or so they said. I can remember that day starting out innocently enough. Bob had Norma and the girls, and myself, on with him during his show, and he was asking us great questions about the Pirates and Pittsburgh. It was wonderful. Then things erupted. He asked one of my girls if she had a boyfriend or sweetheart. It was all innocent—for a normal father. But not for me. I suddenly saw droves of boys coming to our house and trying to date my girls! I put a stop to that at once. I said, "If any of those boys think they're coming to our house, I've got a shotgun mounted above the doorway pointed at the walkway." My girls were so embarrassed. They said I ruined any chance of dating a nice boy. The sad part was that even though I didn't own a shotgun, I was serious about keeping boys away. Obviously I mellowed as time went on! I guess I was a little overprotective!

Willie Stargell

Willie Stargell was called "Pops" by the Pittsburgh club and for good reason. He was a nice guy and a big brother–father figure to all of the young kids. He led by example and had the best work habits of anyone. I've heard people say that he was like a teddy bear because he was so friendly. Well, I can tell you that he was indeed happy and kind—until he got up to bat. Once he was at the plate he had "the roar of a lion." He hit home runs that people remembered because they were such towering shots—I've never seen anyone hit like that with such consistency. He could also hit line-drive home runs. He was just a home-run hitting machine when it came to side-arm pitcher Ted Abernathy of the Cubs. He hit three home runs off Ted one day at Wrigley Field. Willie was the best representative a baseball club could hope for, as he handled himself well off the field and always obliged signing autographs. He would sign, and sign, and sign. Willie Stargell is a Hall of Famer in the game of baseball and a Hall of Famer in life.

Roberto Clemente

My years in Pittsburgh were a lot of fun for another reason. His name, Roberto Clemente. Roberto could do it all. He could hit for average, leading the National League several times in batting average, and he had one of the best, if not the best, arm in the outfield. During my years with the Pirates as pitching coach I was able to see Roberto put up these numbers: 1965—.329 batting average, 194 hits; 1966—.317 batting average, 202 hits; and 1967—.357 batting average, 209 hits. He, Carl Furillo, and Rocky Colavito had the best arms for outfielders that I've ever seen. He had quick hands, and that's one of the reasons why he was a great outfielder. Base runners respected his arm. Not many base runners tried to score on him and certainly didn't try to go from first to third on him.

Roberto had good power, and he could have hit more home runs than he did if he wanted to. One day he proved that to his teammates. He had been hitting around .360 during the season and the players were kidding him about not hitting more home runs. I was the pitching coach and as such threw batting practice to the players. One day he came over and said to me, "Today in batting practice I'm going to show these guys something. I want you to pitch to me." I guess he realized that I could throw a lot of home runs. Well, when he came up to the plate during batting practice, I threw the ball right where I knew he liked it and with not much on it, and he hit three balls over the scoreboard in Forbes Field. And that's a good poke. A real good poke. He had good power. He could have hit 35 or 40 home runs if he had wanted to, but his batting average would have dropped. Roberto hit the ball where it was pitched. He reminded me of Yogi Berra. He was a good "bad ball" hitter. He could hit the ball that was up above his head. He could hit the ball down the right field line, the left field line, and over the center fielder's head. He could run the bases. He could have stolen 40 or 50 bases in a season if he had really wanted. When Roberto was in high gear, there was nobody better than him. Nobody!

He used to help several families in Puerto Rico. These families were poor and he helped them out, even at the price of depriving himself and his family. I'm talking about real sacrifice. I've been to his home in Carolina, Puerto Rico, and I've seen some of the families whom he helped. The tragic death he suffered on New Year's Eve in 1972 happened when he was trying to assist in an emergency. When they had that earthquake in Nicaragua, he chartered a cargo plane. He loaded that plane down with supplies and was going to fly there and distribute these supplies to the earthquake victims. The over-loaded plane took off well enough from the San Juan airport, but shortly after take-off it crashed in the ocean. They never found his body.

Roberto Clemente was a nice guy. He had it all on the field, and he exemplified everything that is good about life off the field. He always took the young players under his wing and helped them feel comfortable on the club. I think we all can learn a lot about giving and the meaning of charity from studying Roberto's life. He was truly a great human being.

14
My Golden Gate Days

BEFORE I MADE MY GIANTS MANAGERIAL DEBUT IN 1969, I HAD the pleasure of managing the Phoenix farm club for the Giants in 1968. This was their AAA farm club in the Pacific Coast League and that year was wonderful. The games were played in the late afternoon and the weather was hot, but dry. Phoenix was hot, but never too hot. Back then, though, Phoenix was a lot different than it is today. In fact, in the '80s my wife and I went back there for a general managers' meeting, when I was general manager of the Yankees, and she remarked how vastly different everything looked. But some things never change, like the restaurant The Pink Pony. That's a terrific place and it will always be there, I hope. But the city was built-up to where it really looked like a big city. It was a great place to golf. Phoenix was great at that time also because it gave Norma and the kids and me a chance to explore a lot by car on off days. We'd go 100 miles in one direction one day and 100 or 200 miles in another direction another day. I longed to be a manager at the big league level and hoped that I would get that call that all minor league managers pray for.

Well, San Francisco finally gave me the call. I got my chance and I was thrilled. I have Rosey Ryan to thank for that opportunity of a lifetime. Ryan, the general manager, was the one who convinced Horace Stoneham that I was ready to manage in San Francisco in 1969. San Francisco is such a beautiful city. The mere sight of the rolling hills is something that makes a lasting impression. The Golden Gate Bridge, the great food at Fisherman's Wharf and Ghirardelli Square, and the lovely town of Sausalito with all of its shops are great places that make San Francisco such an enjoyable city to visit. Then there's the Muir Woods, which has three-thousand-year-old redwood trees. These great memories are still with me today. I know Norma and the girls loved their two years spent there and so did I. While in San Francisco we lived in Los Altos Hills, in Lenny Gabrielson's home. Lenny was playing for the Dodgers in 1969, and so we rented his home and it was lovely. It was a very hilly area. The Gabrielsons' home was all that we could ever dream of, and certainly all we needed to be happy and comfortable. We could see Stanford University and its chapel from our home. Our family used the back deck and patio every day.

The 49ers play in, and some of the football players lived in, Los Altos Hills in the off-season. Paul Wiggins, one of the 49ers coaches was our neighbor, and my daughter Norma baby-sat for him a few times. The one thing about San Francisco that I should warn everyone about is the climate. The difference in temperature from where we lived and Candlestick Park would be about 10 degrees, and Candlestick wasn't that far away, about 37 miles. Whenever people came to visit us we'd tell them to bring a topcoat. The weather can change very quickly. We had lots of friends from Goldsboro come to visit us, and my girls got a big kick out of being able to show everyone around the city, as if they had lived there forever. Our daughters never got tired of showing off San Francisco. It was a great place to live. They took their driving lessons there, and they knew San Francisco from a car better than any place else except for home. The Horace Stonehams were great to us, and their daughter Woochie was nice to us as well.

Living thousands of miles away from the East Coast was different. Although both Brooklyn and San Francisco were picturesque and beautiful, the houses were different in color and design. At that time in my life California was actually better for my family. In Brooklyn everyone had been close together, which made it easier for Norma to be alone when I went on the road. She had all of the players' wives and her friends, right there next door. Here, Norma didn't enjoy the security, as in Brooklyn, of being right next door to someone, but we had lots of room, and at this stage of our lives we needed it. We had three daughters who were growing up and needed the space. The girls would do things together, and they had fun with and without me. When I went on the road, they would go sightseeing and visiting friends like Art and Fran Santo Domingo. Because we were so far up in the hills, Norma and the girls had lots of fun driving to the ballpark. When you're young its fun to drive up and down those big rolling hills, and it was especially so for our oldest daughter, Norma, who insisted on showing everybody how she knew San Francisco like the back of her hand. The girls also made lots of friends there. Don Rood and his wife Bea lived in Sunnyvale and Art and Fran Santo Domingo and their children lived in Atherton, which wasn't that far away, and we all did things together. We had a lot of company. Our house was large, and the girls could have their young friends come and visit from Carolina.

I told everyone who came to visit to bring a topcoat. I remember when our friend Bill Kemp with wife Betty, son Billy, daughters Betsy and Sallie, came to visit us in July, and we told them about bringing their coats. This was July, and here I'm telling Bill that he'd better bring a topcoat. I was right! The first game they went to was an afternoon game, and the second game they saw was a night game. I didn't get to see what took place, but apparently the Kemps told Norma that they wouldn't need their coats, so they left them in the car. From what I understand, in about the middle of the game they had to leave the ballpark and go to the car and get their coats because they were so cold. I had told them the weather could throw a curveball, and it did.

Our daughters were now going regularly to the ball games. We didn't give them lots of money to spend like some parents. We wanted to teach them to be frugal so we gave them only enough for a box of popcorn and a drink. I think they got to know the vendors because sometimes they'd get a refill that Norma would tell me about and we'd laugh. Norma always gave them food to take along that was more nutritious. She cut up apples and oranges for them that they'd take to the ballpark. Norma didn't want our daughters filling up on junk food. We even gave them a dress code. They had to wear skirts and look nice. In fact, Tommy Lasorda commented to me once about how he always remembered the girls "coming to the ballpark in their dresses with their white gloves on." In fact, Norma made a lot of the girls' clothes. She can sew and make dresses with the best of them.

One time a *Sports Illustrated* reporter came to interview me and my family. My daughter Norma had her friend Betsy Kemp from North Carolina visiting us. Norma wanted Betsy to be a part of the interview. She ended up being a part of the interview as a kind of "fourth" daughter, and it was fun. Another time when we were all in the city, my daughter Norma and Betsy were walking behind me. My daughter relates what happened next. "These two good-looking guys were coming toward daddy and didn't even look at us and kept looking at dad. They turned around walking toward us to stare at daddy, and one said to the other, 'Hey, that's Clyde King. That's the manager of the San Francisco Giants.'" Well, the next thing I knew Betsy came up behind me, took me by the arm, and we went walking

down the street together. I didn't know the reason why. Not knowing what had happened, I later found out this story from Norma.
Betsy apparently wanted the guys to notice her and so she grabbed
onto me.

I can't talk about San Francisco without talking about my prize
players. We had some great ones. We had Willie Mays, Bobby
Bonds, Willie McCovey, Juan Marichal, and Gaylord Perry. Need I
say more?

Willie Mays

I had the privilege of managing Willie Mays during my Golden Gate
days. Willie was certainly one of the great players in the game of
baseball. He could do it all on the baseball diamond. He could beat
his opponents in so many ways. He had great defensive ability and
could make the basket catch, as he did in the World Series when he
played for the New York Giants. Willie had the ability to hit both for
average and for power and finished his career with a lifetime batting
average of over .300 and with 660 home runs. He could also beat his
opponents with his strong throwing arm and his speed on the base
paths. He didn't need a third-base coach when he was on base
because he had great instincts running the bases and was rarely
thrown out taking the extra base.

Willie was a generous fellow, sharing with his teammates and his
manager some of the things he received from making appearances
and endorsements. He gave me a watch and a beautiful sweater that
I still have to this day. Willie Mays has left his mark on baseball as
have many other great players. I consider it a real honor to be the
only manager to manage both Willie Mays and Hank Aaron. What a
great privilege indeed!

Bobby Bonds

I knew the first time I saw Bonds that he was special. One of my earliest recollections about him is from spring training while I was managing Phoenix in 1968. Hall of Famer Carl Hubbell was the director
of the San Francisco farm clubs. Phoenix was in the Pacific Coast
League and Bobby was on my roster. We trained in Casa Grande,
about 40 miles from Phoenix where the parent club, the major
league San Francisco Giants, had their spring training. The Giants
started training with us in Casa Grande, but when the spring training games began, the Giants headed for Phoenix stadium. When I

saw this young man and the physical attributes that he possessed, it was something else. I mean he had great legs, a great arm, quick wrists, power in his swing, and I took a liking to him right away. I worked with him just as I did with Boog Powell. I threw him curve-balls in spring training workouts because he had the same problem Boog did hitting the curveball. Then it came time for us to pick our teams. Carl Hubbell was the farm director. We had a meeting with all of the scouts and managers in the minor leagues to decide where each player would go, whether it would be to my AAA club or to the AA or A clubs. Bobby had a good spring, and he had greatly improved in his ability to hit the curveball to the point where I knew he had almost mastered hitting that type of pitch. Well, Mr. Stone-ham, Carl, myself, and the other scouts all met at the hotel we were staying at in Casa Grande. I said I wanted "these" infielders and "these" outfielders. I saved Bonds for last. I said, finally, that I wanted to keep Bobby Bonds. Carl Hubbell spoke up:

"No, Clyde, he's not ready for you. He's striking out a lot and he needs a year in AA ball before he comes to the AAA level."

I said, "Carl, I've spent a lot of time with this kid. I like him. I have confidence in him. I think he can make my club at Phoenix."

He said, "Well, I can't let you have him."

Mr. Stoneham interjected. He said, "Now Carl, if Clyde likes this kid that much, we ought to let him have him." Carl Hubbell didn't like that, and he was miffed at me for days.

Well, we took Bobby on to Phoenix where for the first few weeks I got to see the real impact player he was. My daughters remember playing with Bobby's son, little Barry, at the time, whereas I remember the home run clout and power of Bobby. He was an exciting player. In fact, he was leading the entire Pacific Coast League in hitting at the time he was called up to the Giants. He hit a home run in his very first game, a grand slam. He was on his way to becoming a member of the 30–30 club (30 home runs and 30 stolen bases in a single season). It was wonderful that when he finished his career he had stolen over 400 bases and had hit over 300 home runs. I joined young Bobby the next year when I myself got "the call" to go to the majors. I made my major league managerial debut with the Giants in 1969, and Bobby was one of the reasons for my success as manager. He ran well, threw well, hit well, and had power. He loved to play the game. He was one of the first players to arrive at the ball-park on a given day and always had much enthusiasm for the game. The only advice I ever gave Bobby on hitting was to stay back and not lunge at the ball. He didn't need much in the way of advice. All he needed was encouragement and his bat, glove, and base running took care of everything else. I feel about Bobby as I do about Dusty Baker. They are very special players to me.

Willie McCovey: Stretch

Willie McCovey gave me another reason to love San Francisco. He made managing fun. He really did. I hope he reads this because I want him to know how much I think of him. Some people say that every time McCovey's name is mentioned I get a twinkle in my eye and I look happy. Absolutely. Willie McCovey was a gamer. By that I mean he wanted to win and he'd do whatever he could to win. He'd play when he was hurt and produce. A lot of players will play when they're hurt, but they don't produce because of their injury. Other players won't play if they're hurt. We've got some players nowadays who won't play even if they are only slightly hurt in an area that does not affect their game at all. When I was later with the Yankees, we had guys like Don Mattingly who played hurt with his bad back and wrist, and he produced. Well, Willie McCovey had a back problem but he stayed in the lineup. I'll never forget Willie staying in a game when he had a bad back that hurt him so much you could almost feel the pain yourself. We were playing in Houston. Willie had been having back and knee problems for a while. It was either the fifth or the sixth inning in the game, and he was at the plate hitting. Well, he swung at a pitch and missed, and he just stood there like a statue. He was all locked up. You could see that he couldn't move without sharp pain. I ran right out of the dugout to check on him.

I said, "Stretch, we're getting you out of here. Let's go back inside and get some heat on that back and knee." He looked at me.

He then said, "Skipper, give me a minute. I'll be fine in a moment, and I might come up again later in the game with the chance to help our club win."

He was really adamant about it. I knew he meant what he said. He wanted to be left in that ball game. Tom Gorman, the umpire, understood the situation and he gave Willie all the time he needed, which was much appreciated by me. Willie went on to strike out that time at bat. However, as he predicted, he came up one more time in that game—in the ninth inning! He hit a two-run homer in the top of the ninth inning to give us the lead. Frank Linzy, our relief pitcher, held the Astros in the bottom of the ninth to preserve the win that McCovey had delivered for us. McCovey was a real pro and team player. I wish there were more players like him.

I can remember going on a trip with Willie to Honolulu, Hawaii, to conduct some baseball clinics. Cappy Harada arranged that trip for us, and Willie and I had a great opportunity to talk baseball together. He told me some things about hitters and pitchers and tendencies that I still remember to this day. He told me what he looked for in pitchers. He said that sometimes a pitcher would go way back over his head with his hands when he would throw a fastball. He said the reason for that was pitchers often tried to really put a lot of muscle into their fastball and so they tipped you off that a fastball was coming by bringing their hands farther back over their head so that they would have maximum velocity. In contrast, he said that when a pitcher wanted to throw a curveball he would not bring his hands as far back over his head in his delivery. He also told me that if a pitcher was in the middle of his windup, and you as a hitter could not see much of the baseball showing in his hand, it was a fastball. If the pitcher was going to throw a curveball, then most of the ball would be visible to the batter during the delivery. He reasoned that this was due to the natural motion and grip that a pitcher needed to deliver a fastball versus a curveball.

We also talked at length about pregame preparation. He never lost his cool. If he struck out, he never threw his bat or got angry. Never. He was always in total control. I was hoping that his demeanor would show some of the mediocre players on the Giants, who had temper tantrums, that a real MVP doesn't act that way. He had the right attitude. His Hall of Fame plaque in Cooperstown proves that—because he's there, and our crybaby .220 hitters are not.

Willie McCovey honestly didn't need much instruction. He didn't need any, in fact. Willie had a groove swing, and he and Gil Hodges were two of the best I've ever seen at scooping balls up that were thrown in the dirt to first base. Willie could handle all the low throws from the infielders. In fact, that's how he got his nickname "Stretch." We called him "Stretch" because it seemed like he could stretch halfway across the infield. He had great soft hands. He and Ted Kluszewski could hit pitches thrown on the outside part of the plate and pull them into the right field seats with ease.

Not many players could do that. Hank Aaron could do it. To be able to hit a pitch on the outside part of the plate and pull it into the seats is some feat. Willie was the best at this. Willie was the type of hitter who everyone watched when he went into the batting cage. The younger players used to love to talk with him, especially Ken Henderson (our right fielder), Jim Ray Hart, and Tito Fuentes. They used to sit around with McCovey and talk baseball.

Juan Marichal

Juan Marichal also made managing easy in San Francisco. Marichal did all the great things on the mound and yet, if you were an instructor, you'd never teach a young pitcher to pitch like him. He had that high leg kick and his arm was way down there almost touching the ground, but to each his own. If you can do it well, then do it. He did. Marichal was a fiery guy. He had a little bit of a temper, but overall he kept his temper in control very well. Marichal was a great competitor. He'd get men on in a close game in the late innings, and he'd just reach back and put something extra on the ball. He'd blow hitters away. He was special. He was a gamer too. He went out there and pitched every fourth day. He was a winner.

Touring Japan and the Lotte Orions

There have been times when Norma and I have been able to travel together. The first time we visited Japan was in the fall of 1969. The thing that Norma, I know, remembers about that trip is that we had fresh flowers in our room every morning. We have Cappy Harada to thank for our wonderful times in Japan. He worked for the San Francisco Giants in Community Relations/Public Affairs, and when we moved out to San Francisco he was there to meet us. He introduced us to restaurants and did everything for us. Cappy was Mr. Stoneham's right-hand man and he was a right-hand man for another great military figure, General Douglas MacArthur. He was MacArthur's interpreter and aide in World War II in Manila (the Philippines) and in the South Pacific. When we first arrived in San Francisco he helped Norma and me find our house and got food for us and stocked our refrigerator. He took care of us from day one. He was a great guy, with a nice family, and he arranged for me to go to Japan and instruct the players and give clinics. Cappy was with us all of the time. We could not have gotten along without him.

When we left San Francisco for Tokyo, we first went to Honolulu for three days to rest and to get adjusted to the different time zone so that it wouldn't feel like such a long trip. I'll never forget the press conference when we arrived in Tokyo. They had a tray of alcoholic drinks for all of the media and team officials. At the edge of the tray they had two glasses of orange juice, and they said that the glasses of juice were for Norma and me. They told us that our reputation had preceded us. This pleased us very much.

Tokyo was wonderful. We took a trip on the fast train, called the "Bullet," that was going to Kyoto. We had never ridden on a train like that before. From Kyoto we went to Osaka where they were getting ready for the World's Fair, and everywhere we went people were polite to us. We bought pearls there and they were beautiful.

Watching the Japanese players was interesting. In those days, 1970, the pitchers there did not throw hard at all. They were curveball pitchers and trick pitchers. We did not see a single pitcher there who threw the ball real hard. Today, things have changed. Juan Marichal and Gaylord Perry talked me into using our American baseballs, the reason being that the "grip" was different. Also, the stitches on the Japanese balls were not as pronounced as on the American balls. The Japanese baseballs were not as lively. In Japan, the center-field fence is about 310 feet from home plate, and the right-field fence is about 260 feet because of the use of a deader ball. So, we started using our baseballs; the balls were leaving the park like mad. Our guys were hitting them out of sight and so were theirs.

The Japanese players conditioned 10 months out of the year, and their conditioning was superb. When the season ended, the players would be required to stay in uniform and do exercises. For example, they would lay flat on their stomachs and then get up and run 40 or 60 yards when the coach blew the whistle. They'd do this drill over and over again. They were literally in uniform 10 months out of the year, that's how dedicated they were to their sport.

I told Norma when we went over there that I wanted to be an ambassador for America and for baseball. I wanted to learn to eat with chopsticks, which we did. I wanted to eat everything they put in front of us, and I almost did. Norma could do it. The one thing I couldn't eat was sushi.

We were at a dinner one night with Mr. Nagata, the owner of the Hitachi Motion Picture Company. He owned the Lotte Orions. The Japanese officials had invited us to dinner and we were thrilled. This was before I knew what sushi was. We were at the dinner table, Norma and Cappy sitting beside me. Norma ate everything and loved it all and Cappy did as well. Everyone who knows me well knows that I hate fish. I never have eaten it, and the thought of eating raw fish made me weak. Cappy, who always sat next to me, saw the look on my face when the sushi was placed in front of me. I whispered to him that I really couldn't eat it. He said, "When I finish mine, you slide yours over here and I'll give you my empty dish." That was the only thing I didn't eat.

In 1970 I visited Japan for the second time. The Giants were invited there for a series of games. For the opening day ceremony Mr. Stoneham, the Giants owner, joined us as the two teams walked into the stadium from right field, side by side to home plate. Mr. Stoneham was supposed to deliver the acceptance speech. But knowing he was very shy I felt he wouldn't speak. It must have been "divine guidance" for me to prepare in the event that Mr. Stoneham got cold feet. Cappy helped me write a speech in Japanese. I tucked the speech into my baseball cap. When the procession of players reached home plate, Mr. Stoneham, sure enough, said to me, "Clyde, would you do the acceptance speech for me?" If I hadn't felt that Mr. Stoneham might do that I would have been dead.

When we doffed our caps to the fans, I read my speech, which was inside my cap, in the Japanese language. The fans loved it; they went crazy. There were several thousand people in the stands, maybe as many as fifty thousand. Cappy really made it possible for me to speak the Japanese language and to be a good baseball ambassador. He was invaluable to me and to Norma, and I reflect on those times spent with Cappy with much delight. I really have him to thank for the great times that my family and I enjoyed in Japan—and in San Francisco.

I saw Sadaharu Oh, the Japanese "Home Run King," and I thought he could play in America, but he did have a little trouble with our ace's fastballs. That was because by the nature of the game there he didn't see many fastballs. He could handle curveballs because that was what he was used to seeing. What I also remember about that trip was that for our players, physically, it was a disaster. Our players were not in very good shape because we traveled there in the middle of spring training, and to top it off some got injured. A few players came back battling viruses. The temperature in Phoenix was almost 90° when we left; when we landed in Japan it was 37°.

Fired After 44 Games

My San Francisco days came to an abrupt end. I remember the day I was fired vividly for two reasons: first, the day happened to be my birthday, May 23; and second, my daughter Princie was in college and had her finals the very next day. It seemed like only yesterday that we had finished in second place in my rookie managerial debut in 1969. We were two games out from winning the pennant and maybe going to a World Series! All of a sudden it was my birthday in

1970, and here I was fired just 44 games into the season. This was right after I had taken that Giants ball club to a 92-win season. I wasn't thinking of myself now, but rather of Princie. It was her sophomore year in college, and the press conference announcing my firing was on the six o'clock news. Norma and I were trying to get word to Princie at Westminister College before she saw it on the news that night. She had her finals the next day, and the last thing we wanted was for her to be sobbing and worrying about Daddy that night. Well, Princie heard the news before we could get word to her and went to pieces. She was so upset that anybody would fire her dad. You see, to the public I'm the manager, but to my daughters I'm Dad. For me, as a baseball person, this came with the territory, but for Princie and the girls it was really rough. This was where David Hartman really saved the day.

David Hartman, who later went on to host *Good Morning America,* was at that time a Hollywood actor in the television series *The Bold Ones.* I had gotten to know David because he had asked if he could work out with the Giants during spring training. I had arranged with our public relations department for his workout, and he had a great time training with the team for a few days. He became good friends with Norma and me, and when I was fired he was one of the first people to call me. He had asked me if there was anything he could do for me. I told him that actually there was, indeed, something he could do for me. I asked him if he would call Princie because she was very upset and her college finals were the very next day. Sure enough, David came through and called Princie. I had given David the pay-phone number at her dormitory on her floor, and he called her that very night. They talked for half an hour, Princie later told me, and she said that he cheered her up and that she never forgot his kindness. It meant a lot to me personally because I knew, after having spoken to David and feeling better about the whole situation, that Princie could concentrate on her exams the next day and perform well, and she did.

I remember coming home from that long plane ride after being fired, and walking into the house and, low and behold, the house was filled with friends—even our preacher was there. I looked around the room, surveyed the whole situation, and saw all of the great food spread out there, only there were loads of long faces. I said, "The corpse is alive. Let's turn this thing into a party," and everybody started to laugh. I didn't want everyone standing around feeling sorry for me with melancholy looks on their faces.

I remember that summer of 1970 so well. It was the first summer in my adult life that I had ever spent home in Goldsboro. Every summer since my involvement with professional baseball in 1944 was spent with a ball club. This year was different. Princie and Norma were taking summer classes at UNC Chapel Hill that summer, and I can remember walking down Franklin Street with Princie and Norma. It was a special feeling. I really cherish the summer that I spent with my girls and with my wife. I knew that good tidings were right around the corner for me and sure enough, good news was getting ready to rear its happy face.

15

My Years with the Atlanta Braves

WHAT I REMEMBER MOST ABOUT MY DAYS IN ATLANTA IS TAKING over as manager for Eddie Mathews at the All-Star break in 1974, thanks to Eddie Robinson. Our team was not a very good team at the time. Eddie Robinson was our general manager and I was sort of his assistant. He asked me to take over as manager and I did. After I was fired in San Francisco, Paul Richards, who was the one-time general manager of the Braves, hired me to manage Richmond, which was the Braves AAA farm team, and I did that in 1971 and 1972.

There, a young player by the name of Tony LaRussa was play-ing for us. Tony was an aggressive player. He was a hustler. He got the very most out of his ability as a player. He wanted to play in the big leagues. He asked me if I could help him, and I tried. The Cubs later gave him a chance. He didn't have a whole lot of power, but he was a smart player and used his head on the field and helped us win ball games. He hit .312 that year. He didn't have a real strong arm, but he knew how to get to the bag quickly and make a double play. It's not surprising to me that he became such an outstanding man-ager. I remember when the Yankees were playing the A's in Oakland. Tony came over to me and put his arm around me and told me what a good influence I had on him. He is another of my players that I'm proud of.

In 1973 Eddie Robinson became general manager of the Braves and brought me up from Richmond to be his assistant. I was there in 1973, and in the middle of 1974 I got my second chance to be a big league manager. Eddie Robinson was such a wonderful guy. Not only was he a good player when he played for the White Sox and Yankees, but he was a fine general manager. He was cordial. He was a gentleman. He was suave. He knew how to negotiate with players and was a great judge of talent. Eddie was intelligent, and he really knew how to bring out the best in his front-office personnel, especially me. He never lost his cool and he was a really good listener. You could go to Eddie with any problem, whether it was a baseball problem or a social problem, and he would listen to you and give you great advice. Once a player went to him for advice on hitting and he told that player to go back to his manager, Luman Harris, and ask if it was OK to talk to him. Harris would always say that it was fine, and then Eddie spoke with the player. You see, he wasn't about to talk to anybody behind the manager's back. Eddie was a real baseball fan. He loved to watch batting practice and was always around, but he was not a hands-on guy unless asked. He also loved crab legs and so he gets an "A" in eating from me.

I had a good relationship with our players. We played the best baseball in the National League from the All-Star break onward. We were 10 games over .500 during that streak. The players just gave 100 percent and played well. We had some good players on that team: Dusty Baker, Hank Aaron, and Phil Niekro. Davey Johnson was on that team as well. Darrell Evans was our third baseman, and Hank Aaron, of course, was our right fielder. I enjoyed Atlanta. It was a good city in those days. It was a good place to live and a good place to raise children. I had started my managerial career in Atlanta in 1955 with the old Atlanta Crackers, so it was nice to be back there.

Hank Aaron: A True Legend in the Game

It was nice to manage Hank Aaron. As I mentioned before, I'm the only manager to manage both Hank Aaron and Willie Mays. Hank was a great ballplayer. My first remembrance of him was when I was managing the Giants, and his Braves visited us at Candlestick. I remember how much we feared him. Hank Aaron could beat you in more ways than one. He could beat you with his bat and his glove. When I finally got to manage in Atlanta, I was relieved and pleased. I got to see first-hand, on a daily basis, his power at the plate. He still had a lot of power even in his final years as a player. He just knew how to play the game. He was very laid back. He didn't argue with the umpires. He didn't get himself involved in controversies with the opponents. He just went out and played the game.

Aaron had a strong arm and was a great outfielder. He was also a good base runner. I don't think a lot of people realize that aspect of his game. Whenever I would mention that he was a great base runner in my talks, people would look surprised. It was no surprise to me, having managed Hank. He was a great base runner with great instincts on the base paths. He was also great in the outfield. He had good hands, good range, and he knew how to play hitters. He just knew their hitting tendencies. He also knew how to position himself in the outfield. For instance, if a hitter hit a ball down the right field line, he would move over a little bit toward the line so that he was in perfect position by the time the ball reached the outfield. He knew which hitters could not hit the ball deeply, and so he played them shallow in the outfield. If a hitter was known to hit more balls to right center, he would shift toward center. He was such a smart fielder. I would like people to realize that he was both a smart hitter and a smart fielder because he really did do both well. He could hit for average and hit for power.

Hank Aaron's home runs and the RBIs attest to the fact that he was great. He simply could do it all. I've always said he was the most consistent home-run hitter that I've ever had the privilege to see play the game, and I've seen most of the Hall of Famers. He just hit home runs day in and day out, and they always meant something. Those runs either tied games or won them for us. He had strong hands, great wrists, and a quick bat. He was the only person I know who could literally wait until the last minute when the ball was almost on top of him, and, with his great wrists and great bat, hit that ball right out of the catcher's glove. He was that great a player. He's a credit to this game of baseball, and I think he's handled himself well since he retired as a player. A true legend of the game—my only regret is that I never got to manage him at the beginning of his brilliant career.

A Young Kid Named Johnnie B. "Dusty" Baker

Dusty Baker was a real bear-down type player. He worked on things during batting practice. He didn't just try to hit home runs. He wanted to be a complete ballplayer. I remember him coming out early at 4 P.M. for extra batting practice. Dusty was one of those players who always wanted to come out early and work on things to improve himself. He came to play. He loved the game. He was a clutch hitter. He had good work habits and a great personality. I loved him. I really loved having him play for me. He was a really good outfielder, a good player, and a real hustler. He was a tough out at the plate and came through in the clutch. He could run a ball down in the outfield that you just knew would drop in for a hit, and he'd turn that hit into an out.

Dusty had great instincts. I don't think I ever saw Dusty make a mistake and throw to the wrong base. He had such great instincts on the base paths as well. I don't remember him getting thrown out at third, either. He either knew for sure he'd make it or he'd stop at second base. I've said he was a tough out at the plate, and that's because he always hung in there. If you threw one under his chin, he'd get right back in there, and the next pitch would be a hit or a hard line drive. I'm really proud of him. When I was in the hospital in 1991 after having an operation, Dusty was one of the players who called me on the phone to wish me well and I so appreciated his call. He really cheered me up. Dusty won the National League Manager of the Year award in 1997, and it was well-deserved. I was thrilled when I heard the news. He did wonders with those Giants ballplayers and with that ball club. Dusty is one of my favorite players.

16

My New York Yankee Days

Mr. Steinbrenner and the Meaning of Loyalty

TED TURNER BOUGHT THE BRAVES IN 1976, AND EDDIE ROBINSON was out as general manager. Gabe Paul, the general manager of the Yankees, called me and wanted me to come to the Yankees right away to do some scouting. I told him that I couldn't do that because I had a contract with the Braves and that I was going to honor it. He called the Braves and called me back one night at midnight and said that he had permission from the Braves to talk to me about coming to the Yankees. I told him that I really did not want to leave until the end of the season. He said that they needed me right then and there. I then told him that I would come—now that Eddie Robinson was out, I was a stranger in the Braves organization. I went to the Yankees in September of 1976, and I've been with them ever since.

I came on board just before the playoffs. That was the year we lost to Sparky Anderson's Cincinnati Reds in the World Series. Even though we lost, Mr. Steinbrenner was generous enough to make an American League Championship ring for each of us. The next year was 1977 and that year was special. It was quite a year. The fans were behind us. I was in two prior World Series with the Yankees, only I was playing for the old Brooklyn Dodgers and the Yankees beat us. Now, being with the Yankees, it was special to be a part of the World Series atmosphere on the winning side.

George M. Steinbrenner III

I have worked for Mr. Steinbrenner for 23 years (as of 1999) and counting, and I have enjoyed these many years more than any I've spent in my 56 years in baseball! He is a brilliant and articulate man, a tireless worker, a hands-on type boss, and always—and I repeat, always—knows what is going on with his ball club. The Boss doesn't ask his people to do anything that he would not do himself. He always knows when you've done well and deep down in his heart appreciates your efforts. On the other hand, if you "screw up," he lets you know it loud and clear and in no uncertain terms. After all, isn't this the Boss's prerogative?

One of the nicest things about George is that he does not carry a grudge. Now there are some who will disagree with this, but just look at all those who have left the Yankees on their own, or who were fired, and he has brought them back to work for him again.

Mr. Steinbrenner is one of the most generous men I have ever known. It would be impossible to count the number of young people he has helped through college. I could list, to my personal knowledge, many, maybe hundreds more, that he has helped in some way, but he does not like this to be known. Suffice to say he has shared with those who are in need.

I have never disagreed with his motives but have, once in a great while, disagreed with his methods. However, even then he would turn out to be right more often than not.

George Steinbrenner can hold his own with anybody in any situation. He is an outstanding orator and can speak on any subject. I have said many times to my wife, Norma, and to our baseball friends that Mr. Steinbrenner would have made a great baseball commissioner. If he had been commissioner, baseball would be in a much better position than it is now.

It is a misconception spoken by some people that Mr. Steinbrenner does not know anything about baseball, or that he truly doesn't let his baseball people run the team. The Boss knows a great deal about baseball and has built the Yankees into the greatest sports organization in the world. Just think back to where the Yankees were in 1973 when he bought the team, and where they are now. He restored the "pride and tradition" of the era of Ruth and Gehrig, DiMaggio and Mantle, Berra and Maris to the New York Yankees.

The Yankees are, and have been, since Mr. Steinbrenner took over ownership, first class. When the team would fly into Newark at three or four o'clock in the morning he would have cars waiting to take the players and their wives to their homes quickly to get a good night's rest. Oftentimes on the road he would have food sent to our hotel rooms, knowing that at such a late hour restaurants would be closed. He also made sure we had balanced meals on our chartered plane flights.

Finally, has it been easy working for the Boss for all these years? Yes and no. He expects his people to work 25-hours-a-day and 366-days-a-year, if necessary, because he would, and does, himself. Mr. Steinbrenner expects his people to be totally and entirely dedicated to his organization, and I have been over the years.

I have nothing but complete respect for Mr. Steinbrenner. He is my boss and I respect his authority. As long as I continue to work for him, and I hope this will be forever, I will always respect and admire him for what he has done for me and my family and what he has done for baseball.

My wish is that everyone, especially those who are constantly bashing him, could know him like I do! I do not regret one single year I've been with him, and it has been a real exciting experience.

Several years ago I spoke at the Raleigh, North Carolina, Sports Club and for 30 minutes said nothing but good, positive things about Mr. Steinbrenner and received a standing ovation. They were not standing for me, but they were standing because of all of the nice things they had heard about my boss. Several men came over to me afterward and said, "Are all those things true about Mr. Steinbrenner?" Of course my answer was yes!

So you can see that the Boss is a pretty decent person after all. Yes, I wish everyone could know him like I know him. Then they would feel the same as I do about him. He is the best boss I've ever had—except for Norma.

The 1978 Boston Massacre

Even when Mr. Steinbrenner is impulsive, he usually proves to be correct. The 1978 Boston Massacre is one such example. I was in uniform as a pitching coach during that season, and he told me to get out of uniform and follow the Boston Red Sox for several days in order to get a scouting report to be used for our upcoming four-game series at Fenway Park. I told him I just could not possibly leave the team and my pitchers, as I had several things I was working on with some of the pitchers.

"Let Jerry Walker take over for you. I want you to go and watch the Red Sox and see if you can pick up anything that could help us," he said.

I had that hesitancy in my manner, still not convinced of his plan.

He said, "Who's the boss?"

I replied, "You are!"

He followed with, "Then go." And I did.

During that week I scouted the Red Sox pitching staff so that I would be able to instruct our Yankees players on their tendencies. I also took note of the Red Sox hitters and how they were hitting during that week. I made notes of who was hot and who wasn't. The biggest piece of information that I acquired was quite by accident. After all, nobody tells you their secrets deliberately. I was sitting at Fenway one day watching batting practice. I happened to arrive there really early and nobody was in the stands at the time. It was well before the game, so only a few Sox players were out there on the field. Carlton Fisk was one of the players taking extra hitting that afternoon. He was their biggest clutch player, and any information that we could obtain relating to his tendencies would greatly help our ball club during that upcoming series. My attention was focused on Carlton Fisk as he was taking batting practice. At the time I thought that he was having trouble with balls pitched inside because of a recent hand injury. I was curious to see if this indeed was the case. I said "hello" to one of the players out there to try to get a conversation going.

He saw me sitting in the stands and said "You're out awfully early" in a surprised voice.

I said, "There's nothing to do at the hotel, and I just love to come out early and sit in the ballpark, and watch you guys workout."

He didn't know that I was there especially to watch that batting practice and pick up information that would help us. I observed that Fisk was having trouble with balls that were inside. It looked like his hand might be bothering him. I made a note of this so we could take full advantage of it.

When the Yankees arrived in Boston, I rejoined the team and got back in uniform. I gave my report to our manager, Bob Lemon, who had replaced Billy Martin during the week of July 24th that season. The report explained how we should play the Red Sox hitters defensively. This report included aspects of the game such as the positioning of the infielders and outfielders. As for Carlton Fisk, our pitchers threw mostly fastballs inside to Fisk, and we had good luck with him in the series. The scores from that four-game series were 15–3, 13–2, 7–0, and 7–4. Carlton Fisk went two for nine in that series. Jim Rice went 2 for 11. The two power hitters for the Red Sox were a combined 4 for 20, and those were two of the feared threesome, the third being Carl Yastrzemski. Yaz went o for 11 in that sweep of the Sox. Scouting reports help, though they do not win games; players win the games.

Whether my report had anything to do with our success in those four games is debatable. We won all four games and swept Boston, and we were on our way to a playoff and another World Series, and that's all that mattered.

So you see that even though I did not think that this was the right thing to do, the Boss insisted that I go, and once again he was correct in his decision.

The One Game Playoff in 1978

We ended up in a tie with Boston at the end of the season and won the one game playoff on Bucky Dent's three-run home run in the top of the ninth inning at Fenway Park. During batting practice I went out onto the infield with Bucky Dent and said to Bucky, "If Catfish is pitching you'll play the right-handed hitters over in the hole a little bit more. If Ron Guidry is pitching you play Jim Rice straight away because he's going to be a little slower getting around on Guidry's fastball than he will be on Hunter's fastball." The report showed things such as the Red Sox hitters who would hit and run, the hitters who were first-ball hitters, fastball hitters, high-ball hitters, and curveball hitters, and the guys who might steal or bunt for a hit.

I can still see Carl Yastrzemski in that summer series hitting three or four ferocious line drives that were caught, and I also remember him being quoted by the Boston papers as saying, "I can't believe it. It looks like they know exactly where I'm going to hit the ball before I hit it because they're always standing in front of my line drives," or something to that effect.

October 2, however, will last in my memory forever. It was a special one-game playoff between the Yankees and Red Sox to see who would advance to play Kansas City for the pennant. It was a gem of a game. Lou Piniella made a fantastic play in right field. A ball was hit to him by Fred Lynn that was a bullet. He lost it in that terrible sun that plagues many a right fielder at Fenway. However, he didn't give up, and he ended up making a complete turn-around and fielded that ball and got it back to the infield quickly.

Then came the big blast. Bucky Dent rose to the occasion and hit a home run over the Green Monster in left field that those sitting in

Fenway Park will never forget. This one-game playoff meant everything. The season was on the line. Bucky went to the plate, fouled a
pitch off his foot, and went back into the dugout. He used Mickey
Rivers's bat because his bat was cracked. He came to the plate and
the rest is history. Fenway Park after Bucky Dent's three-run home
run was just exactly like it was when they found out Babe Ruth was
traded to the Yankees, quiet as a mouse. Mr. Steinbrenner and Al
Rosen, our general manager, were sitting next to the Yankees dugout
clapping, and all of us in the dugout were jubilant. Carl Yastrzemski
made the final out by popping up to third baseman Graig Nettles.
That ball seemed as if it would never come down, but when it did we
all poured out on the field to rejoice.

Whoever won the game was going on to the playoffs to play
Kansas City. Inside the right field area were buses for the Red Sox
and buses for the Yankees. If we lost we would have gotten on our
bus, gone back to the airport, and flown to New York. If the Red
Sox lost, being at home, they would take their luggage off their
transportation truck, put it in their cars, and go home. I can remember sitting on the bus, after our celebration in the visitor's clubhouse,
watching the Red Sox coming out with their wives and children and
getting their luggage off their truck. It was a sad scene. I felt sorry for
them. I knew that if we had not won that game, we'd be on our way
home. They had a 14$^{1}/_{2}$-game lead on us, and we caught them and
beat them in this one-game playoff to see who would play for the
pennant. It brought back memories of that 1951 season in Brooklyn
when we had a 13$^{1}/_{2}$-game lead and the Giants caught us. I knew the
feeling. I had been on both sides of the fence. Only now my team
was the one tickled to death that we were going to Kansas City to
play the Royals for the American League pennant.

Well, here it was October 3 and we were in Kansas City. We
couldn't reflect too much on the win we had the night before because
the Royals had been waiting for us. I can remember that many
thought we might lose that first game because of the hectic playing
schedule. Well, we won that first game 7–1. The second night was not
a good night for us, as we lost that game 10–4, but the Yankees, in
typical Yankees tradition, came back at home to win the series three
games to one. At that time the pennant was the best three-out-of-five
series. The World Series that year was special to me as well. The
Yankees–Dodgers rivalry was renewed in New York. I was on the
other side this time. Jim Beattie performed well, pitching a complete
game, as did Ron Guidry. Reggie Jackson again carried us with the
long ball, and the Yankees and Dodgers had played back-to-back

World Series for the first time since 1955 and 1956. It was great to witness it all in person as a coach.

Memorable Assignments

I have had many special assignments and enjoyed each. If I helped a pitcher with his mechanics or with his confidence, I felt it was my job. I've worked with the greats that have worn the pinstripes since 1976, most of the time at Mr. Steinbrenner's request. Well, having said that, here are some interesting stories, or assignments, as I recall them.

Jim Beattie was one such assignment that I enjoyed. It was during the 1978 season. Jim was playing on our Triple A club at the time, and he had been struggling. Mr. Steinbrenner asked me to take a look at him and see if I could diagnose the problem. I said fine and checked the Tacoma schedule to see when I could meet up with Jim to take a look at him. As it turned out, at that point in the season the Tacoma club was playing in Hawaii. Hawaii was in the Triple A International League that year, and teams traveled to Hawaii to play road games. Needless to say, it was a big commute. I reported back to Mr. Steinbrenner and told him that they would be in Hawaii for a week and that I thought I'd wait until they got back to talk to Jim. He said, "Oh, no. You go and do it right away and see if you can straighten this guy out." He always wants you to do it "now." So, I went to Hawaii as quickly as I could. When I got there Hall of Famer Hoyt Wilhelm was the pitching coach. He was cooperative and helpful. What I did for Jim was eliminate his big windup and give him a no-windup delivery. Jim Beattie was a tall guy, about 6'4". He started using this no-windup delivery and I worked with him on his slider a little bit, and he came back and won a game in the World Series for us that year. It was a complete game in fact. His stamina was just fine, and he had adjusted to that no-windup delivery very well. He later became the general manager of the Montreal Expos, in the position to evaluate talent, and he's done a fine job.

Another assignment was becoming the general manager. I remember a couple of tasks quite well; one was the hiring of Woody Woodward as my assistant, at Mr. Steinbrenner's request. It was terrific having him there; he and I picked Lou Piniella as our manager in 1986. Mr. Steinbrenner told us that we could choose between Lou Piniella and Billy Martin. We decided to give Lou the chance to be the skipper. So, we ended up giving Lou Piniella his first managerial job. He did a great job. We finished in second place that season under Lou, and he later went on to win a World Series with the Reds. The Mariners ended up with two of my guys—Piniella and Woodward. They have done very well with the Seattle club.

As a player, Lou Piniella always wanted to learn. He would ask me things all the time about pitchers and what they threw in different situations. As a hitter, he especially liked to talk about hitting because he knew that as a pitcher I would know certain tendencies that pitchers have on certain counts. Lou performed well in the clutch in 1978 during the Boston Massacre and he has performed well as a manager.

Another assignment from Mr. Steinbrenner was Jim "Catfish" Hunter. This Hall of Famer was a pitching sensation, and he didn't need help, really. However, he was having a bit of arm trouble after the season had ended. It was December and Mr. Steinbrenner told me to go to Catfish and see what was up. This was December, remember, the players were home with their families getting ready for the holidays. I told him I would go after the New Year because everybody was busy with Christmas in December. He said, "I want you to go *now*." So Norma talked to his wife Helen by phone and I talked to Jimmy. I told him what my mission was, and he said, "Fine, come on down." So off Norma and I went to Hertford, North Carolina. I told him to find us a motel, but he said, "No, stay with us." We spent the night with them. Now there I was on an assignment to supposedly help a guy who pitched in World Series after World Series, had 20-win seasons, and was destined for the Hall of Fame. It seemed odd to me. However, there I was, miles away from home in December trying to "help" him out. We were up in his attic, and I told him that I needed to see some pictures from his days with Oakland to really look at his delivery. I wanted to look at some pictures of him during his best days with Oakland at the height of his career. His wife, Helen, found many for me. I detected something in his delivery after looking at the photos, and we went into his living room and talked about it. He went through his windup and saw the difference between him at this time and his mechanics in those glory days. Well, whatever help it might have been, he came back and helped us win again. That was just another assignment, all stemming from Mr. Steinbrenner.

Doug Melvin was a batting-practice pitcher with us and I helped him become the director of scouting for the Yankees. He started out working the speed gun for us, then pitching at batting practice. I made him scouting director. Mr. Steinbrenner questioned me about bringing a guy up without a lot of experience, but I got to know Doug real well. I knew that he was intelligent and thoughtful. He didn't make decisions irrationally. He was not a guy who would look at a player one time and determine whether he could play or not. Like me, and Mr. Rickey before me, he looked at players on many occasions to determine their ability. Mr. Rickey always said, "Don't ever get too high or too low on a player too quickly because if you do, he'll turn you wrong side out." Doug was the kind of a guy who gave you an opinion after many looks. He then went on to Baltimore as assistant to general manager Roland Hemond and later he became the general manager of the Texas Rangers. Doug is a great guy. We had a lot of good times together. Doug used to pick me up as he went to Yankee Stadium. That left Norma free with our car to go to the games and to socialize with Doug's wife, Ellen. Doug had a great mind for baseball and has proved it with Texas. These times that we shared with the Melvins were fun. Norma and I lived at the Westchester Country Club in Rye, New York. When the Yankees went on the road, she went to our home in Goldsboro. Westchester was great to us. It gave us a wonderful lifestyle while we were in New York, and our friends Ralph and Ann Branca made the times spent there wonderful.

We also had our friends Barbara and Bob Elmo in that area. They were always attentive to us. Bob has been like a son to me, which is special as I do not have one of my own. I don't know of anyone who does more for other people than Bob and Barbara.

Pinstripe Players and Officials over the Years

Bobby Murcer was a part-time player much of the time I saw him, but I remember once in Oakland he hit a two-run homer for us and it was off their best reliever. I can still see that ball going over the right-center field fence. He was a player whom the Yankees had groomed to take over for Mickey Mantle. He had a distinguished career and was a clutch hitter. Sparky Lyle was another player who made us invincible, teaming with Rich "Goose" Gossage. He could get the job done. People ask me whether or not he was coachable. I tell them the truth, and that is that Sparky just didn't need any coaching. He knew what he had to do, and he always got the job done.

Bob Lemon is also someone I truly enjoyed being around. We won a pennant and a World Series with him. He was a different kind of manager. He was much like Walter Alston. He was low-key. He'd give you the bat and ball and glove and say go play. He'd sit back on the bench and make his moves in a quiet way. He wasn't an ego-type guy. He didn't need to be in the limelight. He would let his pitching coach go out to the mound 90 percent of the time. It was easy to play for him and coach for him. There wasn't any stress or strain or tension. He knew the game. He is a Hall-of-Fame pitcher who once said that baseball is a great kids' game that adults have messed up. He was right.

Bob Watson was such a clutch hitter. He got some big hits for us when we needed them. I'm so happy that he was able to be the general manager for the world champion Yankees in 1996. Bob had a wonderful career in New York. The fans liked him, and I really enjoyed being around him as a coach. He could give you the long ball and the much-needed single when the chips were down.

Don Baylor was another fierce competitor and I'm glad to see he got to manage in the big leagues. He would take a pitcher's best fastball on the arm for the team. He was not afraid of any pitcher. He would take that pitch square off the arm and walk to first base. He wouldn't run out to the mound as players do today. He would just walk to first base and never rub his arm.

Chris Chambliss was another good role model on the field. He was a clutch hitter. The most memorable hit I witnessed in person was that game winner in the playoffs in 1976 that he hit to the deep part of Yankee Stadium. He was like Pee Wee Reese. He was quiet and just did his job.

Barry Halper is another Yankee official whom I truly like and admire. I saw him at spring training in 1998 and visited with him. While the Yankees were on the road one time, he and his wife, Sharon, invited Norma out to their house, and Sharon cooked a Chinese dinner for her. Norma was so impressed when she saw his collection of baseball memorabilia that she could not stop talking about it for days on end. It rivals Cooperstown. It really does. It is an outstanding collection. He's got uniforms and stuff hanging on a rack and it turns on a carousel.

Phil Niekro was a great pitcher who I am happy to say played for me when I managed in Atlanta. He was a strong competitor. He had an outstanding knuckle ball. He was a great team man. He was a lot like Red Schoendienst in that respect. He was the type of person whom a young player could talk to about pitching. In fact, I was responsible for bringing him to New York where he had a real great first year for us and a good second year as well. I just enjoyed managing him. The night that he won his 300th game, he was warming up in the bullpen and he gave me the ball that he warmed up with and said something to me I'll never forget: "Thanks for believing in me." Then he gave me that ball. I'm so happy now that he's in the Hall of Fame.

Don Mattingly is a great player whom I've seen come up through the ranks. I saw him start and finish his career in pinstripes. I have a picture of Don and Yogi and myself that I cherish. He could do it all. He hit 52 doubles one year. He could hit home runs. He could hit to the opposite field. He led the league in batting. Don Mattingly could do everything on the field except run fast. He was a good base runner and by that I mean he had good instincts, but he was not a fast runner. He was an outstanding first baseman. To say he could field well is an understatement. He could hit all types of pitchers, whether they were left-handers, right-handers, hard throwers, or change-up type pitchers. I'm sorry that injuries cut his career short. I might be a little biased toward Don because I'm such a Mattingly fan, but I would vote for him if I was given a vote for the Hall of Fame. Don Mattingly was just super. He was good for the game on the field and good for the game off the field. He never did anything to ever embarrass the Yankees. He could have gone to two or three other teams when he left us, but he chose to stay and finish his career with the Yankees. Don was, again, one of the throwbacks to a bygone era of players who played through pain and helped the team. You couldn't get him out of uniform. Don was a real captain, both on the field and in the clubhouse. I'm so glad that the Yankees had a day for him. It's rare in this day of free agency to see a player play his entire career for one team. "Donnie Baseball" did just that. He was all New York Yankees.

Yogi Berra and I hit it off immediately. Our relationship jelled into a great, treasured friendship when I went to the Yankees. Yogi's a baseball man and so am I. That's the thing that drew us together immediately. We loved to talk baseball. When we were together we didn't talk about golf or playing cards, we talked baseball. Yogi's got a great wife in Carmen. Norma and Carmen have things in common and get along great together, and I just enjoy talking to Yogi. He's a smart man. He's the best judge of knowing when to leave a pitcher in or when to take a pitcher out that I've ever been associated with in 56 years in baseball. He is the best judge of that by far, and I'm sure it's because he was a catcher, notably a Hall of Fame catcher. Yogi is one of the few great players who became a good manager. He took the Yankees in 1964 and the Mets in 1973 to pennants. Yogi was great at detecting the little things that showed that a pitcher was tiring. When Yogi was a coach he did everything, and I mean everything, to help every Yankee manager. He would take the heat off of their shoulders. He would talk to players and do the job of motivating these guys to work out properly.

Yogi had called me during the winter and said he wanted to make a reliever out of Dave Righetti. He said that Dave could come into a ball game in the ninth inning with a man on third and strike out the hitter because of his good fastball. If he came in to relieve in the eighth inning and the game went into the tenth or eleventh inning, Dave was strong enough and durable enough having been a starter to stay in there and pitch right on through those innings. I told him we could try it. Dave went along with the idea and went on to become the "Rolaids Relief Man." Dave used to come in and challenge hitters with his best stuff. He wasn't afraid to throw his fastball to anyone. His best pitch was his fastball, and he threw it for strikes. This is just another remembrance of something that involved my pal Yogi. I'm happy that Yogi is back with the Yankees.

Reggie Jackson and I have often talked about non-baseball related matters. I've told him that I thought he should get married. Reggie was an intense player. I went to former Dodger Junior Gilliam's funeral with Reggie. Reggie spoke at the funeral and did an excellent job.

Reggie was a tough out. They called him "Mr. October" because when the game was on the line, he was ready to produce. He wanted to be at bat. He wanted to be a hero. In 1977 he was a hero. He had three home runs in one World Series game, and I was upstairs in Yankee Stadium when he hit them. I had done the advance scouting that year, and I was proud of Reggie for his great performance. I was at the ballpark that night to see him hit those three home runs, the last one a great shot to dead center field into those special stands out there. I once told Reggie, "If you would concentrate when there's nobody on base like you do when men are in scoring position, you could hit .300." I think one year he did come close to hitting .300.

Catfish Hunter's best pitch was his fastball. He had great control and could throw that fastball through the eye of a needle. Catfish once pitched a nine-inning game against Baltimore and threw only one breaking pitch the whole game. He won the game. Imagine that! He was a real money pitcher. If it was the last game of the World Series or a game needed to win the pennant, Catfish would be one of the guys who could deliver that win for the team. Catfish loved to tell a story about "Old Bob" from Hertford, North Carolina, and it went this way: Old Bob was a fisherman and every time he went fishing he brought back a boatload of fish. Nobody in the town could understand how Bob caught so many fish. They couldn't believe it, because whenever one of them would go fishing, they wouldn't catch a thing. Everyone tried to prevail upon Bob to let them accompany him on his next fishing expedition. Bob wouldn't have it. He said that he fished alone. Finally, the game warden, pleading with Old Bob, said, "If you just let me go with you once, I promise I won't tell anybody where your secret place is; I won't tell them how you do it or anything about our fishing trip. I'm just dying of curiosity." Old Bob finally relented and allowed the game warden to accompany him. They boarded Bob's boat and took off to a rather isolated place, and then Bob just dropped an anchor into the water. He reached into his tackle box and took out a big stick of dynamite about 12 inches long, lit it, and threw it in the water. There was a tremendous "boom" that almost capsized the boat. Bob took a net and started filling the empty buckets with dead fish. The game warden was just sitting there shaking his head.

He said, "I'm sorry, Old Bob. I know I promised you, but I'm an officer of the law and I'm going to have to do something about this. This is illegal."

Old Bob reached into that same box, took out a piece of dynamite, lit it, handed it to the game warden, and said, "Now are you going to fish, or are you going to talk?"

Tommy John pitched so many good games for us and I've got so many great things to say about Tommy that I don't know where to begin. First let me say that his wife, Sally, is just a fantastic person. She's a strong woman and a real leader. She's a take-charge person who's pretty and intelligent. Their children are all talented. Their son sang in the Broadway production of *Les Miserables*.

Tommy was the kind of pitcher who never gave up. Infielders loved to play behind him because he pitched quickly. He made a pitch and got the ball back and was ready for the next pitch. He was serious. He was competitive. When I took over as manager we had just played a doubleheader the day before and our bullpen was shot, the coaches told me. My first day on the job as manager of the Yankees we had another doubleheader. Guidry and Gossage were the only two rested pitchers we had. The coaches told me that this was a tough day and that I came aboard at the wrong time. Guidry pitched the first game and pitched eight innings, and Gossage came on in the ninth and we won the game. The second game was Tommy's game. I asked Tommy when he went out if he could do us all a favor and save our bullpen and he quickly interrupted, "Skipper, you don't worry about it. You give me the ball. I'll do it."

This is the way Tommy was, and this was after his arm operation. The fact that he could win 286 games in his career is a tremendous feat, but to do that after having gone through what is now called "The Tommy John Surgery" procedure is really phenomenal. I went back into that dugout and he took care of the game. He shouldered the responsibility of that game for us. He did it for the team. He was a team player.

I also remember when his young son, Travis, fell out of that third-floor window. Tommy's and Sally's faith in God was unbelievable. It sustained them through this terrible ordeal. Travis is fine today. I know that Tommy will do a good job as a broadcaster. I'd like to see him in the Hall of Fame as a pitcher. I think he deserves it.

Danny Kanell, the young up-and-coming quarterback for the Giants football team, is a celebrity whom I've known since he was a youngster. When the Yankees had spring training all those years in Fort Lauderdale, his father, Dan Kanell, was our team doctor, and we became friends. Dr. Kanell is still one of our orthopedic doctors. I used to see young Danny play football, baseball, and basketball games when he was in high school. We used to sit and talk about baseball a lot. He was a catcher and a shortstop in high school and he was as big then as he is now. He probably could have made it in both baseball and basketball if he had wanted to, as I always thought he was equally good in each sport. Pastor O. S. Hawkins, our pastor at First Baptist Church in Fort Lauderdale, would go with me to see young Danny play his high school games. I'm sure it's exciting for Danny to be a professional athlete. He is a fine Christian with great values. He's grown up in a Christian home and his values are sound, and I expect him to be a great role model for everybody, even when his football career is over.

Bill Dowling is another Yankee favorite of mine. Bill was the general counsel in 1986 and then became the executive vice president of the New York Yankees in 1987. Bill is a member of the New England Society and through his membership, I had the opportunity in 1997 to deliver one of my baseball speeches to a unique audience. Although I had spoken at baseball conferences at universities and I had likewise spoken at corporate gatherings, I now was given the rare opportunity to speak to a group of judges and attorneys. The group is made up of lawyers from the Brooklyn and the greater New York City area who have a bond with New England. Bill graduated from Boston College Law School and therefore had ties to New England. I was so well received when I delivered my speech, and I enjoyed reminiscing about my days spent in a Dodgers uniform and my tenure with the Yankees as special advisor.

President Richard Nixon was one of the biggest Yankees fans. One of the big thrills for me was getting to meet President Nixon at the White House. He was one of my favorite people. I know he took a lot of flack. I don't think that it's fair. Anyway, he was a great baseball fan and I knew him as a baseball fan, not as a politician. In fact, it was during my days with the Yankees as GM that I really became well-acquainted with him. He was a regular at Yankee Stadium. He used to say to me when he would first come upstairs to the press level where the Yankees offices are, "Is that charming lady from North Carolina going to be here tonight?" If I said yes then he would immediately say, "Well, I want to sit with her." Norma spent more time with him than I did. I had to concentrate on the game, so she was the one who got to talk with him. She will tell you that he was a gentleman, and, in fact, when our daughter Princie was working on his election campaign, he asked for the names of our other daughters because he wanted to send each member of our family a book autographed by him personally, and he did. I remember during my GM days with the Yankees that he would always write me a note. If the team wasn't doing well, he'd write me a note of encouragement. If the team was doing well, he'd write me a note of congratulations. He always wrote me a note whenever the ball club made a change. It was wonderful to hear from him, and I know Norma really enjoyed the talks she had with him at the stadium. I remember that he once said, "Trade any player, but don't trade Don Baylor. He's my favorite."

My General Manager Days

I had been doing special assignments for Mr. Steinbrenner. I traveled a lot with the team, and he asked me to be general manager. The first time he asked me I said no because I really wanted to spend more time with my family. Well, he asked me again and this time I said yes. Mr. Steinbrenner had been so good to me and to Norma. I took the job with pride. He even told me that I could go home when needed and still be GM. It was perfect for me. I enjoyed my days as GM. I enjoyed making trades. But in my heart I was a uniform man, not an executive. The time I was there I enjoyed it. The hours were long, but I did like the work. We made some good trades. Dealing with Billy Martin was an experience. I signed a five-year contract. I told him that as soon as I could get a young man to take over, I wanted my old job back. I was now in the same managerial position as Branch Rickey, only I was no Branch Rickey by any stretch of the imagination. My heart was always down on the field. Mr. Steinbrenner agreed with me. Mr. Steinbrenner had a friend in Tampa, a writer, who suggested Woody Woodward to him. At that time Woody was working with the Reds. I talked with Woody and he decided to come aboard. Woody was a good man, and when I thought he was ready, I stepped down and Woody took over. I've done everything in baseball that you can do, except be an owner. I've enjoyed it all.

Brian Cashman became general manager of the Yankees in 1998, and I know that this young man will do a terrific job. He has a great ability to develop cordial relationships among baseball executives around the league. When Brian first came aboard as an intern, I realized right away that he was a bright, articulate young man not afraid to carry out any assignment. He was very warm and friendly. I never will forget that one day I was going to drive Norma to the airport when suddenly I was called away on Yankees business. Brian was pleased to take her to the airport for me, and they had a nice visit. I know that Brian will be an asset to the Yankees organization. He has worked for the Yankees for years and knows all areas of the baseball operation.

1998 World Champions

The 1998 Yankees is one of the greatest teams I have ever seen. Their pitching is what placed them in the top of their class with David Wells, David Cone, Andy Pettitte, and Orlando Hernandez. They were solid up and down the lineup and in the field, and they played like a team. Right fielder Paul O'Neill is a real pro in every sense of the word. When he doesn't perform well, he takes it to heart and shows emotion. I don't think there's anything wrong with him showing his emotions and, although I never kicked a water cooler when I played, I myself took to heart a poor performance. He works hard and plays hard and is always thinking at the plate. He thinks about what pitch is coming and how he's going to approach the situation. Paul is a team player. He has a terrific arm in right field and has had many years of great offensive seasons because of his approach to the game. He is a throwback to the old days when a player would put his team first. Joe Torre and his coaches did an outstanding job in 1998, as they did in the two previous years. Seldom do you see a manager and his coaches work together as well as they do. Joe has the perfect temperament with his laid-back approach, and he is always in control in all circumstances. However, he can be demanding and tough when the situation calls for it. He never expects one of his players to do more than he is capable of doing. He requires dedication, hustle, and 100 percent effort. On top of all of these things, he knows the game inside and out and, having been a great player, he understands where his players are coming from. He is the glue that holds the team together.

A young Clyde
(Courtesy of Clyde King)

My parents, Maggie and Claude King
(Courtesy of Clyde King)

The 1944 UNC basketball team; I am number 15.
(Courtesy of the UNC Sports Information Office)

Norma, 1945
(Courtesy of Clyde King)

Norma and I in our Brooklyn home during the 1947 World Series
(Courtesy of Clyde King)

Me, Pee Wee Reese, Carl Erskine, and Duke Snider packing up and
saying good-bye after the last game of the 1951 season
(Courtesy of Clyde King)

On a movie set with actor Robert Stack
(Courtesy of Clyde King)

Two autograph-seekers approach (left to right) Harmon Killebrew,
Roger Maris, Jim Gentile, and me following a 1961 home-run hitting
contest. They asked me to pitch because they thought that I knew how
to throw home runs!
(Courtesy of Clyde King)

Chatting with Ted
Williams at Gillmore
Field in 1957 while I
was managing the
Hollywood Stars
(Courtesy of Clyde King)

My 1960 reunion with Fidel Castro when I was managing the Rochester
Red Wings
(Courtesy of Ramoncito Fernandez)

Talking to the Lotte Orions during the San Francisco Giants' 1969 tour
in Japan
(Courtesy of Clyde King)

Yogi Berra, Don Mattingly, and I in the Yankees clubhouse after a game
(Courtesy of Clyde King)

Discussing game strategy with Reggie Jackson
(Courtesy of Clyde King)

This is my boss,
George Steinbrenner.
*(Copyright © Carl M.
Hofheinz)*

With the legendary Mel Allen at Yankee
Stadium
(Courtesy of Clyde King)

With (left to right) Janet, Norma, Princie, and Normie at my 1983
induction into the North Carolina Sports Hall of Fame
(Courtesy of Clyde King)

Joe DiMaggio and I shortly before his death
(Copyright © Carl M. Hofheinz)

17
My Favorite Book
The Bible

A STRONG FAITH IN GOD HAS BEEN A MAJOR FORCE IN MY LIFE
since I became a Christian at the age of 12. I have spoken at chapel
services before UNC and Duke football games to impress upon these
young athletes and their coaches the importance of total dependence
upon God. Urging them to trust God, not just on the football field,
but also in their lives off the field and away from the stadium. I tried
to instill in my players, wherever I've managed, the importance of
attending church. I started this back in 1956 with the old Atlanta
Crackers. My first effort was not very fruitful, as only three players
showed up at my invitation. At the second invitation I added, "If
you meet me at 8:30 in the morning in the hotel lobby, I'll treat you
guys to breakfast, and then we'll go to church." Can you believe it? —
eleven showed up. What a difference a free breakfast will make, or so
I thought at first. Then, however, I said to myself that a free breakfast could not be the reason for the increase in attendance. Here's
what I found out later on from Mrs. Daniels.

We had a center fielder for the Crackers by the name of Jack
Daniels who was a great ballplayer. He was a good hitter, good base
runner, and had a good arm in center field. His wife told Norma one
time at a game that she was glad her husband was going to church
with me and the other players. She said that her husband never ate
breakfast. This told me that it wasn't me buying him breakfast that
did the trick, but the excuse he used. He had to have an "excuse" to
go to church so that when he was asked by the other players why he
went to church with Clyde King, he could say, "Well, he bought me
breakfast." He really had a desire to go to church and just needed an
excuse to do it. I really believe that this was the start of baseball
chapel. Even though we didn't meet in the ballpark, it was the idea

of getting this group of players to go to church that was the important driving force in creating a concept known as "baseball chapel." It certainly was the start of baseball chapel in Atlanta for the Crackers team.

There is no doubt that the power of prayer and faith in God is the reason that I'm the person that I am today. I believe in family values, and that the father should be the spiritual leader and the head of his family. Baseball has a rule book that tells you how to play the game. There's also a book, called the Bible, that tells you how to live the game of life. My favorite book is the Bible because it contains everything anyone needs in order to live a sucessful, happy, healthy, prosperous, and enjoyable life.

These are some of my favorite Bible verses, most of which I will paraphrase. Of all the Bible verses, Philippians 4:13 is my favorite. It says "I can do all things through Christ who strengthens me." It is impossible for me to tell you how many thousands of times I've claimed this powerful verse.

Another is Second Chronicles 7:14—"If my people who are called by my name will humble themselves and pray and seek my face and turn from their wicked ways, then I'll hear from Heaven and forgive their sins and heal their land." What a lesson this teaches. It is an answer to our universal problems, as well as our personal ones. Just think, God is saying if we, His people, will humble ourselves, pray, and seek His face, and turn from our wicked ways, He will heal our land. This is the solution to straightening out this old world of ours. Just think what a change this would make in our nation if the president, Supreme Court justices, members of congress and the senate, governors, and every city mayor would pray this verse each day.

Another is Romans 12:6, which says that God has given to each of us the ability to do certain things well.

Another verse is Romans 13:10, which says that love does no wrong to anyone.

Proverbs 27:6 is another great passage. It says "Wounds from a friend are better than many kisses from an enemy."

Second Peter 2:19 says that you are a slave to whatever controls you. This can be drugs, alcohol, sex, gambling, pornography, envy, adultery, greed, lust, and I could go on and on, but I think you get the point. The Bible tells us that we are slaves if we are controlled by any of these things.

Proverbs is one of my favorite books because it has wonderful truths to live by.

Proverbs 6:32: "The man who commits adultery is an utter fool, for he destroys his own soul."

Jonah 2:2: "I cried out to the Lord in my great trouble and He answered me." Now, God will do this, for sure, if we are patient. Being patient has been one of my problems in my prayer life.

This next verse is one we all need to obey. It is Ephesians 4:26 and it talks about anger. "Don't let the sun go down while you are still angry." In other words, don't go to sleep without settling your differences with your spouse, or your mother, or a friend, otherwise sleep will be difficult.

This passage is about decision-making, which in baseball, or in life, could affect the lives and careers of others. To me, choices can either make you or break you. So we should seek God's help about the choices we make. It is Psalms 25:4 that says "Show me the path where I should walk, O Lord, point out the right road for me to follow." God will do this if you let Him.

A humorous example of this verse is in an incident that occurred with Yogi Berra and his life-long friend Joe Garagiola. Joe was driving to visit Yogi at his Montclair, New Jersey, home. He stopped to phone Yogi for directions, and said, "Yogi, I'm at the Montclair Library, how do I get to your house from here?" Yogi replied, "Just come this way and when you get to a fork in the road take it." Now, I'm sure Joe was more confused than before he asked Yogi. We can be absolutely sure that God will give better directions than Yogi gave, and He will always point us to the right road to follow.

The Bible talks about prayer hundreds of times and prayer is so very important to me. I depend on it 24 hours, day and night, to sustain me. The following is an example of answered prayer. Several years ago I faced a serious, critical point in my professional life. Mr. Steinbrenner had mentioned that maybe I should retire, and this really concerned me deeply because I did not want to retire. I was deathly afraid that my baseball career might be over. However, I could have gotten another job with at least three other major league teams. But I would not have done so. I had previously told Mr. Steinbrenner at his son Hank's wedding that I would never work for another organization and that I wanted to remain with him forever. He said, "That's fine, you and Norma are family. If you ever leave the Yankees it will be your choice, not mine." The fact that now I could possibly be asked to retire scared me. So Norma and I started praying and asking God to handle this situation for us. We asked that "His will be done," just as Jesus had done in the Garden of Gethsemane. We promised we would accept His answer whether it be to retire or to continue to work. Several weeks went by and we had not heard from Mr. Steinbrenner. He had said he would let us know by December 15. Norma and I were walking out the door on our way to our Sunday school Christmas party on December 15 when the phone rang. I went back inside to answer it. Guess who was on the phone? You guessed correctly, it was Mr. Steinbrenner, and he said, "Clyde, I want you to continue to work for me." Norma and I were overwhelmed with joy and I no longer feared having to retire. You see, God does answer prayers. Sometimes He says yes, sometimes He says no, and sometimes He says wait. Although it took several weeks God did answer our prayers, and we gave Him the praise and glory. My natural inclination was to be impatient and question why I had not heard from Mr. Steinbrenner, but Norma continually urged me to remember that we had turned this over to the Lord. She reminded me that he had never failed us before. What a great lesson she taught me about being patient.

I told the following story about a boy named Joey at one of my football chapel services, and a big 300-pound guy cried. I was managing in San Francisco. Don Rood, who worked for the Pocket Testament League, went around the world giving away pocket Testaments in the language of whatever country he happened to be in, and he was the one who helped me start baseball chapel in San Francisco. He was a minister. He did our first baseball chapel when I was manager there. One Saturday afternoon Gaylord Perry lost an 11-inning decision to the Dodgers. It was a tough loss—physically, psychologically, and all around. We were in first place at the time. This was in 1969. I got dressed after the game and I left the clubhouse at Candlestick Park and was going to my car to go home when Don came over to me. He said, "I want you to do me a favor." I said, "Fine, call me tomorrow and I'll do it." He said, "No, I want you to do it today." Don Rood is a good friend and I knew he wouldn't push me like that after a tough loss without a good reason. He said, "I went by the hospital this morning on my way to the ballpark and I visited a friend of ours. He's a little guy named Joey. He's 12 years old, and he's in the hospital and he's got bone cancer. He's just skin and bones. I went by to see him, and he found out that I knew you and he said, 'Mr. Rood, please get Mr. King to come to see me.' The doctor told me this morning that he's got two weeks to live." I said OK immediately and went back inside and called Norma and told her to put dinner on hold because I was going by the hospital. While I was in there calling Norma, Don called the hospital and told them I was coming. I went by our equipment room and got a cap—a San Francisco cap with the "SF" on it, the smallest one in our equipment room. On the way there I just said a prayer and asked God to guide me in whatever transpired with little Joey.

When we got to the hospital they had rolled out the red carpet. Six of his nurses were in his room. All the patients on that floor who weren't bedridden were in his room. Two doctors were there and when we walked in they were waiting for us. Little Joey was propped up in his bed with pillows behind him, and he looked deathly ill. I went in and the doctor said, "Mr. King, he's not doing very well. Maybe five or six minutes and I'll give you a nod when you've had enough time with him. We don't want to tax him too long." So I went over and gave him a hug. I had the cap in my hand behind my back and I gave it to him, and I never will forget that the cap was so big on him that it turned to the side a little bit. I told him that all the Giants were pulling for him. Well, we started talking. And we talked and talked. Thirty-eight minutes later the doctor gave me the nod. The doctor allowed the time because Joey was getting along so well.

We left and every other day I would make a little tape recording to Joey from Willie Mays, or Willie McCovey, or Juan Marichal, or Gaylord Perry, or somebody on the Giants. Hal Lanier, Dick Dietz, all of the players said little messages to Joey that were about 90-seconds long. "Hang in there Joey. The game's never over until the last out. We're pulling for you. Be tough," and things to that effect. I'd take it by the hospital and play it for him. He got out of the hospital that summer. He went home. He spent the summer at home, and through the winter, and the next spring his parents brought him to Phoenix for spring training. I brought him in the clubhouse to see the players who gave him the messages, and he passed out. We were scared to death. I called the trainer right away and we sent for our team doctor, but before the team doctor could get there the trainer said, "Don't worry." Apparently, Joey was so excited to see these players that he fainted. Our trainer revived him. Joey was now 13 years old.

A year passed. Then spring training was over and it was June. We were playing in Cincinnati. I walked into the Netherlands Plaza Hotel and went to my room, the phone was ringing. It was Don Rood. He said, "I've got some bad news. Joey died." I was heartbroken. I told all of the players. They were all extremely sad. They wanted to do something. Don had said later on, "Let me tell you what happened. He asked his mother to bring a tape recorder to the hospital. He knew he was dying." Don told us that "little Joey said that he didn't want to die, but that he wasn't afraid to die, and if this had happened a year ago he'd be afraid to die, but now that he had gotten to know Mr. King and the Giants players and he had become a Christian and he knew he was going to Heaven, he said he wanted his Dad, Mom, his brother Bob, and his sister Nancy, to meet him in Heaven. He asked his mom, "Just before they close the top to the coffin please put the cap that Mr. King gave me in there with me." Ninety-seconds later he was dead. He had gone to be with the Lord in Heaven. What an inspiration Joey was to me.

Joshua, Chapter 1, Verse 9, says "Be strong and courageous. Do not be afraid or discouraged, for the Lord, your God, is with you wherever you go." Even on a subway. I'll explain. This happened to me back when I was general manager of the Yankees. It happened in in a New York City subway. We played a night game at 8:00 at Yankee Stadium. We had an hour rain-delay. It was a regular nine-inning game and it was a slow one. It took over three hours to play the game. I was upstairs in the club box and Yogi was the manager. Mr. Steinbrenner said, "Tell Yogi and the coaches to come up. I want to have a meeting." I called Yogi and told him to bring the coaches up. Mr. Steinbrenner does this every so often. We had lost the game and he wanted to talk. Well, we had our meeting and it lasted about 20 to 25 minutes, and by that time it was 20 minutes to one o'clock in the morning. Mr. Steinbrenner said, "Clyde, I'll give you a ride to your hotel downtown," which he often did. He was really good to me. I said, "No. I can't. Murray Cook is coming by in the morning at 8:30." Murray was the general manager of the Montreal Expos and we were going to talk about a trade for Andre Dawson. I told Mr. Steinbrenner that I had work to do to get ready for that meeting. He said, "OK. If you can't do it tomorrow, I'll have a car waiting for you downstairs."

So I did about a half hour's work. Now it was about 1:30 A.M. in the South Bronx. All the fans were gone. Mr. Steinbrenner had said that the security guard downstairs would make sure that the car was there for me. So I went downstairs. It was the first time in the history of Yankee Stadium, I think, that there was no security guard downstairs. If Mr. Steinbrenner knew this he would have fired the security guard. First time ever, no security guard. No car. No nothing. I was going to call a cab, but the phone at the security desk was not working. What alternative did I have? The phone in my office was turned off because the Yankees cut their phones off after a certain time of night. I could not bypass the closed switchboard to get an outside line. I was literally stranded. So, my alternative was to either go back up and spend the night in my office or do what I ended up doing.

I went out the front door, went around Yankee Stadium to where center field is, walked up the steps to the elevated "subway" train at 161st Street. Now it was almost two o'clock. That time of night there were not too many people, but even at that hour people do ride the subway. I waited to pick a subway car that had several people in it. I was by myself. I had my World Series rings on. I saw a car that looked like it had about 20 people in it. I ran down to that car and jumped inside. There are seven stops between Yankee Stadium and the Grand Hyatt at Grand Central Station in New York City, where I was staying. The first stop we made I would say eight or nine people got off. By the second stop every one of them got off. Here I am in that car by myself at two o'clock in the morning with five stops to go to reach the Grand Hyatt. There are three big guys standing outside the subway. They look in and see me. One guy holds the door and the other two guys come inside. The biggest of them was wearing those metal wrist bands worn by gang members. One stayed by the door and one sat on one side of me and the other sat on the other side of me. Not right next to me, but a few seats down from me. The subway ride began. Three or four people got on at the third stop. The fourth stop those three people got off. The minute they got off, the guy on one side of me got up and started toward me and the guy on the other side got up and started toward me. I just said a prayer. I said, "God, protect me. I know what's going to happen. I just ask you to surround me with your love and protective care." Two of them were converging on me, and they were just a few feet away. Well, the doors between the cars of the train opened and two big policemen came in carrying their night sticks, and I mean these were the biggest policemen I've ever seen. They had to be 6'4" or 6'5" and they were walking up to me, and the minute those guys saw the policemen they sat down. Was I ever happy to see those cops! They got right in front of me and one said, "Mr. King?" and I said yeah, happy to see them.

He said, "What are you doing on the subway at this time of night?"

I said, "We had a late game. Sit down, sit down; let's talk."

And they sat down one on each side of me, and the one on my right said, "We know what's going on. Where are you going?"

I said, "I'm going to the Grand Hyatt."

He said, "We're going to ride with you."

The next stop, the three guys got off. Two stops later we were at the Grand Hyatt. They walked me out of the subway, up the steps through Grand Central, into the street, and through the front door of the Grand Hyatt to the elevator door. They said good night and saluted me. I told them as we were walking that if they ever needed tickets or anything, to call me and I'd take care of them. They never contacted me. They were guardian angels. God answered my prayer. I might have only been mugged, but they might have killed me because, knowing me, I might have fought back and that would not have been the smart thing to do in that situation. Instinct sometimes takes over your better judgment, but it never came about because of those two policeman. I had courage, but it wasn't my own courage. My own instinct would have had me bolt out and probably get killed. I got strength from God. The subway part of Joshua 1:9 was my part. "Be strong and courageous. Do not be afraid or discouraged when the Lord, your God, is with you wherever you go." Even on a subway.

On the subject of criticism, try Proverbs 15:31. It says "If you listen to constructive criticism, you will be at home among the wise." This is *constructive* criticism. I'm talking about criticism to help you. I'll give you a couple more. Hebrews 11:1, it's about faith: "Faith is the confident assurance that what we hope for is going to happen." You could put it this way, that what we wish for is going to happen. That's faith.

Here's another one that will fit in with courage. Isaiah 41:10: "Don't be afraid for I am with you. I will strengthen you and I will help you in all instances." God helped me on the subway that night. Here's another about patience. Habakkuk 2:3: "If it seems slow, wait patiently, for it will surely take place. It will not always be delayed." Here's one on the topic of persecution. Matthew 5:11: "God blesses you when you are mocked and persecuted, and lied about because you are my followers." God blesses those who endure persecution.

Philippians 4:6 on the subject of worry: "Don't worry about anything. Instead, pray about everything." I hope that you all can learn from these passages and I'd like to leave you on this note.

It's Deuteronomy 6:7, on teaching: "Repeat again and again to your children. Talk to them when you are at home and when you are away on a journey." This is so important. Teaching your children is one of the most important things you can do in life.

When I Have Changed My Old Cross for a Crown

This Christian outlook was instilled in me from an early age. The following letter from my mother, written two weeks before her death, illustrates my family's spiritual outlook.

To my dear children when I have passed away:

I don't want you to forget Mother's prayers. I want you all to love one another and help each other in every way. If one is sick, see after them. If in trouble, care for them. If all is well, keep in touch with them.

I haven't anything much in this world to leave you all, but I am leaving the prayers of God's blessings on every one of you. If you will only let Him bless you and give Him your hearts and live for Him, it is worth ten thousand of all the world can give you.

I am so glad that when Jesus said, "that whosoever," He included us all. He has done His part and we must do ours.

I am glad for what I know this morning. I have a home in heaven and that all is well with my soul.

Children, I have spent many lonely hours since you have been gone from home, and shed many a tear that God only knew, but almost every hour there was a prayer in my heart for you. And I know that Jesus heard and answered them, and I knew that He was with you to take care and protect. I have always leaned on that everlasting arm.

So now, if any one of you is sick and in trouble or ill health, I want you to always trust in the best friend you can ever have.

Now I don't want you to think of Mother as being dead, because I am going to live on in that city where there will never be a heartache. Remember, I will be watching and waiting for every one of you.

There were many things to take you from home here on earth, but there is nothing to keep you from heaven but sin. So give God your heart and live true, and remember that without holiness, no man shall see the Lord. Don't think you can't live it. *Jesus will carry you through.*

Now I don't want one of you missing up there, for I gave you, every one of you, to Jesus when you were only babies. You are, every one, too precious to be lost. I want you all there; that is my prayer until death.

I want Estelle to copy this for every one of you seven.

Won't that be a happy meeting when we all meet, and then we will know that we will live together for ever and ever? Never say good-bye any more. Ah, it makes me happy to think of that blessed day.

—*Mother* [Maggie King]

Dr. Norman Vincent Peale

Mr. Rickey encouraged in me a real love of spiritual things. During my Brooklyn Dodgers days, as a player not only did I have Mr. Rickey to look to as a model for Christian living, but I had the privilege of getting to know Dr. Norman Vincent Peale. Dr. Peale had a profound effect on my life early in my baseball career. Norma and I met Dr. Peale in Brooklyn through Carl Erskine and his wife Betty. Carl took us one Sunday night to hear him preach. We went to his church at Marble Collegiate on 29th Street in Manhattan. We always went on Sunday night and we would sit with Mrs. Peale. That's how we got to know both of them, and we became good friends. They were very cordial and godly people. Being with them was like being with family. Dr. Peale came to Goldsboro to visit with Norma and me, and he was so influential in my early life in Brooklyn.

He was a great man of God and a great baseball fan. He kept up with the game. He knew the players, their averages, their families. He loved the game of baseball. Norma and I would go to his church on Sunday night when we were home. We couldn't go in the mornings because we had to be at the ballpark early on Sunday. The Marble Collegiate Church, which is a Dutch Reform Church, is a great old church. It was the kind of church that had the doors on the pews. You walked in and sat down in those little pews, just like in Williamsburg, or at the Old North Church in Boston. It was wonderful, and after each sermon on Sunday night we would go back to Dr. Peale's study. Pee Wee and Dottie Reese went back with us, as did Carl and Betty Erskine. We would want to talk to him about his sermon, but he would want to talk to us about baseball. He always asked us to tell him baseball stories. He enjoyed the game. It was exciting for him. He attended the games at Ebbets Field regularly.

I had a problem with playing baseball on Sunday when I first broke into the big leagues and when I first went down to Richmond during the 1944 season. I didn't play on Sunday by choice. I had been raised by my mother not to do shopping on Sunday and not to go to a movie on Sunday. The team at Richmond was nice enough to honor my request. Dr. Peale told me the story in the Bible in which a shepherd went looking for his sheep on the Sabbath when one of the sheep went astray. He told me that it was OK to play on Sunday because it was my profession and it was what I loved. The moral to the story is that it is between you and God.

Dr. Peale was a loyal friend to Norma and myself. We became avid readers of *Guideposts*, which Dr. Peale created. The editor of *Guideposts* was Len LeSourd, a friend of mine. Len wrote a feature article on me in 1959 and then wrote an anniversary article 10 years later in 1969 when I was out in San Francisco managing the Giants. The relationship between Dr. Peale and Len and our family was strengthened because Len married Catherine Marshall. Catherine was a famous writer who wrote *A Man Called Peter*, upon which the movie was based, and *The Helper, Something More*, and *A Closer Walk*. Catherine had been married to Peter Marshall, the Chaplain of the United States Senate. Catherine's book *A Man Called Peter* was based on the life of her late husband. Years later Catherine married my friend Len, and that's how Norma and I got to know Catherine. She was a wonderful person. She passed away some years back and Len passed away in 1997. Norma and I feel privileged just to have known such wonderful people.

Even up to the last couple of years of his life, if Dr. Peale saw anything in the paper about me or my family, he'd send it to us. He was a great man and a great role model for me. Dr. Peale was a great orator, great person, a great pastor, and a great writer. He wrote the book *The Power of Positive Thinking*, a world-wide bestseller. He believed in positive thinking in sports. He helped me a lot in my life, but I still could use some help with patience. He told me often that it was important to be patient with yourself and with others. He said to me that if I couldn't learn to be patient with myself, I'd never learn to be patient with others. It's been a struggle for me all my life to be patient!

My First Public Prayer

When I was managing the Atlanta Crackers I got my initial taste of public speaking. First, however, I had an opportunity to say a prayer publicly. This was when my family and I were staying at a hotel in Atlanta in 1956, and we attended the First Baptist Church of Decatur, Georgia. It was a great church with a large congregation. Louis Newton was the pastor there and he was known as the "Pope of Atlanta." It was time for the girls to go back to school and I had gotten them in the car, packed, and Norma had just driven off for Goldsboro. It was a Sunday morning and they had to go to school the next day. The church was right across the street from our hotel and I waved good-bye to Norma and went across the street to the church. The service was about to begin and the church was full. I had to sit in the back row. I had to step over three older ladies sitting there on the aisle to get to an empty seat. About three or four minutes after I sat down Louis Newton and the choir came in and began to sing. After the choir finished their singing, he announced to the congregation, "We're honored to have Clyde King, the manager of the Atlanta Crackers here today and I would like him to say our morning prayer."

At that time I had never said a prayer publicly in a church and I was stunned. The only way he could have possibly known I was there was that one of the ushers at the door handing out morning programs recognized me and relayed to him that I was there. I was all the way in the back of that church and he could not possibly have seen me in that large congregation. I got up and I was going to say the prayer right where I stood. He said, "No, Mr. King, come down to the pulpit." So, I stepped over those three ladies again, walked all the way down that long aisle up to the pulpit, and stood in front of the microphone. I did the best I could. I'm sure that my prayer was not a very good one, but I'm sure the Lord led me to say what I said. I went back to my seat and I was embarrassed.

The next day, team owner Earl Mann asked me to go to his Rotary Club meeting with him and I did, and after it was over a gentleman approached me. He introduced himself and said he owned a clothing store. His name was Brewer and he told Earl, "I want you to bring Clyde by the clothing store, I want to give him something." So, after the meeting was over we went by and as we walked in he said to me, "I want you to pick out a suit," and he showed me a rack of suits. I noticed that all the suits on the rack were $150. Now this is 1956 and a $150 suit then would be like a $1,000 suit now. I never had a suit like that in my life. I said, "Oh, no, this is over my head. This is not the kind of suit I buy. Show me where the $60 suits are." He said, "No, I want you to have one of these suits." I said, "No, I can't do that." He said, "Well, I was in church yesterday when the pastor called on you to say a prayer and I had a feeling that it was unsolicited. I was so impressed I want to do something for you." I said OK and I picked out a gray suit with stripes in it that I wore for years and still have. It was so pleasing for somebody to appreciate what I did under stress and strain and for him to do something like that for me really touched me. And of course, that was the beginning of my praying in public. I've been speaking in front of congregations ever since.

Just as I always tried to find the right home when the kids were with me during the summer, I always tried to find the right church in whichever city I was working. We always went to a Baptist church and we've been in some great churches.

True Meaning of Charity

I think the true meaning of charity is to give with your heart. It reminds me of a story that happened to my family and me some years back. We were sitting at home one night having dinner when the phone rang. It was a man calling who said that he had worked at the visiting clubhouse at Candlestick Park. He said he was stranded in Florida, that his car had broken down, and that he had no money. He had a little baby, and asked me if I could send him $50. He promised he would repay me. Fifty dollars was a lot of money back in the early 1970s. I got off the phone and I had a family vote on whether to send the man the $50 because we didn't know if his story was legitimate. Well, my wife and my three girls all voted. Janet was in high school and Norma and Princie were in their twenties. I had always tried to help people out when I could. I felt that it was my Christian duty to do so. Norma, Normie, and Janet voted not to send the money; only Princie agreed that we should. So I asked Princie to go with me to Western Union to wire the money. I wanted to give her this privilege because she felt that we should help this stranger and his family. Sometimes you have to give in faith and in trust that God would do what's needed to be done. Although the money was never returned, the lesson was a good one for my children and wife.

At that time admitting that you went to church was like coming out of the closet in a religious sense. Nowadays the players are open about their religious ties. When I went to San Francisco, baseball chapel was strong. I met Don Rood there and, as I already mentioned, he was with the Pocket Testament League, and he performed some chapel services for the team. The first year we had 8 or 10 players attend regularly, and the next year we had 15 or 16. Today, most teams have baseball chapel, and I think it's a great way for the players to attend service on Sunday.

Bishop Bevel Jones

I now come to a man whom I deeply admire—Bishop Bevel Jones. Norma and I first met him when I managed the Atlanta Crackers in 1956. He had sold Coca-Colas as a kid at old Ponce de Leon Park in Atlanta and now was a young pastor at the Audubon Forest United Methodist Church. It was because of his encouragement that I became a public speaker. Although I had spoken with Dr. Peale as a Dodgers player and had given my little prayer in public at the First Baptist Church, this was my first public talk at a Sunday service. I am so thankful and grateful to Bishop Jones to this day for my introduction into public speaking. After that testimony, and because of his confidence in me, I was able to speak on other occasions at various religious outings. His telephone call to Dr. Peale was the reason why I was written up in *Guideposts* in 1959. I was on hand when the Decatur First United Methodist Church turned 150 years old and shared that memory with Bishop Jones. In 1984 Bevel Jones was elected Bishop and I know that he treasures that honor.

On another note, I knew that Bishop Jones was a sports fan and, particularly, a New York Yankees fan, and when I was general manager for the Yankees in 1986 I arranged to have the Yankees welcome him and his wife on the big scoreboard at Yankee Stadium. I took him into the Yankees dugout and clubhouse and introduced him to some players. Having him there with me was such a treat! I really enjoy his company, and Norma and I treasure our friendship with the Joneses. Bishop Jones later retired and took a position at his alma mater—Emory University. He and his wife, Tuck, are still our good friends.

When I think of Christmas I can't help but think of our Christmas decorations. We like to decorate our tree with angels. We must have hundreds of them. People always ask me when I started collecting angels and I say, 52 years ago as of November 29, 1998, because that's when I met a 5'6" tall angel—my wife Norma!

My Israel Visit

During January of 1998 I had the privilege of revisiting Israel, this time with a special group of people. The group's name is "Journey in Faith," and I became involved through my friend John Lotz, the Associate Athletic Director at the University of North Carolina. He called me and asked me if I wanted to go, and I said yes, of course. He then put me in touch with certain key people in Washington, D.C. I later found out that the group was comprised of three generals, one admiral, the director of the CIA under President Carter, Stansfield Turner, General Ron Griffith (who was General Schwartzkoff's right-hand man during the Persian Gulf War), and influential people from various areas of life such as the media industry, and CEOs from the corporate world. The group invited people whom they dubbed as "leaders" in various walks of life. The trip lasted eight days. Nancy and George Bradley were our leaders.

We drove to Raleigh-Durham airport, flew to Atlanta International Airport on Friday night, had a meeting there and interviews with CNN, and then flew to Frankfurt, Germany, and then on to Tel Aviv, Israel.

The first place we visited in Israel was the Sea of Galilee. This was where Jesus "walked on water." The two trips that I had previously made to this area were under calm sea conditions and warm sunshine. This time there was a rough storm, which made it more real to me, much like it was when Jesus was there and his boat was about to sink. The waves on this trip were quite high and although we were not in any danger, it reminded me of the story of Peter. Afterward, we went up to where Jesus fed five thousand people with two fishes and a few loaves of bread at the Mount of the Beatitudes. That was a wonderful site. What struck me most about this place was that the miracle that he performed was right where I was standing. The weather had cleared and the sun was shining, and it was an awesome feeling to know you're in the land where Jesus was—where he walked and where he preached and where he healed people. It was unbelievable. It makes the Bible come true to a person like me.

This feeling of the Bible coming to life was especially true for me in Jericho. When you're in the same area where the "walls came tumbling down," it makes the Bible stories come to life. What was also interesting to me was to see the tree that Zaccheus had climbed to see Jesus. Jesus came by and told him to come down out of the tree. The reason he was in the tree was because he was short and was afraid that he wouldn't be able to see Jesus with all of the people around him. So he climbed up in a Sycamore tree for a better view. Jesus saw him up there and invited him down and said that he would go to his house for dinner. Seeing the tree made a deep and lasting impression on me.

When we went to the Garden of Gethsemane, where Jesus had rested after eating the Last Supper and was on his way with Peter to the Mount of Olives, we saw olive trees that were about three thousand years old. That's where Jesus went into the Garden and prayed and asked God, his Father, to let the cup pass from him, if it would be His will, and he said "not my will but Thy will be done."

We visited the Old City of Jerusalem, and it was a big thrill to be where Jesus had been. The last time that I visited Israel, I went down in the dungeon where he sat, and I sat there for four hours and just prayed for those on the prayer list. We went to the Wailing Wall where Jewish people go and pray and where they write prayers on little pieces of paper and stick them in the cracks of the wall. That was interesting as well. What struck me most about the Wailing Wall was that it is still standing today despite all of the wars and conflicts that have gone on in this area, and that it is part of the actual wall left from the Old Temple.

We went to the Garden Tomb and saw the place where Christ was laid when he died. Then we went to Golgotha and saw in the hillside the large indentation of a skull. This place is where Jesus was crucified. They used to crucify the criminals upside down, but they did not crucify Jesus upside down. Another thing they did when they crucified prisoners was break their legs. However, in the Bible it says that Jesus' legs would not be broken, and they weren't. Then we had communion right by the Garden Tomb with our group, which numbered about 32. Reverend James Hutchens led us in communion.

Our routine was as follows each day: we would get up at six o'clock in the morning and return at six o'clock at night. Each night we all gathered before dinner and spoke about what we had seen that particular day and what effect it had on us. We had to share with each other how what we saw would help us in the future to live better lives and to help others have a better life. It sealed in my heart and mind the things that the Bible teaches us, such as loving thy neighbor and keeping the Ten Commandments. We had some brilliant people in our group who had some great insights. The central part of all of our thinking was that Jesus sacrificed for us and how much he loved us by giving his life for us. When he was in the Garden praying, he didn't want to go through it, but he was willing to accept what God wanted him to do, and that was to die for our sins. The group was very open about their feelings. It makes you realize how little we do in our lives to help other people, compared to what Christ did to help others. Everything he did on earth was to help someone else. He went about doing the Father's work. We can't be ashamed of the Gospel. I don't go around shouting it from the rooftop or wearing it on my sleeve, but I'm not ashamed to talk about it if the occasion arises.

Coming from a Christian home as I did, the background was there. Mr. Rickey had a big part in my learning about religion. I know that any sacrifice we make we can't outdo the Lord. We can't out give Him and we can't do more for others than He did for us.

The Via Dolorosa was another place that was interesting to see. The story surrounding it is that Simon of Cyrene came to help Jesus lift the cross when he fell while carrying it. Each time I have been there I have stopped and prayed. Jesus carried that cross and fell several times on his way to his Crucifixion. In one area, where the soldiers were waiting to find out his fate, the games that the soldiers carved in the stones are still there. It's amazing to stand on that stone and to realize that soldiers were drawing games on the stone. You realize that this is actually where the soldiers were playing games as Jesus was about to be crucified. Jesus said that he is the leader, but that a leader must be a servant as well, and that's why he insisted on washing the feet of the disciples, his followers, that night. He said he was not so great as to not humble himself and wash the feet of the servants. I believe that to be a great leader you must first be a great follower. He followed his Father, God, and it made it easier for people to follow him.

Tiberius, which is near Capernaum, is where Jesus taught when he left Nazareth. He spent four or five years teaching. They've still got an olive press there, and they still have portions of two buildings where he taught and preached. It's really significant. There are stones there with inscriptions on them from Christ's day and age.

We saw the Dead Sea as well, where there is no life because of the concentration of salt in the water. Remember that the Bible said some day there will be life in the Dead Sea. To see people out in the Dead Sea, buoyed up by the saltwater, just laying back like they were laying on their couch and not sinking is amazing. One guy was out there reading the paper. We had six members of the group baptized in the River Jordan, where Jesus was baptized by John. We saw the area where they found the caves containing the Dead Sea scrolls as well. It was a thrilling sight. The caves are still there. We saw Bedouin people and their sheep farms, and it was amazing to see the tents they lived in with their charcoal stoves and their cots, and to see them riding their camels. I got on a camel and Norma rode one as well. We saw the area where the Good Samaritan story took place. That's an intriguing story and I can think of many friends who are Good Samaritans.

We stayed at great hotels. We stayed at the Holiday Inn and Tiberius Hotel. The thing that I'll never forget about my trip was seeing the Bedouin children from the wilderness come up to you and hold out their hands for money. It was sad. It makes you want to cry because they are the sweetest little guys you ever saw. At the end of the trip everyone was wistful because we all got along so well with each other. We hated to separate, and I know that I'll keep in touch with a good number of our group.

While in Israel, and on my previous trip there, I was deeply moved by my visit to the Holocaust Museum. It brought back memories of my visit to the concentration camp at Dachau. I saw some photos in this museum in Jerusalem of places that I have actually seen in person in Dachau, such as the "dormitories" and the torture chambers, and the crematory ovens. It had a deep impact on me. I'll carry these memories with me to my grave. I tried to imagine what happened at those terrible places during Hitler's reign in Germany and parts of Europe. To see the actual places where Jews were packed so tightly that they couldn't even turn over as they tried to sleep and to see the hooks out in the center of the concentration camp where they would hang the victims, just brought tears to my eyes and made me have "chill bumps" all over. Even though this occurred some 50 years ago, it seemed like it happened yesterday and it made me feel just awful. When I saw the gas chambers and crematories, where millions of Jewish people were gassed and then cremated, I could almost smell the burning bodies. I was deeply upset and moved as an older gentleman saw me and came over to me.

This gentleman was a Holocaust survivor. He saw the anguish on my face and he showed me the tattoo number on his arm. He explained how everything transpired with regard to his personal situation and told me how he escaped being killed. He said that since he was young and strong he was able to work, thus escaping the gas chamber. He described to me how children were beaten to death and thrown into trenches in a mass grave. He told me that sometimes children who were still alive were thrown into these trenches. I don't think anyone could ever witness anything worse than this. It is impossible, in my mind, to witness anything worse. It just goes to show you how cruel man can be, especially when he doesn't have God in his life, as Hitler obviously did not have God in his life. If he had, he could have never conjured such thoughts. Satan was Hitler's master, I am sure.

I'm just glad that the world has come to a point where that cannot happen today. I want to go to Washington, D.C., and see the Holocaust Museum there because I've been told by several people in Israel that the Holocaust Museum in Washington is just as moving, or even more so, than the one in Israel.

Our trip to Israel was very special, in spite of the fact that I cracked a rib. My friends might think I cracked my rib while climbing the ancient ruins, but it wasn't anything that glamorous. Rather, I turned to talk to someone on an escalator and fell!

18

Me, the Golfer

I LOVE THE GAME OF GOLF. I TOOK IT UP IN MY MID-TWENTIES
when I was playing for the Dodgers. Looking back, I wish I had
started in high school, but then it might have left me with less time
to play baseball and basketball, my favorite sports.

Since I fell out of the tree house we were building for my grandchildren, I have gotten away from golf somewhat. I broke several
bones and injured my left shoulder, and I can't get the club back as
far as I used to be able to. This has taken some of the fun out of the
game for me.

Golf brings people together. It gives you and your partners a
chance to visit while walking the fairways together. I have heard of
big business deals being made while playing golf. In fact, I have a
friend who did just that. He told me that he had tried for months,
but failed to make a deal until he took his prospect out to play a
round of golf.

Over the years, I've enjoyed playing many outstanding courses
in America. It has been fun and exciting playing in celebrity tournaments such as Michael Jordan's, Phil Rizzuto's and Yogi Berra's, to
name a few.

Once I was playing in Pinehurst on the number two course with
my friends Ralph Branca, Ed Worley, and Jack Scott. This is one of
the toughest courses around. Ralph is a good golfer, as was Jack. Mr.
Worley was like my second father when I was growing up in Goldsboro. He was known as "Mr. Baseball." Ralph was my golf tutor. He
helped me in many ways, especially in club selection.

We were playing from the middle tees, which was a big advantage. We were pretty evenly matched when we got to the eighteenth
green. I had about a five or six putt, the distance I hate, for a score of

75. Up to this point we had been marking our own balls on the greens. This time Mr. Worley rushed up and marked my ball for me and kept the ball, which was unusual. I did not think anything strange about this, but I should have. My putt was closest to the pin, so I was to putt last. The others finished their putts, then Mr. Worley replaced my ball. If I made this putt it would be the best score ever for me on the number two course. After lining it up, I stepped up and stroked it and immediately the ball started to wobble from side to side. My heart was in my throat—I almost had a heart attack! He had put a trick ball down instead of my ball. They realized that I was very upset and they wanted to concede the putt, but I refused. After taking a couple of minutes to collect myself, I made the putt for a 75. Wow!

There is nothing better than being out on the golf course on a beautiful afternoon with good friends for a friendly game of golf. Golf is a great way to get some exercise if you walk instead of riding a cart. However, you must be very careful that you don't become addicted to the game and start neglecting your family and your business. Better still, play once in a while with your wife. Take your children with you and let them caddie for you. This is a wonderful way to spend time with your family.

During the off-season, when I was playing regularly, I would take our daughters to school and then head for the golf course. Often I would play 36 holes, and once played 54 holes. It was so dark after my tee shot on the 54th hole that I could not find my ball. I confess that I rode a cart the last 18 holes. I did not play on weekends, though. I reserved that time for my family.

Golf is a game that requires extraordinary talent. If you are a player on the PGA tour, you must shoot 12 to 15 under par in order to make much money. My friend Clarence Rose, a pro golfer in my North Carolina home town, is an outstanding golfer. He is a fine young man with a wonderful family, and he makes sure he spends quality time with his family. In a tournament a few years ago, he shot in the 60s three of four days and made about $12,000. So see, you must really be good to win money. I am happy to say that Clarence won the Sprint International Tournament in 1998.

When I was managing the San Francisco Giants, my friend Dick O'Connor took me to play the Pebble Beach course. I was really excited, and my goal for the round was to par number 18. I drove off the tee in good position, then used my driver again and was short of the green, but in good position to use a five-iron to the green. Sure enough I made a par! I shot an 80, but if I had shot 100 it would have been OK, because it was such a thrill to play Pebble Beach and par number 18.

I remember playing in the ProAm of the Phoenix Open, and Tommy Aaron was my partner. Now, this is Tommy Aaron the golfer, not the late baseball player. He was the professional and I was the amateur. Tommy hit from the back tees and I hit from the middle tees. We were playing well and he had helped me line up several putts I wouldn't have made without his knowledge of the greens. We came to the eighteenth tee, trailing by one stroke. Tommy hit a good drive down the middle, and so did I. This was a par-five hole, and he hit his second shot just short of the green for an easy chip to the pin.

I was about to hit my second shot and he said, " What club are you going to use?" I said, "A one-iron." He said, "Clyde, why don't you use a four-iron and lay up. Then we will both have a chance to chip and one putt for a birdie."

I replied, "OK," but I put my one-iron back in the bag, shook the clubs around, and took the one-iron out again. Tommy had backed away and thought I had the four-iron in my hand. I hit that one-iron and the ball took off and was going right at the green and then, suddenly, it took a sharp turn to the right and landed in the sand trap next to the green. It was a terrible lie, and it took two shots to get it on the green. I took two putts, for a bogie six. Tommy chipped, but two-putted for a par, and we finished second. I have that beautiful plaque hanging on the wall in my den.

In the clubhouse, Tommy said, "Clyde, I've never seen anyone hit a four-iron as far as you did." I did not have the courage to tell him I didn't use the four-iron. We lost by one stroke. We might have tied if I had taken his advice. Until this day, if Tommy remembers playing with me, he does not know that I messed up by not listening to someone who knew a lot more about playing golf than I did.

In all the years I've played golf, I've made two holes-in-one. My first hole-in-one came on February 13, 1963, at Pinehurst while playing with my friend Bob Warren. The second hole-in-one came on February 17, 1970, at the Mesa Country Club in Mesa, Arizona, this time playing with my friend Sherman Stone. It has been almost 30 years since I made my last hole-in-one, and the chances of making another one seem rather dim.

Norma and I were visiting my friend Alex Lineberger and his wife, Emma, in Winston-Salem, North Carolina. Emma is an artist and Alex is a good golfer. She painted a beautiful mountain scene that hangs above the mantle in our den. It contains six things that I really like in life—there's a church, a red barn, mountains, snow, children, and a horse-drawn sleigh. Alex was an avid golfer and we played a lot of golf together. Like Ralph Branca, he was a good teacher and helped me with club selections. During our visit, I noticed that he had the *Golf Digest* magazine on his coffee table and started to read it.

Alex said, "I saved that magazine for you, and I want you to see how many of the 100 best courses in America you've played." After checking them out, I discovered I had played 52 of them, including the Olympia in San Francisco, Oak Hill in Pittsburgh, Westchester Country Club in Rye, New York, Muirfield in Columbus, Ohio, and Grandfather Mountain in Linville, North Carolina. To me, there's no prettier eighteenth green in America than the one at Grandfather Mountain. When you're coming up the eighteenth fairway, you'll never see a more beautiful sight. Hugh Morton did a great job in designing this course.

Every year after the baseball season was over the PBR (Professional Baseball Representatives), a group of baseball scouts, have a golf tournament. One year it was at the Tanglewood course just outside of Winston-Salem. I won my first golf tournament there. It is a great course. The professional seniors play there now.

I once had a most unique putter, a pickle putter. It was a gift from the folks at Mt. Olive Pickle Company, North Carolina, for having spoken to their group. It was terrific. I loved that funny-looking thing. The putting area looked just like a pickle—it was even green. My other favorite club was an old chipper. This was a 35-year-old chipper back when I used it 25 years ago. I used it for all kinds of shots, from 150 yards out to chipping at the green. It took the place of a five-iron, a seven-iron, and a nine-iron. There is a sad story concerning these two favorite clubs.

Atlanta Braves general manager Eddie Robinson and I had gone golfing. When we got back to the ballpark, I was going to bring my clubs up to the office and then take them home after I finished work. He said, "Clyde, why don't you just leave them in the car so that you don't have to haul them back and forth?" I did, but we both forgot about them. The next day Eddie had to go out of town to visit one of our minor league teams. He parked his car overnight at the Atlanta airport. When he returned from his trip a couple of days later, the golf clubs had been stolen from the trunk of his car. My pickle putter and chipper were gone, and so was my golf game. No clubs could ever replace these favorites. I still miss them. Eddie was very apologetic, and still apologizes every time we see each other.

Playing in Yogi Berra's Celebrity Golf Classics is always fun. I've had some great times with Yogi on the golf course. His tournament benefits underprivileged boy scouts in the Montclair, New Jersey area, where Yogi lives. It's a great day of golf for a wonderful cause. Yogi and his wife, Carmen, are very active in community activities, especially those helping people in need.

Finally, I thought I would list a few of my favorite golf courses that I've had the privilege to play on over the years. Here are my favorite golf courses, not in any particular order: Pinehurst, Number 2; Pineneedles, Grandfather Mountain, Pebble Beach, Westchester Country Club, Doral, and Walnut Creek, my home course.

19

BAT

THE IDEA OF BAT WAS THE BRAINCHILD OF PETER UEBERROTH. BAT stands for Baseball Assistance Team. At the time that this Baseball Assistance Team was formed, Equitable Life Insurance decided that it wanted to get back into baseball as a sponsor. They were allowed back into baseball on the condition that the company do something for charity. At that time you had to give about $5 million to be a sponsor and so Equitable came up with the idea of an Old Timers' series. The plan called for an Old Timers' Game to be played in each of the 26 major league cities. For each game that was played, ten thousand dollars was donated and placed into a fund called "BAT." The fund would then be administered by ex-ballplayers. The goal of the fund was to distribute the money raised to former major league ballplayers and their widows who were in need. Former players, such as Ralph Branca, would supervise where the money went and to whom it was given. That was in 1986.

The preliminary meetings were held in February of 1986, but as late as July a board had not yet been formed. In August, however, a board was born. My pal Ralph was elected as the first president, and he served for about three years before moving up to the position of chairman. When Ralph became chairman, Joe Garagiola became president. Joe was extensively involved with broadcasting at the time, and this was great for BAT because it allowed BAT to get some much-needed media attention. NBC's *Today Show* allowed Joe to talk about BAT, and this publicity really helped BAT gain a broad corporate audience.

All of the legal work necessary to set up this fund was handled by the commissioner's office. The baseball people involved in forming this charity applied for and received an Internal Revenue Code 501C-3 designation for BAT. Next, parameters were established as to what BAT could do as a charity and how it was to be done. Ralph's role as chairman is underestimated. He is invaluable to BAT's success because of his important contacts with the major corporations and securities companies that have become involved in BAT. The bylaws lay out what can be done and set up the grant committee, which processes grants for IRS purposes. Everyone who wishes to qualify as a recipient must get a special form to fill out. On this form the applicant must state his financial situation, his family situation, why he's applying, and what type of support he needs. If an applicant has unpaid medical bills, drug or alcohol problems, or rent or living-expense needs, BAT needs to know. Some guys get in a hole for one reason or another and run up credit-card bills. BAT will bail them out, but not too often, usually only once. The money distributed by BAT usually covers basic living expenses, such as rent and medical bills. Getting back to Ralph's role in BAT, as chairman he is the organizational head, and he never takes any credit for his good work for BAT, but he deserves the credit.

Often people ask me who is eligible to be a recipient of BAT. Minor leaguers, front office personnel, and other executives with four years of service qualify. Former major leaguers and umpires (when their services qualify), as well as their widows, are within BAT's arms. BAT also encompasses all players from the old Negro Leagues. Ralph and the board members felt that those players didn't have the opportunity to play in organized baseball so they deserve to be within the arms of BAT. Ralph calls it the baseball family.

BAT's biggest supporter was Equitable Life Insurance Company, who sponsored BAT for five years and gave $260,000 a year. Then Upper Deck—the baseball card company—came in and contributed for five years, until the company ran into financial problems.

The BAT dinners started in 1989. Bob Friedman, from Goldman Sachs, called up Ralph and suggested that BAT should have a dinner as a fund-raiser. It was at that time that Ralph became instrumental in organizing the dinners. Rusty Staub ran the first few dinners and they were quite a success. When Ralph took over as chairman, he started the practice of having a ballplayer seated at every table to act as host for the table. BAT dinners have grown from 445 people in 1989 to 1,700 people in 1999. 1999 was a successful year for BAT as well. We raised much awareness about diseases such as leukemia, which affects some of the ballplayers' children. There are two price strata of tables—you can buy a $5,000 table and sit with a ballplayer or you can buy a $10,000 table and sit with a Hall-of-Famer table host. I think the best part of the evening is when players get together at a private cocktail party and reminisce. It's only for players and their families. It runs about one hour. That's followed by a cocktail party for everyone, including fans, and that runs an hour and a half. All of the players, including Hall of Famers, sign autographs, and you can get them all. Ralph will tell you that people love that part of the night, it's this part that sells the dinner and makes it a success.

One time at a dinner someone came over to Ralph and told him to go rescue Sandy Koufax and Nolan Ryan because they were literally up against the wall with people crowding them for autographs. Things can get a little out of control when autographs are involved. The dinners are terrific, though. I've missed only one dinner and that was January 1998, because of my trip to Israel.

Ted Williams still comes to the BAT dinners even after his massive stroke, which I think shows Ted's love of the game of baseball and his love of charity. Ted Williams was instrumental in the Jimmy Fund in Boston, and he is just great with the BAT dinners. In 1998 he spoke to the crowd and he was wonderful. Ted can always electrify a crowd, including a crowd of his peers. Ted's a loyal supporter of BAT and gives every ounce of his strength to help his former colleagues. Joe DiMaggio came even after his fall in which he broke a rib. Henry Aaron came as well. Sandy Koufax is the best at talking to people and signing autographs. Sandy, Ralph told me, was one of the first to be honored at a BAT dinner. When Sandy learned about what BAT does, he joined immediately, and Ralph has told me many times how important Sandy has been to BAT. These dinners raised more than $400,000, thanks to the Clark Foundation, which founded the Hall of Fame and has been a large contributor from the beginning. The dinners are a lot of fun, and they give me the chance to reminisce with my baseball pals.

BAT cannot publicize who it helps. It is done discreetly, as Ralph proudly states, because he does not want that type of personal information to be known. The only time that Ralph, Joe, or Sandy will talk about who BAT helps is if the recipient of BAT's help talks about it first, then BAT will talk. I know that Ralph is happy that present-day players such as Joe Girardi, Jay Bell, and Jeff Conine are lending their help to BAT. Many young players today have their own foundations and that's great, but the old adage that Ralph and I like to repeat is that charity begins at home, and we'd like to see young players more cognizant of their own fraternity's needs. This way, BAT can collect more money to help a greater number of people or increase its support to its current recipients.

Modern-day players should be aware of the players that came before them, especially because modern-day major leaguers make so much money. It's hard for these players today to imagine what it's like to not be able to support your family, but it's not hard for us former players to imagine at all. Minor league ballplayers make less than the average working person by far. BAT has helped old timers who never made much money and minor leaguers who need support to get through the lean years. BAT will pay hospital bills when players need treatment and have no insurance, and it will pay the rent for these players as well, so that they can get back on their feet. If it weren't for those players who came before them, where would the players of today be? They wouldn't be making tens of millions a year.

BAT has given out more than $6 million in 10 years, starting in 1987. It's a great organization, and I'm proud to be associated with BAT. There are many people hurting from the days when baseball paid its players nil. It's great to see guys rehabilitate themselves and have prosperous lives. Ralph won't admit it, but here he is again helping those in need. He and the BAT board members are deeply concerned about caring for those who cannot care for themselves.

20

Goldsboro and My Beloved
State of North Carolina

NORMA AND I HAVE HAD A LOT OF OPPORTUNITIES TO LIVE elsewhere, but we call Goldsboro home. In fact, the doctor who operated on our daughter Princie's eye when she was four years old offered to give Norma and me an acre lot in Atlanta because of our friendship through the years. It was on beautiful terrain in a beautiful section of Atlanta, and we could have it if we would come there and make Atlanta our home. Of course I refused that offer, even though I was deeply touched, and that's because Wayne County and Goldsboro have always been special in my heart. I was born here and raised here. I know the people here, and I love the pace of life here. We have everything we need. We're close to Raleigh, the capital, and we're only 1 hour and 15 minutes away from New York by airplane from Raleigh. We're also close to Atlanta. Each year when the baseball season ended I couldn't wait to get back here.

I like my church here. Norma and I belong to the Madison Avenue Baptist Church and have been members since 1954. Our children grew up here, and all three of our daughters were married in this church. It's just a great place to live. We live in an area called Stratford Acres. There isn't any traffic by us, and all we can hear on a still day are the airplanes from Seymour Johnson Air Force Base. In fact, many of the fighter planes in the Persian Gulf War came from here in 1991. It's just a great place to live. I wouldn't live anywhere else.

I believe that community is important. I've said this so many times. I think that a person's hometown is important to them, and that organizations such as the Chamber of Commerce, the Rotary Club, the Kiwanis Club, and the Lions Club can make a difference because they are a channel through which you can contribute to your community. I've said this before: anybody who lives in a community and doesn't support the institutions of that community is a parasite. They're eating out of someone else's dinner bucket. I think that North Carolina is a great state and that Wayne County is an ideal place to raise a family. I remember during a clinic in Japan, there was a little guy sitting in an army truck with his head between his knees. He looked awfully sad, and I went over to him and tapped him on the shoulder and said, "Son, where are you from?" He said he was from Anderson, South Carolina, and before I could say anything else he said that he'd give a million dollars and be willing to work it out at a dollar a day just to go home. That's the way I feel about my country and my state and town and my community. Someday I won't be here, and I'm trying to set an example for my children and grandchildren and sons-in-law in supporting my community, because you just don't have a successful community without personal involvement.

I've been involved with the North Carolina Sports Hall of Fame, and in 1997 we went on a walk to raise money for the Museum of History. I try to be involved as much as I can. I've been involved in prison ministries at Seymour Johnson and other prisons. I've gone around the states to minister to inmates and have had some wonderful experiences and some not so wonderful. Here in Goldsboro we'd go out every Tuesday night and we'd mix with the inmates and do Bible study. We were told not to get too close to the inmates and never to ask what they were in prison for. The warden told us that if they ever got to trust us, they'd tell us without our asking.

One incident that happened to me during spring training is as follows. I got a call from an inmate. I knew who he was, and I asked him what was up. He told me that he had escaped from prison. He said he was scared and didn't know what to do. I told him to turn himself in to the authorities. He said he didn't want to turn himself in because he was scared that the authorities would put him in solitary confinement, and he was afraid of being beaten up by the other prisoners. I asked a lot of friends what to do. My friends said to back off, that the FBI would get after me. I spoke to my wife Norma, and she said that she was afraid that the inmate would come to our home. I decided to try and find somebody who could help. I called Ollie Toomey, a close personal friend and important person in the Goldsboro area, and he put me in touch with a prison official in Raleigh who told me not to let the prisoner tell me where he was. When the prisoner called me I had already told him that I didn't want to know where he was and that if he called me back the next day at the same time and same number, I'd have an answer for him. Well, the prison official in Raleigh told me that if the prisoner called back the next day that I should find out where he was and let the official know. The prisoner called me and told me that he was in Virginia Beach. I told the official where he was, and he went to Virginia Beach, met the prisoner, and took him back to the prison. The prisoner was put right back into his routine and not placed in solitary confinement. This was an answer to a prayer.

I started working with Walt Rabb, the baseball coach at UNC. I've always tried to work with the UNC baseball players, and I still attend football and basketball games there. I've been acquainted with baseball coach Mike Roberts, and Mack Brown and Dean Smith. I did some physical work with one of the quarterbacks when he was having trouble with his arm. The university meant so much to me in the early years because it gave me my college education. I met Norma there, and it's just a special place for both of us. This is why the state of North Carolina means so much to me and why I built my house and made my home here. It had to be in North Carolina and in Goldsboro.

We had lived in the city of Goldsboro for many years in a little house that was on a lot that was 50 by 150 feet. We lived in this house for 25 years. It was at 408 South Oleander Avenue. As mentioned earlier, I had used the $4,200 bonus that we as Dodgers received for being in the 1952 World Series against the Yankees to put a down payment on this house. The house had two bedrooms and a bath, and we paid $11,500. One memory I have is of the time Norma bought some new carpet for the girls' bedroom and the door wouldn't close. The carpet was so thick that the door would drag over it. Norma had asked me many times to take the door off and saw off the bottom so that it would close. Well, it was a Saturday afternoon and I was watching my Tar Heels play football on television and Norma came in and asked me again to do it. So I said that I would do it at the half. So the half came and I went in and took the door down and laid it out on our wrought-iron steps. I sawed it off maybe an inch or an inch and a half. I was quite proud of my sawing, and although it wasn't exactly straight, it was reasonably straight. The piece fell off on the ground, the sawing was done, and I took the door and tried to reinstall it. I put the door back on its hinges and the door still wouldn't close.

I said to Norma, "The door still won't close. You're going to have to get somebody that knows what they're doing to cut this door down."

She looked up at the top and then looked at me and said, "The reason it won't close is because you cut off the top!"

I tell you I took that door down again and went back and nailed that piece back on the door. Norma had seen enough. She stained the wood and fixed that door, and when we sold our house you couldn't even tell that the door had been sawed off. Thank goodness we have our handy son-in-law Jesse in the family now.

It was in 1977 that Norma and I moved into our new home in Stratford Acres, about eight miles east of Goldsboro off Highway 70. We had been planning this home for a long time. Everyone would ask us what kind of home we were building, and I would always say, "We're building a combination of all of the homes we've lived in all these years in baseball." We've lived in so many different towns and houses that Norma tried to arrange this house to be a combination of all of our previous homes. I'd be asked constantly when we planned to move in. I would answer, "As soon as we can," because we were so anxious to have a new and larger home.

Our dream house was the third house to be built in the Stratford Acres area. It's adjacent to Walnut Creek, our country club, of which we've been members since its inception. It's got a great golf course. It's a beautiful club built about 30 years ago.

I built my house the way I always dreamed of building a ball club, from scratch. I started with a solid foundation. I tripled the piers underneath the house because I knew that we would have grandchildren someday, and I built it for them to be able to jump and play. I knew how I used to be as a kid when I'd go to a home with stairs—I loved to jump off the stairs onto the floor. I put several extra piers underneath the house where the stairs would be, so that when the children jump off them, it doesn't shake the house. Goldsboro means so much to me because it's where I have my family, where I grew up, and where I'm having the privilege of seeing my grandchildren grow up as well.

Goldsboro is the home of great restaurants. A great Goldsboro landmark, and national landmark, is Wilber's Barbecue. It's a world famous barbecue place. It's been written up in *The Wall Street Journal* and *Southern Living* and numerous culinary books as the number-one barbecue restaurant in the country. People go out of their way to eat at Wilber's. People who are just passing through this area by car stop there all of the time. Its founder is a man by the name of Wilber Dean Shirley. He does a lot of great things for our community, and he's very generous to our charities. Andy Griffith used to teach school here in Goldsboro years ago, and he loved Wilber's. Ava Gardner is from Smithfield, just a few miles from Goldsboro. Actress Ann

Jeffers was born in Goldsboro. When they were all in Hollywood and would come to New York for a function, they'd call Wilber and have him put some barbecue on a plane and send it to New York. Years ago we had a substation here for Piedmont Airlines, and Wilber would put the barbecue on the plane. Somebody in New York would meet the plane and get the food, and they would have a barbecue party in their hotel in New York. We had a friend by the name of Sonny Carter, an astronaut, and when he flew up from Houston to visit us I took him to Wilber's. He enjoyed the barbecue so much that he took some back to Houston with him. He also took Wilber's barbecue on the next space flight. So, it can be said that Wilber's has been in outer space. Sonny unfortunately died an untimely death. He was going to make a speech, but the private plane that he was traveling in crashed and he was killed. He circled the Earth twice without incident, but he was killed on a private plane. President Clinton has been to Wilber's, as has President Bush. Johnny Grant loves Wilber's as do all of our hometown heroes. Another great barbecue restaurant is Ken's Grill in LaGrange, North Carolina. Ken's Grill has outstanding barbecue and fish stew. Ken and David Eason really know how to serve delicious food. Yet another is McCall's in Goldsboro.

One great memory I have about my grandchildren is of the time when the girls were little and we bought them a battery-powered Corvette. It was pink, and it was a real miniature car. This Corvette had everything. It had a pedal and steering wheel and we started teaching the children at a young age to drive it. They'd get in there and they could mash that pedal and speed off. They could drive that car wherever they pleased. Once in a while they'd run into something. We've got a big garage, and we'd take the cars out and let them drive around in there if the weather was bad. We built a swing and we have our birdhouses, and we also have our tree house.

We've got a basketball goal that our son-in-law Jesse A. Blackman built. Jesse is married to my oldest daughter, Norma. Jesse is simply the best medical doctor around. He is educated, caring, and really knows medicine. I have been around team physicians for years, and I can see that Jesse listens to his patients and understands their concerns. It fills me with great regret that medicine has become so filled with paperwork. I think Jesse is so valuable to his patients because, through all of the modern computers and paperwork, he always puts his patients first and foremost. If it's possible to combine the friendly, old style of medicine with the modern drugs and apparatus, then Jesse has done it. He is up on the "computer age" of medications and still has the old-school touch of class about him. Normie helps Jesse a lot in his medical practice, and has become a computer whiz. Several companies have tried to hire her, but Jesse will not let her go because she is so valuable. Jesse and Normie have two children—Jesse A. Blackman, Jr. and Elizabeth Graham Blackman. They usually go by their nicknames of JAy, or Jay, as it has been modernized, and Egie, which stands for E. G.

Our oldest grandson, Jay, is a graduate of the University of North Carolina at Chapel Hill. He's a great basketball player, and I go out there and play one-on-one or "horse." He's 6'5" and he is some player. He was one of the managers of the Tar Heel team under Dean Smith that went to the Final Four in 1997.

Jay also shared another great memory with his grandfather. During my tenure as a manager in 1982, Jay was able to be the New York Yankees batboy! For one game in which he was the batboy, Joe Garagiola was on the air, and Joe thought that it was so neat that my grandson was the batboy. In a flicker of an eye, as I saw him on that lush green grass at Yankee Stadium, I suddenly remembered all of those backyard games of catch Jay and I used to have when "we" were kids. I say "we" because whenever I played with Jay I felt like a big kid.

My granddaughter Egie attended Appalachian State in Boone, North Carolina, and later transferred to UNC at Wilmington where she is deciding on a major.

My middle daughter, Princie, is married to Doug Evans. They have three children—Blythe, Miranda, and Sam. Princie is quite a gal. She is up on everything—government, politics, and local affairs. She is a great teacher and a wonderful cook. One of the great things about being a grandparent is being around little kids. I remember I had taken Sam to a Kinston Indians game to introduce him to baseball and he loved it. Baseball is a great family game. I know that Sam will remember the time he slept over at Coach Whitfield's house last year. George Whitfield was just inducted into the hall of fame here at Chapel Hill as a high school baseball coach. I really enjoy watching Sam play baseball or basketball. He has great ability for a kid, and he might be a better athlete than his grandfather. I really cherish the times I get to spend with him and play catch with him. It's great to know that I am his "coach." I really treasure our backyard games of catch and our basketball contests in the driveway by our goal. This is what life is all about.

Being a grandparent is great because you get to tuck your grandchildren in at night and tell them stories. I'd sit in my recliner and tell Miranda some of my boyhood stories. I limit them to two stories each night, but Miranda always asks for one more. Grandchildren are the best audience anyone could ever want in life. I always tried to come to Miranda's piano recitals and her soccer games. Soccer is very popular in our schools here in North Carolina. Sometimes her soccer playoffs were when I was working, but I'd make every game that I could when I was home. I wanted to take them to football games at UNC while they were young so that it would make a lasting impression on them. Miranda is a whiz on that piano. Her teacher keeps giving her harder and harder songs to play. I just enjoy it, it's the best concert in the world, listening to my Blythe and Miranda play piano. Now Miranda has taken up the violin. Blythe is now taking guitar lessons. Wow!

Blythe is a fantastic piano player! She really is. She can play Beethoven's "Moonlight Sonata" and she can also play popular music to the point where you can close your eyes and feel that you are at a concert. When Blythe plays at her recitals I get a little carried away. I know it's a little embarrassing, but after her piece is done and everyone is clapping, I'll add that extra, "Yeah, Blythe, go Blythe!" I just love her piano playing, and being a grandparent means cheering for your grandchildren even at the expense of embarrassment. She competes in state music competitions and I know she has a real talent for music. She and Miranda will be great musicians.

Another great joy of being a grandparent is driving lessons! I love taking Blythe out in my Jeep and teaching her how to drive. I let her motor around our property and it's great. I did the same thing with Blythe's mom and her aunts. In the summertime I take the grandchildren to the mountains. They love visiting Grandfather Mountain. Blythe, Miranda, and Sam met Mildred the Bear, the main attraction at Grandfather Mountain, when they were young.

I think the time that was most scary for Princie's children was when we were in a car accident. I was taking them home early one Sunday morning so that they could attend their church back in Wilson. A lady driver smacked us in the side and the radiator went up in smoke. I think they thought that the car was on fire. We came through the accident unharmed. Blythe rose to the occasion by unbuckling her little brother Sam and pulling him out of the car. The interesting thing was that it happened right in front of the fire station. I had to get a new Jeep—mine was totaled.

My youngest daughter, Janet, is married to John Peacock. Janet is a great mother, as are Norma and Princie. She was a cheerleader and homecoming queen at Country Day School. Like her sisters, she is involved in many community projects. Her husband had been the vice president of the chamber of commerce in Charlotte, North Carolina. That chamber was responsible for bringing NBA basketball to Charlotte, the Charlotte Hornets. It also was responsible for the NFL granting an expansion franchise to the city. The Carolina Panthers have certainly taken North Carolina by storm, and they've played well since their inception. Johnny is now the president of the Wayne County Chamber of Commerce. The Peacocks have an uncanny ability to make friends wherever they live. I think it's because of Johnny and Janet's stellar personalities. They have three daughters—Mary Clyde, Hadley, and Mallory. I love attending their soccer games, and I love attending Mallory's voice and dance recitals. When I think of Mallory, however, I'll always think of our backyard softball games, but not for the reasons you might think.

They say that kids imitate their elders and they're right. If these ballplayers don't think they have an effect on children, they're wrong. When Janet and John lived in Charlotte, they had a house with a huge backyard. The backyard was converted into a softball field, with painted white lines, bases 40 feet apart, and a real pitcher's mound. Well, Mallory would get up to the plate and she would go through the "major league routine" as I dubbed it. First, she'd tap the plate three times with her bat. Then came the routine of using the bat to knock the dirt out of each cleat, and finally she'd spit! Just like a pro! She learned this routine from watching ballplayers on television. Last, of course, she'd cream my best pitch down the left field line for a sharp double!

Mary Clyde is named after her grandfather and is a cheerleader, like her mother. If I know Mary Clyde, she'll be a homecoming queen also. She plays the piano and a mean flute. Hadley plays a wild saxophone, and Mallory sings and dances. Listen to Grandpa brag a bit: each of my grandchildren are good to excellent students, and make As almost every report card.

People who say that dogs are not intelligent don't know dogs very well. John and Janet have this white Maltese dog and they couldn't figure out what to name the dog. Hadley insisted on the name Charlotte, because they were living in Charlotte. John and Janet didn't really want that name so they coaxed Hadley into compromising. They named the dog Scarlet. Apparently this dog became Hadley's personal dog. I came over to their house soon afterward and decided to play games with Hadley like all grandparents do with their grandchildren. I made like I was a bandit and started growling, and that dog quickly jumped right over everyone and came in between Hadley and myself, as if to protect her. Nowadays, when I play with Hadley, Scarlet knows I'm kidding. You see, dogs do have intelligence and a sense to protect someone.

We have a tree house that I built with our three wonderful sons-in-law—Johnny Peacock, Jess Blackman, and Doug Evans. They built it amidst our trees, as we have three and a half acres with tall oaks and pines. It's a real one-room house up in the trees. It's not a fort, but a real tree house. There's a full-size bed in there, intercom system, and it's got carpeting and windows, a porch, chairs, and a fan. It's heated for the winter. There's a radio in there, and eventually, we'll put a television in there as well. Our grandchildren have slept in that tree house and many great little memories surround it. However, I would not categorize my fall from that tree house back in 1991 as a great memory.

We built the tree house without first building the steps that would lead up to it. We started out by using the raised patio porch, and then we used ladders to construct the tree house. Jess and I were working underneath the porch when it started to rain. I ran inside and brought out some plastic and placed it on the porch above us. We finished work and went inside. The next day I went back outside to take the plastic cover off. I climbed up on that ladder by myself and tried to pull the plastic off. I pulled, and pulled, but it wouldn't come off. So, I braced myself and really jerked it hard. It suddenly came loose and I fell over backward. I fell out of that high tree house and onto the ground, landing flat on my back and breaking six ribs. I also broke my shoulder, my collar bone, and I damaged one kidney and my left lung. Jesse said that if I hadn't been a former athlete in such great physical condition, I would have been killed. This happened at age 66.

The fall was so hard it knocked my shoes off. I hit the ground and my shoes flew off and landed 8 or 10 feet from where I fell. I got up, and needless to say, I couldn't straighten up. I staggered toward the house. Norma and her friend Mary Lou were inside and when I got near the house Mary Lou said to Norma, "I hear Clyde calling and he's hurt. It looks like he's having a heart attack." Before I even came inside they had called 911. The rescue squad came in less than 15 minutes and took me to the hospital. Jesse was already at the hospital waiting for me. I went right into intensive care and they started taking care of me. When a first rib is broken, which is the strongest bone in your body, there are likely to be serious complications. You can't tell right off the bat if there's heart damage or other damage. I recovered, however, and received much fan mail both kidding me for being up in a tree house and wishing me well in my recovery.

The one lingering effect of that fall is that I can't swing the golf club as far back as I'd like, because my shoulder is now an inch lower. I can't bring the club behind my back to the point where I can hit the ball as far as I used to, so it's not quite as much fun for me to play golf anymore. Being the competitive person that I am I can't just go out on a golf course and play around, because I know that before falling out of the tree house I could play the game well. When Norma called Mr. Steinbrenner to tell him about my accident he said, "What was he doing in a tree house?" He told her that only three types of people play in tree houses—kids, fools, and Tarzan. Later I asked Mr. Steinbrenner which of the three did he think I was, and he said maybe all three.

The fall happened because the tree house didn't have a rail around it. We decided to build steps and enclose the top. Jesse came over here and built those steps by himself. I still don't know how he did it. It's just as sturdy as can be. Jesse didn't want anybody else getting hurt, so he built a guardrail around the elevated porch and the steps leading up to it. It was then that I realized that any one of us could have fallen before, but at the time we were building the house no one thought about getting hurt. In fact, I'll never forget the day the tar paper was being put on the roof, and my sons-in-law Johnny and Doug were up there without any guardrail, and it started raining. It was dark, and I stood on the ground praying that they wouldn't fall. They covered that roof with the tar paper and the rain didn't affect the inside because it was now sealed. That house is as sturdy and as strong as anything. It's a testament to family projects. I spent last Christmas Eve out there late at night. I wanted to start the fire early in the morning on Christmas Day, and so I went out of the house without disturbing anyone and slept there. It was great. I got up early and started the fires in the fireplaces before the others awoke. It really felt like Christmas Day.

We've also got a tricycle and bikes for our grandchildren. Our son-in-law Johnny taught all of them how to ride the bikes. He'd run alongside them and hold them up until they'd get started and then turn them loose. We've got bikes like stairsteps. We had five bikes at one time. I started teaching the kids driving. I taught Jay and Egie how to drive, and now we're teaching Blythe, Miranda, and Mary Clyde.

Another nice thing that Goldsboro did for me was to make me a hometown hero, along with Johnny Grant, at Applebee's restaurant. The advance-man from the Applebee's chain came to Goldsboro and asked people who should be the hometown hero. Applebee's has a hometown hero section in every one of their restaurants. Well, the local Goldsboro people he asked apparently said I should be, because the next thing I knew he was asking me for memorabilia. When he came to me I told him that in my mind Johnny Grant should be the real hometown hero. He told me that everyone agreed that both Johnny and myself should be the heroes. Johnny Grant has been the honorary Mayor of Hollywood for years. He's been on all of Bob Hope's trips for the USO when they've gone to entertain the troops. When someone gets their handprints in the famous Mann's Chinese Theater in Hollywood, he's the guy who's always there next to them. He's a real hometown hero to me. He was the number one disk jockey on the West Coast with KTLA. He and Gene Autry started out together. He knows all of Hollywood, and he's just a wonderful person. In fact, he was nice enough, since we've known each other from our high school baseball days in Goldsboro, to include me in his video of his 50 years in show business. He brought a crew to my house, and it was wonderful to be a part of it. At Applebee's restaurant, I now have a booth with a collage of my memorabilia that I loaned to Applebee's. It's a great feeling to walk in there and sit in that big booth and have dinner. Johnny Grant has his place there as well, and we were both there for the opening. I told the executives at Applebee's that I would only be associated with a family establishment and if there were any bar fights or anything not in the spirit of family, then my memorabilia comes off the wall. It's a great place, and they have kept their word about it being family-oriented and friendly.

Hugh Morton is another great man I want to talk about because he has done so much for the state of North Carolina. Hugh, I've often said, has done more to put this state on the map than anyone else. He is the owner of and conceived the idea of Grandfather Mountain. Orville Campbell, the owner and editor of the *Chapel Hill* newspaper, introduced us to Hugh 25 years ago. Grandfather Mountain is a resort area east of Asheville. It's famous for Mildred the Bear and the mile-high bridge that people love to visit and walk across. Poor Mildred isn't around any more, but she is on display. She was a gentle, wonderful bear. I thought Mildred was great for Grandfather Mountain because she gave people the opportunity to be photographed with a real bear, and not a bear that would attack someone. Grandfather Mountain has nature trails and a beautiful zoo with otters, bears, and cougars. The otters are just fantastic. Besides this, Grandfather Mountain has the best picnic areas around with the best views in the state. In 1996 Hugh asked me to speak at "Singing on the

Mountain." Gospel groups come from all over the southeast on a Wednesday and it runs through the weekend. I spoke before seven thousand people. The platform was up high, and the people sat in the valley. Billy Graham, Jerry Falwell, and a lot of other renowned speakers have spoken there as well. Hugh is an environmentalist and really cares about North Carolina. He's a PR man for our state and does a lot of charity work. Grandfather Mountain also has the best museum around. There's a VIP area where pictures of famous people, such as Mickey Mantle, Walter Cronkite, Dean Smith, and Charles Kuralt, adorn the walls. Newt Gingrich was there in 1997 as well. Anybody who comes to the western part of North Carolina would surely be missing something if they didn't visit Hugh's place. I know one member of my family who will never forget Hugh, and that's my granddaughter Mary Clyde.

Hugh took pictures of Mildred the Bear with her paws around our grandaughters, and he used one picture on his poster. I remember him calling us, and Janet and Johnny in particular, and asking if he could take a photo of Mary Clyde for his posters, and we were tickled to death. Janet and Johnny were only too happy to oblige, as they loved the idea of having their daughter on that poster, which is still the poster advertising Grandfather Mountain. In fact, the resort hotels in North Carolina all have this advertisement for Grandfather Mountain and there's my Mary Clyde! Grandfather Mountain is a real wonderful place to be, both in the wintertime and in the summer.

My daughter Princie has a fond recollection of Hugh Morton because he brought the battleship *North Carolina* back to North Carolina in 1960, running a little campaign to accomplish this goal. He enlisted the schoolchildren of North Carolina when Princie was in the fourth grade. She was nine years old, and she gave all she had, which was 10 cents, toward that campaign. She was thrilled. After the campaign was over, each schoolchild was sent a membership card, and the card stated that the child had contributed to the campaign to bring the battleship *North Carolina* back to be berthed in Wilmington, North Carolina.

Julia Morton, Hugh's wife, is an outstanding woman. She is a learned Christian lady, and she and my wife Norma love to talk about Bible studies and Christian books. Hugh lived in Wilmington during the early years and then went to Grandfather Mountain in the summers, before moving to Grandfather Mountain permanently.

We love our little place at Echo Cottage. It's really a treat for my grandchildren to come there and get up in the morning and actually be so high up in the mountains that the clouds roll right by the porch. They can literally touch the clouds, and it's so much fun for them. We go to Little Switzerland every year during the summers. It's so much fun because we can go down to the local stores, buy the morning paper, take our swim at the Chalet, and just enjoy being in the mountains. My wife's sister married Jim Duls, and his family had a house in Little Switzerland. His sister Luisa wrote a book about the history of Little Switzerland. It's a great book about that area.

The Switzerland Inn is a great place to stay at, and it has a first-class restaurant owned and operated by the Jensen family. Jake Messer's general store is a unique place to shop and have lunch. Dr. Curtis Johnson and his wife, Kaye, operate a fabulous bookstore that you can browse in for hours.

I remember Charles Kuralt as a down-to-earth guy. He once told me of his ambition, when he was growing up in Wilmington, North Carolina, of wanting to be a major league baseball player. He loved meeting people. When I say he loved meeting people, I mean ordinary people. You seldom saw him interviewing executives. He interviewed the people who lived off the earth. I thought it was great, the way in which he ran his show *On the Road*. He taped a documentary of North Carolina that I thought was magnificent. He was a great ambassador for the state of North Carolina and a great ambassador for the field of journalism. He was a consummate professional and that's why his *On The Road* series will endure forever.

North Carolina is home to another great man—Billy Graham. One time John Lotz, the associate athletic director of UNC, arranged for Norma and me to have a visit with Billy Graham and his wife, Ruth. John's brother, Danny, is a dentist in Raleigh, and he's married to Ann Graham, Billy's daughter. We got to know Ann through that connection. She's such a good speaker that there's a waiting list for the Bible study that she conducts. She and Danny invited us to their daughter's wedding in Montreat. Their daughter was married in the same church in which both Danny and Ann and Billy and Ruth were married. Three generations of Grahams have been married in the same church. I went to that wedding alone because Norma was on a trip to the Greek Isles at the time. Then in early December Danny's other daughter got married in Raleigh and both Norma and I went to that affair. We saw Billy there and discovered that unfortunately he was battling Parkinson's disease. At the last wedding they made an announcement that Billy was there against his doctor's orders. He came in with a cane, and it made us sad. When Norma and I spent the afternoon with him a few years ago, he told us about his Parkinson's disease, and he asked me to pray for him. I couldn't believe that he asked me. I told him about my prostate operation, and he prayed for me. Ruth gave Norma one of her books and autographed it for her, and she treasures it. What an inspiration Billy and Ruth are to Norma and me, and millions of others.

North Carolina is home to the Tar Heels, my alma mater, and I would just like to say how proud I am of the wonderful program Dean Smith has turned out all these years. It was sad to see him retire. Dean made UNC the best college basketball program in the country and the cleanest. UNC has an excellent graduation rate, and Dean chose players who would represent the school and community very well. So many NBA greats have learned from Dean Smith. Michael Jordan, whom I've gotten to know over the years, is just fantastic about giving back to UNC. I know he credits Dean Smith with the wonderful times he had at UNC and for all Dean taught him, not just about basketball, but about life. Michael has become the greatest in the game of basketball, and when I reflect on him as a young college kid I can't believe time passes so quickly. It seems like yesterday that he was on the court at UNC. Coaches George Karl and Larry Brown came under Dean Smith's tutelage, as well, and have done well in the NBA as head coaches.

I remember one World Series when George Steinbrenner let me invite some close friends from UNC to a game—Orville Campbell, my close friend who owned the *Chapel Hill* newspaper, and Dean Smith. Dean then invited me to a tournament at Madison Square Garden. That just shows you what type of guy he is, always trying to reciprocate. He is a gentleman and the epitome of a level-headed, decent person, in and out of basketball. Bill Guthridge has taken over, and I know he's going to do a terrific job. I'm big on Antawn Jamison and Vince Carter. I know they'll do well in the NBA.

I do think that any team that signs a player after his sophomore, or junior, year ought to be required by the NBA league officials to pay that college a large financial settlement. I think it would deter NBA teams from enticing young players to leave college before they complete their education, or at least not until after their junior year.

21

What Babe Ruth Means to Baseball

BABE RUTH WAS BASEBALL. EVERYONE KNEW ABOUT RUTH, no matter where you lived. Our neighbors who didn't follow baseball knew all about Babe Ruth's power. When I was a kid and one of my friends would hit a real long home run, our neighbors would talk about it being a Ruthian-type shot. I knew he had tremendous home run power. I loved the power hitters. We had a player here in Goldsboro playing for the Goldbugs. His name was Eddie Ignasiak, a left-hand-hitting first baseman who hit home runs. I would go to watch the team play just to see him hit. I'd stay on the outside of the park and try and catch any foul ball hit over the stands. I couldn't afford to buy a ticket, so I tried desperately with my brothers, Claude and Billy, to catch one of the foul balls hit behind the home plate stands or wherever during batting practice, because if you presented a foul ball to the man at the gate, he would let you in free. That's how we got into the ballpark.

I would picture Ruth in my mind whenever I'd see Ignasiak play. This is what really started my interest in Babe Ruth. When I was a kid we could get the results of New York Yankees games on the radio. The first thing I would look for in the papers the next day was to see if Ruth had hit a home run. I would turn right to the sports pages to see what Ruth did day in and day out. Ruth had that type of impact on the game of baseball and on baseball fans.

I was a Yankees fan and a Ruth fan. I was so glad to have been involved with all three of the New York teams during my baseball career because I knew the impact that these rivalries had on the game of baseball. My next hero after Ruth was Joe DiMaggio. I remember I wrote a fantasy paper on DiMaggio and how he hit a ball out of Goldsboro's Griffin Park onto Ash Street that went so far it landed on top of the Wayne Bank Building and then bounced off of that into the Neuse River. This would have been a three-mile home run! My teacher underlined that part of my paper and told me that I really was fantasizing, the objective of the assignment. I've got a picture of Babe Ruth going out of the dugout at his final appearance at Yankee Stadium; it's from a writer friend of mine. It's amazing to me that Ruth could catch, pitch, and hit. He started out as a left-handed catcher, then was converted to a pitcher, and then a right fielder. As a right fielder he used that great pitching arm, because to play right field you need a real durable and strong arm. Ruth did it all well. I believe that he forever changed the game. I think that Arnold Palmer did for golf what Ruth did for baseball. Arnold Palmer kept golf going after legends like Ben Hogan and Bobby Jones were gone. Ruth took baseball into new dimensions. Ruth, more than any other player, got people interested in the game of baseball. Ruth could eat hot dogs and then hit three home runs. I think that Babe Ruth's number 3 should be retired throughout all of baseball as well.

I think Babe Ruth is the greatest ballplayer of all time; he brought positive attention to the game like it had never had before. Ruth loved children, and he made baseball a kid's game back in an era when kids needed a hero. Babe Ruth and kids are synonymous.

At the age of eight his mother and dad gave up on him. He was such an incorrigible youngster that they couldn't discipline him, and in 1902, they sent him to St. Mary's Industrial School in Baltimore. There, he came under the influence of a guy who changed his life. He was a Christian Brother, Brother Mathias. He took a special interest in Babe and recognized right off the bat that this was a special youngster. At St. Mary's he learned to read and write. He learned right from wrong. He even learned a trade, tailoring, and Brother Mathias stayed close to him. Also, fortunately, they played a lot of baseball there. They had 800 kids in that school, and they had 40 teams of all ages. And Brother Mathias made sure that Babe was active all the time because he needed some way to vent that energy that he had inside of him. Babe was later quoted as saying, "I was a bum during those days."

He was a street urchin. Many times he left that school, and they went and got him and brought him back. But he was under the influence of a quiet, 6'6" soft-spoken, but strong, man who had strong convictions and who felt a need to look out for Babe. He turned his life around, really. He taught him all of the things that he needed to know. One day, the St. Mary's pitchers had been having a rough time. They were in a slump. Babe sort of laughed at them and kidded them, and Brother Mathias said, "We don't have that on our team."

He told him, "We don't have teammates criticizing each other. If you know so much about pitching, you get out there and pitch."

Babe said, "Well, I've never pitched before."

Brother Mathias said, "You go out there and pitch. You think you know how to do it better than your teammates, you go out and do it."

What a career that started! Brother Mathias was his first pitching coach. Babe became a pitcher and he never lost a game that he pitched for St. Mary's. He had a great fastball and a good curveball. He was left-handed and, being a left-hand catcher as well, he was versatile. When you think of the versatility of this great athlete, it's amazing. He played first base; he played the outfield. He pitched and he caught. What else could he do? He hit home runs, and he could steal bases if the situation called for it.

He went on to pitch and play and hit balls over outfielders' heads and over the fence for several years. He finally got the attention of the newspapers in Baltimore, and they started to write about this youngster with great talent. St. Mary's was playing this one big game coming up against St. Joseph's. It had been billed as a great event. Babe Ruth was going to pitch. However, the morning of the game he reverted back to his childhood antics and jumped over the wall and left St. Mary's. He vanished for four or five days. Nobody even knew where he was, but the Christian Brothers went out and found him and brought him back. Brother Mathias punished him by having him stand alone for five days in the schoolyard during the games, while they were teaching him discipline. That discipline really touched the Babe because he learned then that he could not do wrong and get away with it, and what a great lesson that was for him. And don't you know that Brother Mathias didn't hold that against him. As soon as he had stood for five days alone, he put him in a game against Morrison, their archrival, and Babe won the game as a pitcher. He hit two home runs, a double, and drove in four of the six runs. They won 6–0. And by this time there was a gentleman in Baltimore named Jack Dunn, who owned the Baltimore Orioles, a minor league team, who had heard about this young player and wanted to talk to him.

He came to see this game that Babe won 6–0. He asked Babe if he wanted to sign a contract. Babe said that he did and signed the contract for $600 for the first season. Babe later said that he thought that was all the money in the world. He couldn't wait to get going. By this time he was 18 years old and the Brothers had enough confidence in him that they let him leave on weekends to play with the semipro teams. When he was 9, he was playing baseball with teams made up of kids 12 years old. When he was 12, he was playing with kids 16 years old at St. Mary's, and he was always ahead of his teammates. Jack Dunn offered him that contract, and Brother Mathias stood at the gate at St. Mary's and saw Babe Ruth walk away for the last time to catch a train south for spring training. It brought tears to Brother Mathias's eyes.

He said to him, "George, you'll make it. Don't ever give up. Don't look back. George, you'll make it."

How true that was; what a great career he went on to have in baseball. You know it reminds me of all of the pictures I've seen showing Babe with children, either on his lap or in his arms. I think that came from the fact that Brother Mathias paid so much attention to him when he was eight years old. It really gave him direction and guidance. So many people talk statistics, but I think to love Babe Ruth is to talk about Brother Mathias and his role in guiding young Ruth. I spoke about that aspect of Brother Mathias in a speech about Ruth at Hofstra University on April 29, 1995. In that speech I drew a parallel between Brother Mathias and my freshman basketball coach Al Mathes, who as I described earlier helped turn my life around.

I wish that we could raise the level of baseball back to where it was in the days of Babe Ruth, the level that he raised it to in the 1920s and 1930s. Wouldn't it be great if today we had a baseball ambassador like Babe Ruth was back then? Mark McGwire and Sammy Sosa gave baseball a great shot in the arm by the way they handled themselves during the exciting home-run race in 1998. These two fine young men are certainly heroes, and I hope they will be role models as well.

22

Baseball Is a Great Game—
Let's Not Ruin It!

THERE ARE SEVERAL GREAT SPORTS, LIKE FOOTBALL, BASKETBALL, golf, tennis, and I could go on and on, but baseball is the greatest of them all. Baseball has been my life since I was a young child. Without a doubt, it kept me off the streets and out of poolrooms that would have had a negative influence on me. When I stop to reflect on my life, I realize that I played some sport almost every day of my life, whether if be baseball in the summer or football and basketball in the fall and winter. So you can see, there was no time for me to hang out on street corners. I've been involved in organized baseball since I was 19 years old. In the days when I was playing I had to supplement my income by holding other jobs during the off-season, and I had many of them. One year I drove a laundry truck delivering dry cleaning. One year I took school pictures. I went around to the schools and into the classrooms and took the school pictures. Another year I refereed basketball games. In those days, in 1951, I won 14 games and lost 7 for the Brooklyn Dodgers and had six saves, and I made $13,000 with two kids to support at the time. I had to have extra jobs in order to support my family.

Having said this, I am deeply concerned about the future of this game. There are several things that need to be addressed and changed if baseball is to remain healthy and prosperous. The selection of a baseball commissioner has been too long in coming. There were several candidates, in my opinion, who would have made a fair and strong commissioner. Jim Bunning would have been one to consider, as would Rudy Giuliani (Mayor of New York), George Will, John Schuerholz, Orrin Hatch, Tal Smith, Colin Powell, and George Bush, Jr. (Governor of Texas).

Now that Bud Selig has been appointed, the owners and players should strongly support him. The owners must come together as a unified group in order to become more compatible and to be willing to work together. The division among owners must cease. I'm a believer in the old saying "together we stand, divided we fall." This could be changed to read "together we succeed, divided we fail." The players' association relishes in the fact that the owners are not going to unify. The unions, therefore, will have the upper hand. Let's stop fighting each other, declare peace, and make both sides get rid of their egos for the good of the game.

There are some brilliant, articulate, commonsense owners who are genuinely interested in the good of the game and want to keep it above and beyond reproach at all times! To this I say Amen! Our presidents over the years have ended their "State of the Union" addresses with "God Bless America." In addition to this, I say "God bless baseball."

The Major League Baseball Players Association is very much aware that "unity is strength and division is weakness." Their hope, I'm sure, is that owners remain as they are, which makes their job much easier. So I say to the owners, renew your love for the game, learn to work together for the good of baseball, and in so doing your investments will be safer, more secure, and better protected. Baseball could survive without the players' association, without the umpires' union, and without player agents, but it could not survive without the owners. So, until the above-mentioned groups realize that baseball is bigger than they are, separately or combined, baseball will continue to struggle, and the threat of a strike, or a lockout, will remain with us. It took the class of Sammy Sosa and Mark McGwire and their pursuit of 62 home runs in 1998 (breaking Roger Maris's record of 61 home runs) to rejuvenate baseball. To these men I say "God bless."

One of the worst additions to baseball in recent years is the player agent. First of all, player agents have eliminated, almost entirely, the relationship between the owners and their general managers with the players. The owner seems to have no voice concerning his employee (the player). Players nowadays hide behind their agents and don't have to face the ones who pay their salaries. Most agents—not all mind you—have very little, or no, regard for the welfare and health of baseball. They are totally consumed with how much money they can get for their clients (players). If baseball were to "fold," today or next year, they could care less because their players have their million-dollar, guaranteed, long-term contracts. Even if their salaries stopped, they have already made enough money to live comfortably for the rest of their lives. When a player has made three, or four, or ten million dollars, over 3, or 4, or 10 years, how much more money does he need? Maybe he just has to have a sixth car, or a third boat, or another 50 suits, or another 50 pairs of shoes. Whatever it is that is causing the players and their agents, and the players' association to continue to gouge the owners, it had better level off, or stop, soon. If not, baseball could go broke, or declare bankruptcy.

I have a poster in my clubhouse that was given to me by my friend George Whitfield. I think it's an example of just how much the game has changed. It's a *Sports Illustrated* cardboard poster of the 1968 National League Champion St. Louis Cardinals starting lineup and it's a beauty. The title of the poster is "The Highest Paid Team in Baseball History." Here you have all of these great baseball players sitting at their lockers with their jerseys hanging down beside them and right next to their photo is their yearly salary. The entire team's salary totaled $607,000, and that's peanuts to what a single star makes today. That 1968 team included Hall of Famers Bob Gibson, Lou Brock, manager Red Schoendienst, and others such as Roger Maris, Dal Maxvill, Curt Flood, Orlando Cepeda, and Mike Shannon. Roger Maris, the home run king, made $75,000 that year. Dal Maxvill, their shortstop, made $37,000. Red Schoendienst made $42,000. Orlando Cepeda made $80,000. Curt Flood, their center fielder, made $72,500, and pitching legend Bob Gibson made $85,000, and he was the highest paid player.

It is inconceivable to me that players have the power to tell the owners when they can schedule games, or when a rainout must be made up. It is unbelievable, yes unbelievable, to me that an agent will call a general manager, or owner, and question a decision to send his client to the minor leagues. It is as if the agent knows more about operating the club than the baseball people.

Are you ready for another one? A relief pitcher has an incentive clause in his contract that pays him $15,000 if he's in a certain number of games. The club is in the final two weeks of the season battling for the division title, and the agent calls and says that the manager should get his pitcher in three more games before the end of the season so that he can get his bonus of $15,000. It doesn't matter to the agent that his pitcher has pitched terribly of late and that is the reason the manager hasn't been using him. The fact that the club is fighting for the division title doesn't concern the agent. Also, it doesn't bother him that by using this pitcher the team's chance of winning might be jeopardized. So, I hope you can understand that this agent—not all agents—doesn't "care a hoot" about the team, or baseball. All he cares about is getting his client the extra bonus money. I ask you, does baseball need this kind of attitude? Fans will answer this question. My answer is—it does not.

I must now talk about the umpiring situation. Major league umpires of today are much too aggressive, less tolerant, have short fuses, and are far less cooperative than they should be. I saw a minor league game recently, and I was very impressed with the umpires. They were energetic, on top of every play, and handled every situation very professionally and fair. Also, they were in good physical condition! The first-base umpire became involved in an argument with a manager, but he did not do what many major league umpires do—throw out his chest and get nose-to-nose with the manager. He calmly let the manager have his say, then he had his say, which was calm and not agressive. The argument was over and the ump did not follow after the manager as he went back to the dugout, as so many major league umpires do today. No one was ever "shown up" and no one was thrown out of the game. I wish major league umpires would take a lesson from these young men, and handle themselves as they did. If the umpires ever decide to strike, I say "let them," then bring up umpires from the minor leagues, such as these three. If a team can bring up a young 20-year-old player, why couldn't a young umpire perform just as well at the same age? Some umpires today have become lazy and complacent simply because they know that they are like the supreme court justices, as their jobs are safe and their tenure is forever.

I would suggest that if an umpire fails to do a competent job, he should be sent down to the minor leagues, or released. After all, "What is good for the goose, is good for the gander." If a ballplayer fails to do a credible job he is sent down to the minors, or released. The same should apply to umpires.

Another interesting little twist that took place a couple of years ago was the lowering of the pitcher's mound. Some fans might wonder why that makes such a difference. Well, from the point of view of a former pitcher, let me tell you that at first I wasn't in favor of lowering the pitcher's mound from 15 to 10 inches. However, the "Lords of Baseball" were convinced that it would make the game more exciting for the fans. They convinced me that it was what the fans wanted. To be fair, it's penalizing the pitchers, but if it's what the fans want, then I'm all in favor of it because baseball is the fans' game.

Another thing that is of concern to me is the concept of teamwork. The old Brooklyn Dodgers had their regular lineup of Campanella, Reese, Robinson, Cox, Furillo, Hodges, and Snider. The only position in which a change was made daily was in left field, as managers chose between Andy Pafko and Gene Hermanski. Everyone usually stayed healthy as well. Today, lineups seldom remain the same from year to year on any given team because either players get injured, or are traded, or are lost due to free agency. I hope that the old-fashioned phrase "team loyalty" doesn't become lost in this age of mega millions. I know that Tony Gwynn knows what team loyalty is all about, as does Cal Ripken, Jr. and Kirby Puckett, and I always say God bless these men who have stayed loyal to their teams. Tony Gwynn has been so loyal to San Diego and Cal Ripken has been so good to Baltimore. Kirby Puckett had to suddenly retire because of his eye injury, which deeply saddened me. He went to work in management for the Twins. I hope the young players take a lesson from these men who remain loyal to their teams. Among others, Stan Musial and Ernie Banks played their entire careers with the same teams.

Lastly, the modern schedule needs to be addressed. I can remember years ago there being only two exhibition football games and a 10-game NFL schedule. When they increased the NFL season games from 10 to 16, they added six weeks to the football season. Nobody complained, however. The fans loved the extended schedule. Baseball used to play a 154-game schedule and now they play a 162-game schedule, with an extra wild-card playoff spot. However, in total it comes to only about an additional two weeks a year. The NBA is playing games into June, and when the Rangers won the Stanley Cup in 1994, Mayor Rudy Giuliani called Mark Messier "Mr. June." Baseball, thus, in its defense, has received some unfair scheduling criticism. However, I do see continued television wars over air-time because each league is running into the other's season. Football and baseball schedules have some overlap, and college hoops start before football is finished. However, regardless of what the players or executives think, if the fans don't mind the overlapping schedules, then it's fine by me.

The five-man pitching rotation that so many teams employ is another aspect of the game that has changed. Years ago, you pitched every four days. Today, you start a game, get knocked out in the second inning, and then you wait four more days before you pitch again. This means, however, that you have pitched, maybe, two innings in 10 days, and that's not good. I know managers can work the rotation around so that they can slip a pitcher back into the slot before their next start, but I'm a four-man rotation person. I think your arm stays stronger, and you have less arm trouble. Years ago, pitchers pitched batting practice between starts. Nowadays they won't let the pitchers throw batting practice. Managers prefer to have their pitchers throw in the bullpen or on the side instead. However, that's not the same as throwing batting practice. It's as if a hitter were to throw the ball up in the air and hit it instead of taking batting practice. As far as I'm concerned, a pitcher throwing in the bullpen is much the same as the batting scenario I've just described.

Relieving today has gotten more specialized, and I think that it's great that relievers are finally getting the credit they deserve. In my day I was a reliever, and I loved coming into ball games that were "on the line." I always felt I performed better in these close situations, and I always wanted the ball when the game was on the line. If I had my wish, and I were the general manager of a brand new expansion team, my first pick for that 25-man roster would be "the stopper" or "closer." You need men like Goose Gossage, Sparky Lyle, or Rollie Fingers. Several great young closers have come on the scene, such as Mariano Rivera, Trevor Hoffman, and John Wetteland.

The game of baseball is rapidly changing both on and off the field, and although I've voiced some concern, I have a positive and optimistic attitude in my heart. I love the game of baseball. I do know that what I've said needs to be addressed by the owners and players. If this is done with care by both sides, our game will remain the national pastime.

23

Norma Gets the Last Word

THE ONE WHO MEANS MORE TO ME THAN ANYONE OR ANYTHING in my life is my lovely wife, Norma. Norma is a lady in every sense of the word. She has a sweet spirit, a beautiful smile, a soft voice, and a countenance about her that is infectious. She is intelligent, and I rarely make a decision without consulting her. She truly has a great woman's intuition. She is absolutely beautiful both inside and out. She is my lover, my best friend, and my "Sweetie"! Therefore, it is only fitting that Norma has the last word!

Baseball has been great to Clyde and me. We love the game, and the game has been good to us. I've been privileged to have been involved with the game of baseball and, more importantly, to have met the wonderful wives that I have over the years. Clyde and I have had a rich life because of baseball. Baseball has taken us from North Carolina to Brooklyn, to Hollywood, to San Francisco, to Atlanta, and then back again to New York. We've been to Japan and have had the chance to travel to Israel and Europe and it's been great. I never thought when I became a wife that one day I'd be eating with chopsticks in Japan. It's been a dream come true for Clyde and me to have met the hundreds of people that we've met over the years. We've met the top executives in the game, stayed in the best hotels, and been treated like "Kings." I'd like to tell you what it was like for me to be a baseball wife, and I hope that many women across the country will find reading my perspective on the game of baseball interesting— and inspiring for those of you young ladies who are thinking about careers in sports or sports management.

Clyde and I met while students at the University of North Carolina at Chapel Hill. I was a physical education major and went to most of the football, basketball, and baseball games. Many of the players were in my classes. I loved sports and they were a great part of my college life. In 1943 and 1944 girls only played intramural games, and I enjoyed playing basketball and participating in other sports. I did my practice teaching in modern dance and softball. It was so much fun, and I am grateful that I chose physical education as my major.

During my last semester at Carolina, Ben Ward, a mutual friend from Goldsboro, introduced me to Clyde. On our first date we went to a Carolina–NC State football game in Raleigh. I think Clyde was impressed that I could keep up with him as we ran across the railroad tracks and into the stadium. We enjoyed the game, and that was the beginning of the story of our lives together in the sports world. I had watched Clyde play basketball and baseball and knew that he was the star pitcher on the team, but I did not know that he was absolutely the nicest, kindest, and most special person—just as he is today. Clyde had already been signed to a professional baseball contract by the Brooklyn Dodgers, but he was back in school for the fall semester. I graduated and went on to teach, and he went to play ball in the spring. Our courtship was mostly by long-distance phone calls and by letters. Even so, it was exciting, and we fell in love.

When Clyde proposed, I accepted, and we set our wedding date for November 29, 1946. Everything had to fit in with his career, so I finished my contract in health education at the YWCA in Syracuse, New York, where I loved my work. Then I went home to Roseboro, North Carolina, to complete plans for our wedding. My parents gave us a beautiful wedding in the Baptist church where I had grown up. It was like a dream for us. Clyde was a great witness to me and told me before we were married that he loved me more than anyone in the whole world, but that Jesus Christ was first in his life and then me. Somehow God gave me the grace to understand and appreciate that commitment, and so our married life together was built on Jesus Christ. What a blessing and what a difference it has made. We had a lot to learn to make a good marriage, but our love for each other had a strong and firm foundation.

After our wedding and honeymoon, we took an apartment in Goldsboro, and of course we spent a lot of time with my parents— it was only 50 miles away. Clyde played a lot of basketball that winter, and I went to every game. We had such good times being together and sharing. Everything we did was fun and the time passed quickly. The time came for Clyde to leave for spring training. The Dodgers were going to Havana, Cuba, and they would stay there for about six weeks. When Clyde went to Havana, I went home and spent the time with my family. I'll never forget how I thought my heart would break having to be separated that long! But I learned something that I have lived by for all these years. Clyde told me that he hated saying good-bye to his mother because it made it so much harder for him to leave when she would cry, and so he always made his good-byes to her as quick and short as possible. So from that day forward I always sent Clyde wherever he had to go with a happy face, and I always made his homecomings as special and as happy as I possibly could.

I had lots to keep me busy—I still had lots of thank-yous to write for the wedding gifts and the many nice things that had been done for us, and I spent time with friends. Also, Clyde was so good to write every day and share with me all of the things that he was doing—his pitching progress, his time with friends, and the experiences and excitement of being in Havana. Time passed quickly, and I had so much to look forward to in my first year of marriage and baseball life. I had no idea of what my life was going to be like as a baseball wife!

You can imagine how thrilled and pleased I was for Clyde to make the team! So, my parents put me on the train in Fayetteville, and I was on my way to be with my wonderful husband and spend the baseball season in Brooklyn. What a place to be and what a thrill to be a part of that Dodgers team! Even though I had been to New York City and visited the sights, I was still a little nervous about just what it was going to be like and how I would fit in and adjust. Clyde told me exactly what to do and made all the arrangements for me. We stayed at the St. George Hotel, where most of the players and their families stayed until they found apartments or houses for the season. It was a great hotel, and I did a lot of swimming in the salt-water pool there while Clyde was at Ebbets Field for workouts.

To be with Clyde again was like another honeymoon. Little did I know that would be the pattern of our baseball life. The first morning we went to the dining room for breakfast and there sat Dottie and Pee Wee Reese and their two-and-a-half-year-old daughter Barbara. They had been in Havana with Clyde, and when Clyde introduced me, they invited us to sit with them. We became friends immediately, and thus we began a friendship that has meant so much and is just as strong today. I could not have found a better friend than Dottie had I searched the world over. They already had found a place to live, in the Bay Ridge section of Brooklyn. They helped us find a house on Lafayette Walk at 94th Street, which was not too far away from them. Dottie knew most of the players and their wives and she introduced me and made me feel at home. We spent every road trip together and I had a wonderful summer. I thought she knew everything and she did. She was just as pretty from within as she was in physical beauty, and I learned all about being a good baseball wife from her. There again God gave me the very best! To this day, I am indebted and grateful to Dottie.

Dottie Reese taught me to knit and encouraged me with my sewing, and she let me use her machine. There were so many interesting and fun things to do which we both enjoyed. We would go into New York City, have lunch and shop, and other wives would join us. Dottie was an excellent driver and always drove her car, as she knew her way around. When our husbands were at home and we'd have a free night, we'd go to see a Broadway play, and we managed to see the best ones. We would also get together at our house or theirs and play bridge. In fact, they taught me to play. Sometimes I would go to the baseball games alone when Dottie stayed home with Barbara. Dottie was very careful to have a sitter for Barbara that she knew and trusted.

One of those times when I went to the game alone was when I met Rachel Robinson because our seats were together. I was glad to get to know her and was able to introduce her to the other wives after the game. What a lovely lady! All the Dodger wives were friendly and we enjoyed the times we were together. We lived far apart and only saw each other at games and special occasions. It was a very special group. I knew it at the time, but not until 50 years later did I realize again just how special the Dodger wives were back then.

On the celebrations of Jackie's 50th Anniversary of breaking the color barrier in baseball, I looked back and realized the important role that the Dodgers players, and their families, played in racial integration. The summer was filled with excitement as history was being made. We were privileged to be a part of it. Jackie certainly was successful in fulfilling the role that Mr. Branch Rickey had given to him, and his teammates recognized him to be an athlete of great skill and ability.

The Dodgers won the National League pennant in 1947 and played the Yankees in the World Series. We didn't win the World Series, but we went home for the winter with a grateful heart to have been a part of a great team and receive a World Series check of $4,200.

Going home for the winter and separating from all our baseball friends was much the same as going home from college and leaving all your classmates and friends. It's a sad and lonesome feeling even though you knew you'd be together again in the spring. Clyde and I were happy to have loving families to go home to, and we made the rounds.

We decided that we would buy a car with part of our series check. It was our first big purchase. It was wonderful to have our own car and to be able to travel whenever and wherever we wanted. As you can imagine, we went back to Chapel Hill for all the Carolina games. It wasn't long after we were at home that I went to the doctor and learned for sure that I was pregnant, and the baby would be due about June 15th. We were both so excited, but it surely wasn't any fun having morning sickness. As time progressed, I felt fine and had a wonderful pregnancy.

As spring training of 1948 drew closer, we were more uncertain as to where I should plan to have our baby. Dr. Charles Powell was my doctor and I felt so confident and secure with him, but he assured me that I needed to be with Clyde more than I needed him. Dottie and Pee Wee told me to go with Clyde and that if anything happened—like Clyde being sent to the minor leagues—they would take care of me until I was able to be with him. The Dodgers were training in the Dominican Republic and so Clyde was off again, and I went home to my parents. My mother was an expert seamstress and had taught me to sew years before. We bought beautiful material, and, with her instructions, I made by hand the layette for our baby. Clyde was so proud of me and I was proud of myself.

Soon it was time to meet Clyde in Brooklyn. We were fortunate to be able to rent the same house. Dottie and Pee Wee found a house about three blocks from us. We were all set and glad to be able to spend road trips together again. Dottie helped me find Dr. Stanley Hall, who was a super doctor and gave me just the care and special attention that I needed. Dottie planned a baby shower for me and invited all the wives. I think almost every wife came and brought generous gifts that were just what I needed. I still remember how much fun it was to open each gift, and then I put them in our nursery in final preparation for our baby. On the night before I went into labor, we had dinner with Dottie, Pee Wee, and Barbara.

At about six o'clock in the morning on June 17th, my pains were getting closer. Clyde called Dr. Hall (he had to drive in from Long Island, but had promised me that he would), and we left for Methodist Hospital. Dottie went with us and helped get me settled in my room. Clyde couldn't be with me any longer. Husbands back then didn't get to help deliver the baby like they do now, and so he left and went to Ebbets Field, where he had received a message to see Mr. Rickey. And guess what? Mr. Rickey was telling him that he was being sent to Montreal, the Dodgers AAA farm team. As they were talking the phone rang and it was Dr. Hall calling to tell Clyde that he had a baby girl! Well, Mr. Rickey sent Clyde immediately to the hospital to be with me and told him that he could stay in Brooklyn as long as was needed before reporting to Montreal.

Well, there we were with a beautiful healthy baby who we named Norma, and Clyde had to be leaving! The Reeses were now caring for a new mother and baby. I would have been devastated, but they assured me that they were perfectly capable and willing to take care of us. So Clyde went off to Montreal, and I stayed in the hospital for 10 days—that's the way it was back then. Dottie came to see me every day, and they sent me a fresh gardenia corsage every day. I cried every day until a wonderful nurse told me that I should be ashamed of myself because there were mothers who had their babies during the war and they didn't know if they would ever see their husbands again, but I was going to be with mine again soon. I guess I did a lot of maturing right then! I went home to Dottie's house and thank goodness Pee Wee was on a road trip. Dottie had everything ready for us (crib and all). I couldn't have had better care. Dottie was so patient and easy going and such a loving and helpful person. She taught me all that she had learned when Barbara was born.

Clyde pitched a good game in Montreal, and so they let him fly to Brooklyn for the weekend. That was great for him and us as well. I got stronger and we packed up all of our belongings in our car. (A player being sent to Montreal drove the car for us.) Pee Wee returned from the road trip, and I was very nervous that Normie, that was little Norma's nickname, would cry during the night, or bother him in some way. But he was very understanding just like Dottie, and if it did bother him he never let us know it. When the baby was three weeks old, they put us on a plane for Montreal. We were on our way with the excitement and anticipation of being with Clyde again and living in a different country. I was so glad I had studied French!

Clyde met us at the airport and drove us to our home for the summer. We simply exchanged houses with Paul Miner, as he was sent to Brooklyn and took our house there. It was fine as long as Clyde was with us, but very lonely and sometimes frightening to have all the responsibilities of a house and baby alone. Clyde would call me every day on the road and that helped so much. Also, I had to learn my way around, and just going to the grocery store was not easy. We didn't have car seats and all of the safety devices that are required nowadays.

Toward the end of the season, Clyde was told that the Dodgers wanted him to play winter ball in Havana. We decided that I would go home to North Carolina so everybody could see our daughter, and I would have time to reorganize before leaving for Havana. Stanna Dapper, whose husband Cliff was the team catcher, was a good friend, and she said that she would drive with me to Washington, D.C. We had to stop there and stay with my sister, Mary Watson Duls, until the "medical alert" concerning polio was lifted in North Carolina. Anyway, Mary Watson and Jim's house became the stopping-off place for us wherever we were going during all our years in baseball. As soon as the season ended for Clyde, he flew home and had a few days before we were off to Havana. Another great experience!

We drove to Miami and then got on board a ship (taking our car), and we arrived in Cuba the next morning. It was pure luxury and Normie was very good except when we went for dinner and left her with a sitter, and then she cried the whole time. Anyway, Havana was all that I had thought it would be. The ball club and everyone around us were so good to us, and it was such a nice baseball city! We had a beautiful house, a maid, and a sitter who would sit for Normie. So we were able to do things and explore and enjoy our time there. Clyde pitched well, and we were able to go home to North Carolina just in time for Christmas. Nothing could have pleased us more.

Spring training was in Vero Beach, Florida, and Normie and I were able to go with Clyde. It was a pleasure to train in a small town (at that time) where wives could spend a lot of time together. It was a vacation for me as Clyde worked and I played. I loved the sun, ocean, swimming, and all that Florida offered. As soon as spring training was over, we were off again to Montreal, only Clyde went with the team, and I had to drive. Fortunately, Jean Laga, another pitcher's wife, needed a ride, and I was thrilled to have her go with me. Not only was she good company, but she was a great help in taking care of Normie. We drove to North Carolina and spent a few days with my family and then went on to Montreal, stopping for the night in Brooklyn on the way.

In Montreal we found a nice apartment and settled in for the season. A lot of the players were future Brooklyn Dodgers stars, as was Buzzie Bavasi, who went on to be general manager of the Dodgers. It was a good place for Clyde to be and another learning experience for us. It was a good team, and we made lots of new friends. Betty and Carl Erskine, Betty and Chuck Connors, Jo and Tommy Lasorda, and many others—these were just a few of our teammates whose friendships we have always treasured. We spent all of the 1949 and 1950 seasons playing in Montreal. Clyde had developed a new pitch (the slider) and had a very good year. We won the International League pennant and went on to win the Little World Series. Several wives were pregnant, including me, and so Clyde sent Normie and me home on the train, and this time he was left to drive.

I had lots to do to get ready for our new baby. I was fortunate to have my family doctor and my family to help us this time. Barbara Prince (Barbara for Barbara Reese and Prince for Prince Nuffer Dixon, a mutual friend at Carolina whom Clyde had known all through school in Goldsboro) was born on November 1, 1950, and was delivered by Dr. J. Street Brewer. I had an awful feeling that Clyde was going to be disappointed that she wasn't a boy. He was finally able to convince me that he was thrilled to have another precious daughter like Normie. As soon as I was strong again, we went to Goldsboro to live and that has been our home. With two children it was time to settle and make a permanent home for our family—a decision we've never regretted.

It became more complicated traveling with two children, but we managed and things went well. Clyde had a good spring training in 1951 and made the Dodgers team again. We went back to Brooklyn and found an apartment in the home of Mr. and Mrs. Walsh at 180 Marine Avenue. Can you believe, only two blocks from Dottie and Pee Wee, and next door to Bev and Duke Snider. Betty and Carl Erskine were living in our former house on Lafayette Walk. It was absolutely wonderful to be so close to our friends. We did lots of things together. Dottie only had her daughter Barbara at the time. She was great company for our girls, and we shared in so many ways together.

The Erskines and Clyde and I went to the city every Sunday night that the boys were at home, to Dr. Norman Vincent Peale's church. After the game, we'd have to rush to get there. Mrs. Peale would meet us at the door and she would take us to her pew. How blessed we were to get to hear Dr. Peale and to have that precious time with them. It meant more to us than they could ever know and what an example they set for us! We went to their home on Fifth Avenue for dinner and I wanted to be a gracious hostess, just as Mrs. Peale had been. Dr. Peale enjoyed the games and came as often as he could and sometimes even brought their children—Margaret, Elizabeth, and John.

It was a busy year, and the Dodgers were sailing along well ahead in the pennant race in 1951. Clyde was used as a relief pitcher and was having a good year. That year Ralph Branca was engaged to be married to Ann Mulvey in October. Jo Parrott, the wife of Harold Parrott, the team's traveling secretary, had a bridal shower for Ann at their beach home, and it was one of the highlights of the summer for the wives. We were all there and it was a wonderful party.

As the season progressed, we were losing ground to the Giants and the season ended in a tie for first place. We lost to the Giants in a three-game playoff. It was a sad time when Bobby Thomson hit the home run off Ralph, but our concern was for Ann and we wanted her to know that we were all in it together, win or lose, it was a team thing. Ann was sitting in a field box that game, and we couldn't get down there fast enough to let her know how we felt. So, we comforted one another and all went to our homes for the winter. Ann and Ralph had their beautiful wedding—one that was probably the biggest social event in the sports world in New York that year. They went to the Cloisters at Sea Island, Georgia, for their honeymoon and on their way back to New York stopped in Goldsboro to spend a few days with us. During their visit a call came to Ralph wanting him to be on the Ed Sullivan show. So, he flew to New York and was on the show and flew back to Goldsboro while Ann stayed with us. Nobody could have been as good a sport or could have handled it with such grace as Ralph. To this day he is a real hero! We have always been good friends and have shared many happy times together. They became Auntie Ann and Uncle Ralph to our girls.

We had a good winter at home. Again the time passed quickly as we anxiously awaited another season. We traveled to Vero Beach and had a wonderful spring training, and then it was on to Brooklyn. Mr. and Mrs. Walsh made an apartment in their basement and moved downstairs so Clyde and I could have their big house. Millie and Rube Walker took the upstairs apartment where we had lived the past summer. Ellen and Andy Pafko and Mozee and Preacher Roe found places close to us. Ann and Ralph lived in White Plains, but they would come stay with us, so we could all gather for "covered dish suppers" and other things that we did together. The boys could share rides to Ebbets Field and to the Polo Grounds. Those were good times for all of us. Patty Branca was born that summer, and we all enjoyed and loved having a new baby around and we were especially happy for Ann and Ralph.

The Dodgers had a good year and won the pennant in 1952 and, of course, played the Yankees in the World Series. It was a busy time getting ready for the games, and all the celebrations that are part of winning. My sister, Mary Watson, came and took Normie and Princie back to Washington on the train, so I would be free to go to all of the games. It was great to get dressed in the new outfits that I had purchased. I can tell you that all the wives were a lovely group and were, collectively, an asset to the team. Part of the fun and excitement was going by bus from Ebbets Field to Yankee Stadium with a police escort. Some of us had been a part of the 1947 World Series, but the thrill was just as great. Yankee Stadium was big and awesome—as there was so much history there. It was a great series, but the Yankees won in seven games. It was never easy to say good-bye, but the next day we were all packed and on our way to pick up our girls and then head on to Goldsboro.

Clyde had not pitched very much that year because of a sore arm he developed from having thrown so much in the bullpen the year before. We had been home only a week or so, when the general manager, Buzzi Bavasi, called to tell Clyde that he had been traded to the Cincinnati Reds. Well, to me it was like the end of the world had come! I was heartsick to think of leaving our friends. But that was the way it was in baseball, and I knew and understood. I remember many called to tell us that we'd still be friends and see each other whenever possible and would always stay in touch. They all have remained true to their word and through the years we've remained friends. We've attended each others children's weddings when possible and have been to many Old Timers' games and other events that were a reunion for us.

Clyde and I were grateful to have another World Series check and decided that we would use it toward a down payment on a house. We looked for the best house available that we could move into and spend the winter and that would give us more space for the girls. We found a nice brick home that had only been lived in for a few months. It was in a nice neighborhood where many of our friends lived, and it was close to our church (Madison Avenue Baptist), to school, and to downtown. We lived there for 25 years and as our needs grew, we added on to the house at two different times. It was such a perfect place for us, and it was so easy to close up everything and be away for the summer.

The spring of 1953 was spent in Tampa, and then we went to Cincinnati for the season. We rented a nice house in the Hyde Park section, and it was a relief to know that there was life in baseball after Brooklyn. Cincinnati was a lovely city, and Gabe Paul, the Reds' general manager, and others made us feel welcome. On the Dodgers first trip to Cincinnati, and just as they had promised, Pee Wee, Rube, Duke, Carl, and Ralph came for dinner. It was great to catch up on all the news of families and have a good visit. What a comfort to know that our friendships would last forever. It was also great to get to know the players on the Cincinnati team and their wives, and not only did we make new baseball friends, we made Cincinnati friends. Ann Branca's roommate at Marymount College, Patsy Grote, and her husband Tom, became our family there. We loved being with them and their children, and we still correspond to this day.

After the 1954 spring training Clyde was still having arm trouble, so the club told him to go to Tulsa, Oklahoma, and pitch where the weather was warm, and it would hopefully help his arm. After spring training, the girls and I had gone back to Goldsboro until Clyde found a house for us. Rarely were you able to get the same house as the year before. He was very discouraged and was ready to come home. That was the first time that I really had some influence on his career. I persuaded him to go and give it a try and assured him that the girls and I would get packed and would drive to Tulsa and be there when he arrived. The team was on the road at the time.

That was the beginning of many long trips by car with our girls. This was to be a part of our future in baseball. Clyde traveled with the team and we drove alone. So I had AAA plot a road trip from Goldsboro to Tulsa. It was a three-day trip, which meant we had to spend two nights in a motel. My mother was always afraid that the girls would distract my attention, and we might have an accident, but they were great travelers and were always quiet when I needed them to be. Also, I had perfect assurance that I was doing what I should be doing, that Clyde was praying for us, and that it was important and wonderful for us to be together.

The route to Tulsa was new territory for me, and everything was fine until the second day. As we were crossing the Mississippi River Bridge in Memphis, Tennessee, amid heavy traffic, we got a flat tire. Before I even had time to think about what to do, the first car that passed slowed down and the driver hollered to me that he would send help. Normie was fine, but Princie was frightened, and I assured her that everything would be all right and reminded her that Jesus was watching over us. Well, help did come and within 15 minutes the tire was changed, and we were on our way. I followed the service man to his station where he patched the tire, and I paid him and was able to thank him. I just hope the man who sent help somehow knew how much he had helped and how grateful we were.

On the third day of our trip, the weather was stormy. The wind was so strong and the rain was so hard that I stopped on the side of the road. The car would actually sway, and the rain was so hard that we could barely see. We sat there—again, me trying to be brave and comforting the girls. Finally the storm calmed, a bus came along and I pulled back on the road and followed it. What a relief to get through that storm safely. We arrived in Tulsa and located the house that Clyde had found for us. There were tornado watches out, and soon Clyde was calling to tell me exactly what to do for our safety. I remember opening the windows slightly and taking all the precautions that he had instructed. We were a happy family once again when Clyde arrived later that night, and we were ready to enjoy our time in Tulsa. It was easy to get settled, because the house was very clean, and it didn't take long for me to put our clothes away and get everything in order. I do want to say that I always tried to leave a house cleaner than I found it, for my own reputation and for the sake of other baseball families.

The weather was good for Clyde, and he pitched well. So, after two months he was sent to Indianapolis for the remainder of the season. They were in a pennant race and needed pitching help. We had enjoyed our time in Tulsa and loved all of the different activities such as watching calf-roping. The people there were good to us. However, I was happy to see Clyde get promoted. And so, we were on the move again, and it was to be another long trip, so Clyde was given time between pitching assignments to drive with us. It was to be a short time in Indianapolis for the girls and me because Normie would be starting her first year of school and we wanted her there at the beginning. We were fortunate to find a place to live in for such a short period of time. Although I'm not a car-racing fan, it was a thrill to see the Indianapolis 500 racetrack. We went to some of the games and explored the city. Clyde always enjoyed taking the girls to the parks and playing with them at every opportunity. When he went on the road, we went to Anderson, Indiana, to visit Betty Erskine. She had gone home while Carl was on a road trip with the Dodgers. It was about a hundred miles away, and we had a wonderful visit with Betty and their boys, Danny and Gary.

When it was time for us to return to Goldsboro, Clyde was invited to stay with Herb Score and Rocky Colavito for the remainder of the season. They were very nice young single players and they promised to take good care of him, and indeed they did. He couldn't have been treated better! The team did win the pennant and went on to play in the Little World Series. The extra money was $1,000! Herb and Rocky went on to become major league stars.

By the time Clyde came home, Normie was all settled in school, and we were all settled in for the winter. Clyde's mother had suffered a stroke. Goldsboro did not have adequate nursing home facilities at that time, so Clyde made our side porch into a room for his mother so we could take care of her. Almost overnight I became a nurse. We did have a hospital bed, and Leora Moore, my household help, came six days a week to help me. She was also a minister, and I can't begin to tell you how much she meant to us as she read scripture and prayed for Mrs. King and us daily. How fortunate and grateful we were! Clyde would help watch over his mother at night. Normie and Princie were also a great help as they would stand on a stool, talk to her, hold her hands, and comfort her. It was confining and a big responsibility, but also a rewarding and growing experience that made our marriage and commitment to each other even stronger. Mrs. King passed away in early February, and we were glad to have had that special time with her.

Sometime during the winter of 1955 the Atlanta Crackers had purchased Clyde's contract, and so he was off again for spring training. The girls and I stayed at home because of school. As soon as the Crackers were back in Atlanta for the season, I went to visit Clyde and to look for a place to live. Leora stayed with the girls as she has done many times through the years. We did find an apartment and as soon as school was over, we went to Atlanta. I was pregnant and having morning sickness, but I had two good little nurses to take care of me when Clyde would be away. I'll never forget that Georgia red clay, and how hard it was to remove from the girls play clothes and shoes!

Clyde was still having arm trouble and so he was given his release, and we went home again. He was sure that he wanted to stay in baseball, and within three weeks, Atlanta made a change in managers and called Clyde to offer him a job. To be able to start a managing career in AA ball and to work for Mr. Earl Mann was like a dream come true! We learned that Mr. Branch Rickey, who had given Clyde so many advantages and opportunities to learn about how baseball works while he was in the Dodgers organization, had recommended him for the job. We still have a copy of that telegram that he sent to Earl Mann. What a great feeling to know that Mr. Rickey had such confidence in Clyde's baseball ability, and for him to say that Clyde's character would be an asset to any organization was just a great feeling. So Clyde was off to Atlanta to finish the season.

He had been with the team and knew the personnel. They did well and moved up in the standings—ending on a very positive note.

That winter was to be a good one. I had a good pregnancy and on February 7th our third daughter, Janet, was born. I didn't even worry about another girl this time! I knew how Clyde loved his girls and was such a good father that it just didn't matter. The girls were so excited and thrilled with their little sister and were old enough to be a big help taking care of her. When Janet was three weeks old, Clyde was off to Florida for spring training again. We couldn't go, but Clyde was able to devote all of his time to holding a successful spring training, getting his players ready for the season. As soon as Clyde was back in Atlanta, he found a nice house for us on Coventry Road in Decatur. We decided it was better to take Normie out of school in Goldsboro and have our family together. It was a good move because Normie had a wonderful teacher and loved her school.

Atlanta was such a nice city (about three hundred thousand in population at that time—1956) with wonderful people—such an enthusiastic baseball city. We were welcomed with open arms by so many nice people. We had the best church families: First Methodist where Dr. Pierce Harris was pastor and a golfing pal of Clyde's, Audubon Forest Methodist where Dr. Bevel Jones was pastor, and Druid Hills Baptist where Dr. Louie Newton was pastor. They were all outstanding and were a blessing to us. They ministered to us and loved us, and we knew it. When I think back, I thank God for the influence and impact they had on our lives. I would have to say that year was absolutely a dream year for us in every way. I could write a book just about those three people! We would ride down to Ponce de Leon Avenue and think about Catherine and Peter Marshall—we had just read her book *A Man Called Peter,* and Peter had been pastor of a Presbyterian Church on Ponce de Leon near the ball park when Catherine was a student at Agnes Scott College in Decatur. We almost felt a part of what Catherine was writing, never dreaming that in years to come, Catherine would become our dear friend.

The team played well. Mr. Mann was very considerate and good to us, and he has a very special place in our hearts. It was exciting to be a part of that winning Crackers team during Clyde's rookie year as manager. I went to as many games as possible. Fortunately, I had a good baby-sitter who the girls loved. I rarely took Janet to the game, but would always take Normie and Princie to Sunday afternoon games. They received lots of attention from the fans and began to love the games at an early age. All too soon, it was time for me to return to Goldsboro and have the girls ready for the first day of school.

We left early on a Sunday morning. Clyde had packed the car, and we said our good-byes, leaving him very sad and lonesome. He went to church at Druid Hills Baptist and sat in the back row thinking no one would see him since he was a few minutes late. Somehow, Dr. Newton saw him, and he announced to the congregation that Clyde King would be leading the morning prayer and asked him to come to the pulpit to pray. It was a new experience for Clyde, and he was very nervous. The next morning Mr. Cully Cobb took him and Mr. Mann to the Athletic Club for lunch and afterward to Obie Brewer's Men's Shop where he bought Clyde a suit. Mr. Cobb had been in the congregation on Sunday and just wanted to do something nice for Clyde. He wore that suit for years and always with special thoughts of how God works in the hearts of men.

Atlanta went on to win the pennant in the Southern Association and play Houston of the Texas League in the Dixie Series. Clyde was voted Manager of the Year for 1956 and what an honor that was for him! Flying to Houston and being with the players and their wives was a nice reward for all of us, and being a part of that winning team with such good fellowship is a treasured memory.

Clyde and I were so happy to be back home with our girls after the season ended. We'd been home only a few days, when Joe Brown of the Pittsburgh Pirates called to offer Clyde the job as manager of the Hollywood Stars for the following year. This was the AAA club of the Pirates—not only a step-up for Clyde, but a nice increase in salary. It was very difficult to leave Mr. Mann and the Atlanta Crackers, but this was an advancement that Clyde graciously accepted. So came February of 1957 and we were off to Hollywood and another exciting adventure in our baseball life and in Clyde's career.

We had decided that it would be best for us to drive to California together. Changing schools for the girls was our only concern, but that too worked out nicely. Irv Kaze of the Stars had found a nice house in Van Nuys for us to rent, and it was ready for us to move right in and feel at home. The neighbors were so nice and welcomed us with open arms. Clyde helped get the girls settled in school, and we had a few days to get acclimated before he left for spring training in Anaheim—about 30 or 40 miles away. The team would stay in the new Disneyland Hotel during spring training, which would be for about five weeks. Since Janet was only one year old, I was busy taking care of her and getting into the routine of school during the week days. Normie and Princie adjusted easily, though they found themselves sounding very different from the other children—saying "yes, ma'am" or "yes, sir." As soon as school was out on Fridays, the girls and I would drive to Disneyland and spend the weekend with Clyde.

The hotel was new and beautiful and we looked forward to those weekends. We were welcomed guests at Disneyland and what a wonderful place it was to entertain the girls. We have many pictures that help us to remember being some of the first to explore that great amusement park that people continue to enjoy today. It is hard to believe how it has grown through the years and all that it has to offer—it is an education for all ages. We're fortunate now to have Orlando's Disney World in our part of the country.

We found Hollywood to be just as interesting and as much fun as we thought it would be. There was so much to do and so many places to go and nice people to visit. Gilmore Field was a nice old park, and it had a great history surrounding it and a lot of character. The boxes had wooden doors, almost like church pews. It was definitely the place to be, and at every game there were many movie stars in the stands. What a thrill it was to see many of the stars that we had seen in the movies! Some that I remember being at the ball-park quite often were Gene Autry, Roy Rogers, Charles Coburn, George Raft, William Powell, and Jayne Mansfield and Frank Love-joy and his wife Joan Banks and Esther Williams and her husband Ben Gage, who always sat with Mr. and Mrs. Bob Cobb, were regulars as well. Mr. Cobb was the president of the Hollywood Stars and the owner of the Brown Derby Restaurant. Johnny Grant, who had gone to school with Clyde in Goldsboro, was the most popular disk jockey on the West Coast. He knew everybody, and he made sure that we met many stars and were able to visit the sets of movies being filmed. It was truly a chance of a lifetime for us, and we experienced everything that we could work into Clyde's schedule. We also did many things when he was on road trips, all made possible by our many friends.

Dr. Norman Vincent Peale came to Los Angeles to make a speech and invited us to visit with him. While there, he made arrangements for us to visit with his good friends Dale Evans and Roy Rogers at their famous Double R ranch in Chattworth. Dale and Roy were kind enough to invite us out to the ranch on a day when a commercial was being filmed at the stables, and we were able to watch the filming. We arrived at their home and were greeted at the door by Dale. She was making homemade ice cream in order to use some of the cream from the cows on the ranch. All of the household help had the day off, and the children were away at camp. Dale gave us her undivided attention, and I remember she was wearing a red bandanna kerchief around her head. She looked pretty wearing denim. She served us ice cream, and she told us that there was always a chair reserved at their table, and it was for Jesus. She showed us her book, *Angel Unaware*, which I had read, and she told us about their lifestyle and gave us a chance to ask questions and to get to know them better. Afterward, she gave us a tour of the house, and what a thrill it was to go into this special room and to see all of Roy's expensive and beautiful cowboy outfits—many that he had worn in his movies. All were in glass cases and under lock and key. The room was like a museum because there was so much memorabilia. Later, we were shown around the grounds, and the girls were taken for a ride in "Nelliebelle," the jeep used in their movies. Then it was time for the filming to start and our chance to visit with Roy. We were allowed to climb on the fence for a better view. It took a while because every time a noise was made that wasn't supposed to be in the commercial, they would stop and start again. We learned a lot about patience in filming. Roy and Dale were so gracious and gave us a day that we have never forgotten.

Frank Lovejoy and Joan Banks were two of the best and most loyal baseball fans—they rarely missed a game. They invited us to spend a day watching the filming of *Meet McGraw*, Frank's TV series. We went to their home in the morning where Joan served donuts, and then we were off for the day watching Frank. We were driven from one scene to another and were allowed to be close to the action so that we wouldn't miss a detail. Somewhere along the way, sandwiches and drinks were brought for lunch. It was so much fun being a part of it, and Frank was so kind and took such good care of us. Clyde was appreciative of all the attention shown to his family.

Back then children weren't always allowed on movie sets, but the girls did watch some outside filming—Robert Stack was the star, and how gracious and charming he was! That time we were able to bring Janet and our sitter. Pictures were taken that we still cherish.

We were guests on several radio shows like *The Breakfast Club* and the *Dale Moore Show*. Those were great experiences! We also had a fulfilling summer in other ways. We attended Van Nuys First Baptist Church and met many wonderful people, and we were included in activities there like the Daily Vacation Bible School and swimming in our next-door neighbor's pool and tap dancing lessons. I bought a map and learned my way around Hollywood and Beverly Hills so well that I could have given a tour of where the stars lived.

It was a fun, exciting summer, not to mention all that the baseball season had to offer. As the season was ending, it became definite that the Brooklyn Dodgers would move to Los Angeles and it would be the last season for the Hollywood Stars. It was a sad, yet happy time for all those dedicated fans who were so anxious to have major league baseball in their city. As much as we hated to leave, it was soon time for us to pack up and head back to North Carolina. It had been a successful season and a "mountain-top" experience for our family. The Pirates AAA team would be the Columbus Jets for the 1958 season, and Clyde would be the manager. We had to rent a U-haul to take our accumulation of things home with us. After a big farewell party, we departed on our trip across the country where we looked forward to being in our own home again with family and friends—remembering forever our year with the Hollywood Stars.

When Clyde had begun his managerial career, it was another adjustment for our family, as he was involved during the winter months with the organization making plans for the next season. He flew to Columbus a couple of times for that purpose, plus he spoke at the civic clubs so that he could get to know the people and they could get to know their new manager.

Goldsboro was a good baseball town and still had a professional team. There were many who wanted to see Clyde's team play. So Mr. Fred Jones, the president, and Mr. Harold Cooper, the general manager of the Columbus Jets, made arrangements to fly the team to Goldsboro and play a game with the local team on the way home to Columbus from spring training in Florida. It was a huge success and a thrill for many, and Clyde's way of doing something for his home town. After the game, Wilber Shirley treated the players to a dinner of his famous eastern North Carolina barbecue at his restaurant. It was nice for the girls to see their dad—even for a few hours—and it helped make the time seem shorter before we could join him in Columbus for the summer.

As soon as the girls were out of school, we were on our way, traveling through the mountains and getting another flat tire. It was the second flat tire during all those miles that we traveled over the years, and it happened close enough to a small country store that I could drive into the parking area. Two elderly men were sitting on a bench, and they saw what had happened and came over to help. They changed the tire, and when I offered to pay, they wouldn't take anything. They said that they were happy to help and that was their good deed for the day. Traveling in those days was safe, and I never had any fear that anyone would take advantage of, or harm, us, even in such a remote place. God's angels were surely watching over us!

Columbus was a lovely place to be, and we enjoyed ourselves. We had a nice house in the Arlington section. Our landlady left all her good china, crystal, and silver, and told me to feel free to use it, and I did. It was especially nice that I could entertain the players' wives for lunch, and we could visit and get to know each other better. I felt that was one of my responsibilities as the manager's wife.

In 1959 we were back in Cincinnati where Clyde took the job of pitching coach. It was good to be back there and working for Gabe Paul again. Somewhere about mid-season we made another change, and Clyde went to Rochester, New York, to manage the Rochester Red Wings, the AAA team for the St. Louis Cardinals. Mr. Frank Horton was the club president, and Mr. George Sisler, Jr. was the general manager. Clyde had known George's parents years before when he was with the Dodgers and they became good friends. Mr. Sisler Sr. was one of the great men in baseball and is in the Hall of Fame. George Jr.'s wife, Elizabeth, was from Albany, Georgia, and it didn't take long for us two southern girls to become friends. In fact, George said he could always tell when Elizabeth and I had spent time together, because she would be speaking in her southern accent again. They had two daughters, Susie and Nancy, and our children were good company for each other. Frank and Marge Horton had two sons, Frankie and Steven. Our families did many things together and had such fun. Marge and Elizabeth introduced me to everybody, and I was included in many social activities. Rochester was a community-owned team, and many distinguished ladies were devoted baseball fans and became our friends. Clyde couldn't have worked for or with nicer people, and it was four wonderful years that we spent in Rochester.

Frank was running for Congress, and Princie went up and down our street handing out his cards and politicking for him. He won the election and was the representative for many years. We were fortunate to visit them in Washington and were able to learn something about life in the nation's capital—a history lesson our girls will always remember. To this day, Frank always calls Clyde on his birthday.

The summers were short, as they always are when things are going well. Ralph and Ann Branca and their girls, Patty and Mary, came to visit. That was a real treat for us, and so much fun to have them root for our team. They were no strangers to our lifestyle. Even though Ralph had retired as a player, they were still involved with the Dodgers and were very much a part of the baseball world.

Whenever Clyde would have a day off, we would always do something special with the girls. One time we went to Niagara Falls and spent the night. What an experience and thrill for us to see that famous waterfall! We received VIP treatment—thanks to Mr. Horton. Upstate New York has so many beautiful lakes; and I think we visited all of them.

It was always an ordeal getting a house cleaned, packing the car, and traveling home. Wherever we went, we always stopped along the way to take advantage of famous historical spots. On our trips to and from Rochester, we always went through Gettysburg, and I can't tell you how many times we climbed the tower to overlook the battlefields. We certainly were exposed to a lot of U.S. history.

We were usually at home by Labor Day, as that was when school began. That gave me some time to set up my sewing machine and sew for the girls before Clyde came home. I sewed many dresses through the years. It was a challenge and really kept me busy. I would make most of their clothes, and then put my machine away for the winter. When Clyde came home, neither of us wanted our bedroom to be a sewing room. We loved being home and every day was precious.

After our summers in Rochester, Clyde went to work for Bing Devine and the St. Louis Cardinals in 1963. It was a different role for him, and he would be doing a lot of traveling while Goldsboro would be his home base. We welcomed the opportunity to spend the summer at home. That was new to us, and such a relief for me not to have to pack our clothes, close the house, and be gone for three months. We were able to take trips with Clyde when there was no time limit on travel and he would be working with a team for several days. Once we spent a week on the beach at Sarasota, Florida, while he was working with the team there—that was a wonderful vacation for us. Also, the girls were now old enough for camp. For several summers they would spend four weeks at Camp Yonahlosse in the mountains at Blowing Rock, North Carolina. This was such an important part of their lives as they made new friends and had many new adventures such as sailing, horseback riding, archery, tennis, canoeing, swimming, and working on all kinds of crafts. We also spent a lot of time on the farm with my family at Roseboro. My brothers, Hoover and Tommy, found plenty for them to do and would pay them for their work. They loved payday and really learned a lot.

On my fortieth birthday, Clyde was in St. Louis for meetings. He called to tell me to get ready because he was going to the Dominican Republic on an assignment and wanted to take me with him for my birthday. You can imagine that I made plans in a hurry and was ready to go when he arrived! Clyde was so thoughtful to take me someplace special every year—a time just for us. Our trip to the Dominican was such a luxury for me. We stayed in the same hotel that the Dodgers had stayed in during spring training in 1948. I couldn't believe that along with all of this beauty and luxury there was so much poverty! It certainly made me appreciate our country more than ever.

The next winter Clyde managed a team in the Dominican Republic. It was not something that he really wanted to do, because it meant being away from home all winter. His friend, Vern Benson, was supposed to manage, but his wife got sick and he couldn't leave her. When he asked Clyde if he would do it for him, there was no way Clyde could turn him down. The club really wanted Clyde and promised that he could fly home for three days at Christmas. We promised that we would fly there to be with him for Thanksgiving. It was our girls' first trip over the ocean and to a foreign country. They loved every minute! The weather was beautiful and they had a huge pool with a high diving board where the girls could swim and dive all day. Going to the games with everyone speaking Spanish was strange, but they learned some Spanish and Clyde insisted that they use it in their conversation. Each had a story to tell when we came home. Clyde did come home for Christmas. We had decorated the Christmas tree and had everything ready for a big celebration and celebrate we did! All too soon, he was gone and we started planning and looking forward to the end of his season. After a trip to Venezuela to play in the play-offs, he was home again until it was time for spring training.

After two years with the Cardinals, Clyde was asked to be the pitching coach for the Pittsburgh Pirates in 1965. He was to be reunited with Joe L. Brown, the general manager. Harry Walker was the new manager and he had a coaching staff of Johnny Pesky, Hal Smith, Alex Grammas, and Clyde. So we were kind of glad to be back with a major league team and going to the games every day.

However, the girls' summers were now being filled with their own activities. Normie was going to spend two months in Europe traveling with her girl scout troop of 20 girls and their leaders. So we drove to New York City where they boarded a ship for their trip. Ralph and Ann Branca were always so gracious to have us stay with them. On the day of departure, we were there to see Normie safely on board and wave good-bye. Princie, Janet, and I stayed a few days so we could go to the World's Fair before driving to Pittsburgh and to our home for the summer. Normie's scout troop would fly back to New York at the end of the tour, and Ralph and Ann would meet her plane and see her safely on her plane for Pittsburgh. She had a few hours between flights, and so they took her to the World's Fair to pass the time and so she wouldn't miss it. How great it was to have friends like Ann and Ralph who would go to so much trouble to help make Normie's trip so relaxing.

The next summer Princie was an American Field Service (AFS) exchange student to Finland. Again, we went to New York where all of the AFS students gathered to board their ship to Europe. The Brancas, once again, welcomed us and helped us give Princie a grand bon-voyage. This time Normie, Janet, and I were left to drive to Pittsburgh.

We surely missed Princie that summer. We wrote often and could hardly wait to receive letters from her. She always kept up with all that was going on in the world and was interested in everybody and everything! She had a great and wonderful experience with the Finnish family and came home with much to share and tell. We were a little anxious about her flight home because she had to change planes in New York and make her connection to Raleigh-Durham. You can imagine that we were thrilled to see her step off that plane and to have had a safe journey. Princie kept a diary and had learned a lot about Finland, and she was able to talk about her experiences to her AFS chapter at school, and to all the civic clubs. She had learned through the years what it means to represent your family, school, town, and country well. She had inherited her father's speech-making ability. She made us proud!

We had three good summers in Pittsburgh. We made many friends on the ball club. Some players and coaches had children close in age to ours which made it much more fun for them. Forbes Field was one of our favorite ballparks, and it was an intimate little place. The seats were close to the field, and you could see the players and get to know them better. Fenway Park in Boston is like that. The Pirates had many outstanding players and all were friendly and congenial. We enjoyed lots of picnics and times together with the Hal Smith, Johnny Pesky, Vernon Law, Harry Walker, and Alex Grammas families.

Most of the players' wives and children came to the games, and it felt like one big happy family. That's the way it was with the Pirates. Joe L. Brown, the general manager, made us feel important, and it was a pleasure to be a part of that team and organization. The team traveled dressed in gray slacks and black blazers, and what a fine-looking group they were. We are able to get news of the team through the Pirate Alumni Association. Sally O'Leary and Nelson Briles do a good job. They always remember Clyde with a birthday card and a Christmas greeting plus all the newsletters with messages from the players. Vernon and Va Nita Law's son, Vance, was the first player's son whom we knew as a boy to grow up and play major league ball. We followed his career with great interest—I'm sure he never realized that he had such a fan club!

After three years, Joe Brown decided to change managers, which meant that the new manager would choose his coaches. So in 1968 it was time for us to make another move. It turned out to be a move that we could hardly wait to make. Clyde was hired by Mr. Rosey Ryan to manage the Phoenix Giants in Phoenix, Arizona. The Giants was the AAA club in the Pacific Coast League. We were excited to have the opportunity to live in desert country. Our girls didn't mind being so far away from home—adventure and travel had become their lifestyle.

The winter months passed quickly, as Clyde had to learn another team and organization. It meant going to Phoenix and meeting the press and all that is involved in getting to be a part of a city and its people. He came home with glowing reports that made us even more anxious to live there. Our winters at home were always busy. Piano lessons, mixed chorus, scouts, and school and church activities kept us on the go. Since Clyde had to be away so much, he devoted his time at home to us. He was interested in, and a part of, everything we did. When he was away, he was as close as the phone, and we talked often. Normie was already in college and Princie a senior in high school, so there were many needs to be met. When Clyde left for spring training, I had plenty to do to keep up with him in Casa Grande; Normie at Peace College in Raleigh, North Carolina; and Princie and Janet at home. We started making plans for our trip to Phoenix right away. I knew it would be a three- or four-day trip, and we would have to take as little as possible. As soon as Princie graduated and Normie came home, we packed the car and were on our way to Phoenix. Three girls, a French poodle, Clyde's sister-in-law (Dot Crumpler), and I made a full car. Dot's son, David, was living in Flagstaff and she would visit him before flying home. It was a comfort to have her with us. Even though Normie and Princie could have helped, I think I did all the driving. It was an enjoyable trip, but were we ever glad to get to Phoenix!

Clyde had rented a nice home in Mesa, and we quickly felt at home. It was a whole new world for us—the desert, cactus, no tall trees, and hot weather. We were fascinated by all of it and immediately knew that it would be a different and interesting summer. We adjusted to the heat and were relieved not to have the humidity that we had in Goldsboro. Needless to say, Clyde was grateful to have us with him and to have home-cooked meals again. He was also anxious for us to meet his new friends. We were soon to meet two of baseball's grand and elegant ladies, Mrs. Horace Stoneham and Mrs. Rosey Ryan. Mr. and Mrs. Stoneham were owners of the San Francisco Giants and lived in Scottsdale during the winter. Mr. and Mrs. Ryan were long-time friends of the Stonehams, and Mr. Ryan was general manager of the Phoenix Giants. They were so nice to us and made sure that our needs were met. Soon we felt so at home that we decided that if we ever lived any place other than Goldsboro, it would be Phoenix.

As the season progressed, we found many fun things to do. We never missed a game and got to know all the players and their families. Bobby Bonds's son, Barry, was about two years old and little did we know that he would be the second son of a ballplayer whom we knew to become a major league star. Janet would take him for a walk and get cotton candy. His mom was always glad to have a few minutes to relax. Mr. Ryan called Janet "The Little Ambassador."

All of the games were played at night, which enabled us to go places and explore the countryside during the day. The girls loved to go to the Verde River and get in an inner tube and float down the river. We went to Flagstaff, where there were trees that looked like home, and we explored the Grand Canyon. Sunday games were played at six o'clock because of the heat. So life was much more normal for us when Clyde could take our family for services at North Phoenix Baptist Church. During a road trip when the team played in San Diego, we drove there to meet Clyde and spend that time with him. He showed us around the city and of course we went to the zoo—I'm sure we went to the zoo in every city. After the team left San Diego, we visited with Duke and Bev Snider in Fallbrook and Stanna and Cliff Dapper on their ranch. It was such beautiful country and a thrill to get to visit them in their homes. We stopped in Disneyland—it had changed and grown so big! We really hated to leave, but we had other places that we wanted to visit. Our next stop was our old neighborhood in Van Nuys.

We had great difficulty locating our house on Noble Avenue. The freeways had changed everything. Nothing was familiar, but we were satisfied when we finally found the house in which we had lived during that very special 1957 season when Clyde managed the Holly-wood Stars. We happily started our trip back to Phoenix, stopping in Palm Springs. That, too, had changed, but Palm Springs still remains a pretty place. We had been on the road for several days, but we arrived home in time to greet Clyde when he returned from the team's road trip.

During the summer we had made lots of friends and had been able to visit all of the famous places, plus visit the famous restaurants. Clyde played a lot of golf and made a hole-in-one at the Mesa Country Club. Soon it was time for us to leave for Goldsboro, as Normie and Princie would be leaving for college. We planned to travel a different route so we could see a different part of the country. In all our traveling we tried to make the trips educational and interesting. My sister flew from Washington, D.C., to travel home with us. She was so much fun and entertained our children all the way.

We started our trip home by going to the Grand Canyon and then on to Albuquerque and the Painted Desert. Clyde had gone on a road trip before we left Phoenix, so we planned to meet him in Oklahoma City, where the team would be playing, and spend the night. That meant that we could see another game in another ballpark. Every time together was precious—it would be several weeks before the season would be finished and Clyde could come home.

From there we drove to Nashville, Tennessee, where we stayed overnight. The next morning we visited The Hermitage, home of Andrew Jackson, and then had a beautiful drive through the mountains. Once we reached the North Carolina state line, we felt like we were almost home. What a thrill! Even though we had to drive across the state, we decided to go all the way, and we did, arriving at our parents' doorstep about midnight. Mary Watson's husband and sons had come from Washington to meet her. It was a great reunion with many hugs and much conversation before we fell into our beds. After a good night's sleep and mama's delicious country breakfast, the girls and I drove to Goldsboro and were grateful to be in our own home again and to see our friends.

We always came home to a clean house and the yard in good shape. Our yard man, A. W. Gore, kept the grass mowed and took care of things while we were away. It didn't take long to get unpacked. Of course, my first chore was a trip to the grocery store. We had little time to waste because Normie and Princie had to be at school by a certain date. There was much to be done. Princie's school started first, so we had to concentrate on her. Normie was a great help getting Princie organized. It was no easy task trying to remember and be sure that she had everything she would need, as she would be far away from home. Princie and I were going to drive to Murraysville, Pennsylvania, and spend the night with our good friends, Carita and John Anderson. We would then drive on to Westminister College in New Wilmington, Pennsylvania (about 60 miles), the next morning. It was a 10-hour drive, but we had a good trip and everything was fine.

About midnight the phone rang, and it was for me. Dr. Paul Bennett, our family doctor, was calling to tell me that Normie had a kidney stone that had blocked her kidney, and he had to have permission to operate. He explained to me that Dr. Jim Lancaster would perform the surgery, and then he put him on the phone to talk to me. He assured me that he would take care of her just as if she was his very own. I knew he would do just that, and I had complete confidence that Normie would get the best possible care and attention. Then I had to call Clyde in San Diego, where the team was playing, to let him know. He wanted to catch the next plane home, but I told him that I would manage with the help of our friends, and that he should finish the season. It was our first, and only, emergency during our baseball years. Normie had not been feeling well that morning, but never did I dream of a kidney stone. She was having dinner with our friends Betsy and Ollie Toomey and their daughters Georgia and Mary, when she had the attack. They got her to the doctor immediately, and we'll be forever grateful for the way they took care of her.

Well, not only was I concerned for Normie, but I had to think about Princie. I could hardly stand to think of leaving her! What should I do? Carita decided for me that she would take Princie to Westminister, and I would go home to Normie. We went to bed, and I spent a long time praying before going to sleep. Morning came early, and we were up and making arrangements for Carita to take Princie and for me to go home. Everything had to be moved from my car to hers, but soon we were ready to leave. Even though I knew Princie would be fine and that Carita would take care of her, it didn't make it any easier for me to say good-bye. It helped that Princie was brave, and Carita was so gracious and willing to make it easier for her. I'll never forget that day—my heart was so heavy yet so grateful. It was a beautiful, sunny day to travel, and I was calm and peaceful knowing that God was watching over us and trusting that all would be well.

When I arrived in Goldsboro, all was well. I was overwhelmed with the loving care and attention that had been bestowed upon Normie. I still have difficulty finding words to describe how my heart overflowed with gratitude to the doctors, nurses, friends, and family. My brother, Hoover Surles, had come from Roseboro to make sure that the financial needs were taken care of, knowing that Clyde and I were away. Poor Janet had even cut her head on a car door, and my dear friend Grace Warren took care of her and had Dr. Con McDonald make sure that she was all right. Never was I so relieved to be safely at home with Janet, knowing that Normie's operation was successful and she was on the road to recovery.

Now it was time to call Princie and Clyde. I could hardly wait to talk to Princie about her first day of college. She assured me that everything was fine and she liked her roommate. Carita and her son, Bill, had helped unload the car and take her bags to her dorm room and even unpack and put things away. I couldn't wait to call Carita to thank her again and also to let her know about Normie. I was satisfied about Princie and knew that we would visit her at college as soon as possible.

It had been a long and anxious day for Clyde, and I knew he would be in his hotel room waiting to hear from me. I was happy to have good news about all of us. I had phone numbers so that he could call Normie in the hospital and Princie at school, and this would help put his mind at ease.

Normie's concern was that she get well and be able to begin her junior year at the university. We were given a date that would be the latest possible time that she could enter for the fall semester. She was so anxious. She convinced the doctor and us that she was strong enough and ready when the time came. I could do most of her packing and getting ready. She was very organized and her trunk from Peace College was still packed and ready to go. Chapel Hill was only an hour-and-a-half drive, and so she was on her way with high hopes, excitement, and determination. It was a comfort for her to be so close!

Just as we were ready to settle down and get into our normal routine for the winter, Clyde called to tell us that Mr. Stoneham had asked him to be the manager of the San Francisco Giants. We were so excited, as this would be his first opportunity to manage a major league team! His season was over in Phoenix, and he could fly home and be with us until it was time for the official announcement. This was big news, and we had to keep it a secret! We had loved Phoenix, and now to live in San Francisco was almost too good to be true. Thank goodness, it wasn't long before Clyde was off to San Francisco for the press conference which would announce and introduce him as the new manager. It was a very special and happy time for the Clyde King family, for we knew that being a big league manager had been Clyde's ambition and dream. He had worked many years in preparation for this position. He was well-received by the media, and the organization was pleased. We received messages of congratulations from many friends and fans—all were happy for Clyde. He came home filled with enthusiasm and ready to start a new season.

The major league winter meetings were held in San Francisco the first week in December. Mr. and Mrs. Stoneham invited me to go with Clyde as their guest. Mrs. Stoneham was so thoughtful and kind. She introduced me to everybody and entertained me while Clyde was attending meetings. There were always tours, shopping, and special events planned for wives. Mrs. Ryan was there also, and we had the best time being together and doing things that we enjoyed. I was so fortunate to have them to guide and teach me. Of course I fell in love with the city, and I knew that our girls would love living there. We flew home, and it was time to get ready for the Christmas holidays. Normie and Princie would be coming home, and we wanted everything to be perfect. There was much shopping, decorating, and baking to be done. Christmas was so meaningful and special at our home, and Clyde was like a child loving every minute—there could never be too many decorations to please him! He was a good help, and we spent many happy hours getting ready for the celebration of Jesus' birthday.

After Christmas, Clyde's thoughts turned to baseball, and soon it was time for him to leave for Arizona and spring training. It was going to be a long time before we would be together again, so it was important that we make plans for the summer. After much thought and prayer, we felt it would be best for us to fly. Driving would take too much of our time, especially at the end of the summer when the girls would have to go back to school. Also, Clyde had already made arrangements for a car for us when we arrived in San Francisco. Everything was working out just as we had hoped it would. Somehow, when the time was long and we missed each other so much, we were able to meet somewhere, and this time it was when the Giants came east on a road trip. As I'm sure you have surmised, there were years that Clyde and I put our girls' welfare first and made many sacrifices because we wanted their lives to be as normal as possible. That, too, we've never regretted!

The 1969 spring training went well, and the team was winning. The excitement and anticipation of being there to root for their dad made it easier for us to get ready for our trip. In fact, we could hardly wait! As soon as Normie and Princie arrived home from college, it didn't take long for them to unpack and repack their bags—they could only take two bags each and their winter coats. Mrs. Stoneham had forewarned us about the wind at Candlestick Park. We had to get a kennel for our poodle, Matisse. Soon the four of us with our eight bags, one dog kennel, and each of us with a coat on our arm were on our way to the airport for our flight to San Francisco. Our flight was smooth and relaxing—it gave us a chance to nap and get some much needed rest before our arrival. Clyde and Cappy Harada were there to greet us. Clyde had driven the car and Cappy a van. We needed all the space to transport us to our new home for the summer. Mr. John Livingston loaned us his "Beetle" convertible for the girls, and it didn't take them long to learn their way to and from Candlestick and around San Francisco. They were thrilled and couldn't believe all that was happening to them! We had wonderful neighbors and soon felt very much a part of the neighborhood.

Being the manager's family had some advantages, like having our very own box. We loved the games and the girls enjoyed keeping score. Clyde always wanted to see how attentive they had been.

Our days were full, and we visited every area of the city plus everything within a day's drive. When Clyde was on the road, we tried to do something special. One time, Normie, Princie, and Janet went to Yosemite National Park with our good friends, the Don Rood family. On an off day, we would drive to Pebble Beach. Clyde was a good golfer in those days, and it was a thrill for him to play there. I'll never forget how cold the ocean water was there as compared to our beaches at home!

Once after a Sunday afternoon game, we drove to Lake Tahoe. Monday was an off day, so we spent two nights. The countryside was so beautiful. We saw where the show *Bonanza* was filmed and everyone treated us nicely.

We were so glad that our friends from Goldsboro came to visit us, but they had to love baseball! George and Mary Lou Whitfield and their son Geoff came for a visit in July. George had been voted National High School Baseball Coach of the Year, and he was to be presented the award in San Francisco. When I told Mary Lou to bring coats, she thought I was off my rocker—coats in July! They brought their coats and wore them, plus gloves, scarves, and a blanket from the clubhouse. And they were still cold! The wind off the Bay is so unpredictable! Bill and Betty Kemp and their children Betsy, Billy, and Sallie, came for a visit as did Bobby Wolfe. We loved exploring San Francisco, especially Fisherman's Wharf, the Embarcadero, Lombard Street, Nob Hill, Coit Tower, and Alcatraz Prison, not to mention driving across the Golden Gate Bridge to Sausalito and going to Candlestick Park.

Art Santo Domingo and his family were great to be around. He and his wife Fran, and their children, all enjoyed being with Normie, Princie, and Janet. We're still close with them to this day and were happy when they visited us in Goldsboro. Sid and Ronnie Mobell were good friends, and Sid helped Clyde find the house in which we lived. He was a famous jewelry designer and made me some treasured jewelry. Mr. and Mrs. Stoneham were wonderful to us as well. What an outstanding summer that was soon—too soon at that—over. It was time to go home to start school again.

Leaving Clyde was never easy, but this year he was in an exciting pennant race and we knew that the race would consume his energy. For me, it was time to go home and get the house in order and get the girls ready for college.

The baseball season ended with the Giants in second place with a record of 90–72. It had been a good year and Clyde came home with the news that he had been invited to go to Japan and conduct clinics for the Tokyo Orions Baseball Club. Wes Westrum and his wife, along with myself, were all included in that trip. Cappy Harada was there to be by our side. He was our interpreter and team liaison. His wife, Kay, was to go with us, but at the last minute neither Kay nor Wes's wife could go. Clyde and I first flew to Phoenix so that he could play in a golf tournament for Mr. Stoneham. I was Mrs. Stoneham's guest at their home in Scottsdale. Their home overlooked Camelback Mountain. She had a luncheon and invited all of my Phoenix friends and it was great to see everyone again. She had been to Japan before and so she shared her knowledge with me to make my trip more meaningful. We really enjoyed being together, and I can't begin to tell you how I treasured her friendship. She loved our girls and appreciated our family values and lifestyle. She and Mr. Stoneham even took Janet on a trip with their granddaughter, Kim Rupert, to Coronado Beach, San Diego. What a treat for Janet!

Clyde and I flew from Phoenix to San Francisco, where we spent two nights at the Clift Hotel. We took along a large trunk filled with bats, balls, caps, and gifts for the Japanese players. We thought that we would be bringing back an empy trunk, but the Japanese officials had many presents for us.

After our two-day stay in San Francisco we were on our way to Honolulu, where we spent two days. We were taken to Pearl Harbor and went on the Admiral's Boat for a tour, where two navy men told us the details of the bombing of Pearl Harbor. This was an education in history we'll never forget. How we grieved for all the young boys who died for us. We saw a film that had been captured from the

Japanese. We stayed at the Ilikae Hotel and had time to go walking along Hawaii's beautiful beaches. We dined in a different restaurant for every meal, wondering how life could be any better. Cappy made sure that we didn't miss a thing when it came to all of the local historical sites.

Our flight to Tokyo was excellent. We landed at Tokyo International Airport where we were met by dozens of flashing cameras. After going through customs, we went to the VIP room for a press conference. Baseball was so popular in Japan, and the press and baseball people were prepared for us. Knowing that we didn't drink, they had our orange juice ready.

On a Sunday, Clyde, Cappy, and I went to Kyoto on the "Bullet" train. It was a beautiful ride—so fast, smooth, and comfortable. We saw the countryside—the rice fields, the persimmon trees, the vegetable groves, and Mount Fuji, which is snow-covered. We saw all of the important shrines, the Silk Mansion, and visited Osaka. We visited all the buildings getting ready for "Expo '70." Our baseball clinics were a huge success, and we were warmly received.

On our trip home, we stopped in Honolulu again to break up the trip and to allow us more time to see the resort island once again. We arrived in San Francisco within days, and Clyde and I boarded our plane to Raleigh-Durham. It was Thanksgiving Day and we were so sleepy from the time-zone changes that the stewardess couldn't wake us to serve us the turkey dinner. When we arrived home our girls were there to meet us, and what a great homecoming! It was truly a time for Thanksgiving.

We had remembered the girls with nice jewelry—pearls, rings, and earrings that they would wear and cherish forever. Clyde was soon off for the winter baseball meetings the first week of December, so there was much to do before he left. We were so glad to be at home and knew that the time would pass quickly—Christmas and then spring training again. These were interesting and exciting times for us, as our girls were enjoying their college years and were making new friends, but maturing too fast to suit Clyde! He would have kept them little girls forever!

In February, Clyde left for spring training. This year, Janet and I would be able to join him. She had some vacation days from school and we added a few extra days. Janet and I were able to spend some time at Casa Grande before the team moved to Phoenix for the exhibition games. Clyde had the penthouse suite that was reserved for the team manager—a luxury for us. There were two pools—one in the shape of a baseball bat and the other in the shape of a ball. The weather was perfect and we enjoyed swimming every day. We made our plans so that we could see as many ball games as possible. We saw Mrs. Stoneham every day, and it was a good time for us, but soon Janet had to leave for school.

During the 1970 season I flew to New York to meet Clyde when the Giants played the Mets. I saw lots of our friends from the good old days, such as Dr. Peale. I flew home and was busy making plans for another summer in San Francisco, when Clyde called to give me some news.

Clyde told me that Mr. Stoneham was changing managers and he was fired—on his birthday, May 23. It was the shock of a lifetime! What? Why? How? All these questions flooded my mind. As I had time for it to sink in I remembered that Mrs. Stoneham had told me during spring training that a player (and she told me who it was) was coming to Mr. Stoneham every day and was crying on his shoulder. It hurt, and soon the whole world knew that Clyde had been fired. It seemed so unfair! I do want to say that later Mr. Stoneham told Clyde, in my presence, that he made a mistake and that he was sorry. Anyway, the phone started ringing, and we heard from so many friends and people from all over the country. Our hearts were touched by the loving and encouraging messages that we received. Mrs. Stoneham and her daughter Woochie Ruppert called and wrote letters to let us know how they felt—all brought many tears because they shared our feelings and disappointment. Normie and Janet were with me, and David Hartman was so good at consoling Princie that I can't thank him enough. Clyde came home and was a shining example of faith and courage to us. He knew that he had done a good job. He also knew that God was in control, and He has His way of picking you up and using you in His way. I knew it would be hard for Clyde to be out of baseball even for a short time—it was his life's work. I also knew that there would be another job just around the corner. If need be, I could always teach.

The time Clyde spent with Normie, Princie, and Janet that summer was precious to them. Clyde spoke at the Fellowship of Christian Athletes Camp at Berry College in Rome, Georgia. I can't begin to tell you what fun it was for all of us and especially for the girls, being there with all of those fine young men. It was an exciting week, filled with many nice campus walks and good sports competition. I would recommend the FCA to every boy and girl. Clyde has been a member from the beginning and still speaks at meetings whenever or wherever he's invited.

Our next "mountain top" experience was on the top of a mountain! Hugh and Julia Morton had invited us for 10 days at Grandfather Mountain. They own this famous mountain at Linville, North Carolina, with its mile-high swinging bridge, museum, animal habitat, hiking trails, and picnic areas. The view is breathtaking! They had a picnic on July 4th and had invited some of our very best Carolina friends, Orville and Dudley Campbell. It was so great to share good food and friendship, and we felt like we could have stayed there forever.

Paul Richards, the Atlanta Braves general manager, called and offered Clyde the job as manager of the Richmond Braves, their AAA farm team. It was close to home and the Braves were a great organization. The decision was a good one, and we rented an apartment near the ballpark, Parker Field. It was convenient and I was always there when Clyde was at home. We now belonged to the Richmond Braves and we were true loyal fans. They were our team, and Richmond was our city. We spent two summers there and learned a lot visiting all of the historical places. Princie graduated from college and Normie was engaged to be married, so our second summer there was exciting. For graduation Princie had asked for a trip to Finland to be with the AFS family that she had visited years earlier in school. It was a big decision, but she made her own travel arrangements and we let her go, as this was to be her last fling before getting a job.

We spent the summer making arrangements for Normie's wedding on October 7, 1972, to Dr. Jesse Aycock Blackman. Jess was from Fremont, just 12 miles away from Goldsboro and what a fine young man from a lovely family. Our families worked well together planning everything. Princie had a great trip to Finland and arrived home a week before the wedding. The wedding and reception were beautiful and we couldn't have done it without the support of our friends.

Eddie Robinson had become the general manager of the Braves, and he asked Clyde to be his assistant. Clyde's new job would entail much travel as he had to scout the different organizations for young talent. This was a welcome change for Clyde; he could live at home and I could spend some more time with my parents. By this time, Princie had a job at Bush Gardens in Williamsburg, Virginia, as assistant personnel director. Janet and I were free to go with Clyde on his short trips as soon as she finished her school year.

Spring training for the Braves was held in West Palm Beach, Florida. It was fun being there and Janet's spring break fit right into Clyde's schedule, allowing her to have the fun of attending the games. Two of our favorite places, once the Braves left spring train-ing, became Savannah, Georgia, and Charleston, South Carolina. We explored those beautiful southern towns during the day and went to the games at night.

My family, the Surles, always spent Christmas Eve at the home of my mother and daddy. They wanted us to be there and accommo-dated all 21 of us! The Christmas of 1973 was so very special, though we never dreamed it would be the last with my precious mother. In early January she suffered a heart attack and died on March 29th. So it was a blessing that I was able to be at home and spend a lot of time with her. How grateful I am! It was the end of spring training, and Clyde was on his way home to be with us. Janet was a senior at Wayne County Day School and would be graduating in June. She had been accepted to Peace College in Raleigh. She had been very active in school activities and was a cheerleader and Homecoming Queen. It was an exciting time, though it was hard for Clyde and me to realize that our youngest would be in college and away from home!

A lot had happened during the first half of that year, but there was more to come. During the All-Star break in July, Clyde came home to spend that three-day period of time with us. The Braves, during those three days, decided to make a change in managers, and Clyde was going to be the new manager. At that time I had mixed feelings. I was happy for Clyde, but I felt sad for Eddie Mathews, whom Clyde was replacing. This meant that Janet and I would go to Atlanta and stay there while Clyde was there and then go home when the team went on the road. It had been 18 years since our Crackers days in Atlanta. There were major changes, as Atlanta was now a big city.

The team responded well to Clyde as their manager and had the best record in the big leagues after the All-Star break. After the sea-son ended, Clyde went to the World Series and then it was time for the winter meetings in New Orleans, and I was invited. We had a wonderful time and visited with our baseball friends. Dottie and Pee Wee Reese were there. While on spring break, Janet came to spring training and brought her friend Charlotte Maxwell. Our girls always had nice friends, and we always told them that they could bring their friends along on our baseball trips.

My next responsibility was to find a home in Atlanta for us for the summer. We wanted to be close to the stadium and were fortu-nate to find a furnished condominium nearby in downtown Atlanta.

On May 5, 1975, Normie and Jess presented us with our first grandchild, Jesse Aycock Blackman, Jr. Clyde and I were thrilled—

Clyde had his boy—and I can tell you there is nothing quite like being a grandparent! Of course I could hardly wait to go home and visit this beautiful baby and hold him in my arms. As soon as possible, I was on my way to Goldsboro, so I could be there to help Normie when she came home from the hospital. Of course Clyde was just as anxious to see his grandson. Soon they visited us in Atlanta.

During the month of August, my daddy died. I flew home, and Clyde came for the funeral. It was a sad time. Ours was a close and devoted family, and there was so much for which to be thankful.

Soon after I returned to Atlanta, Connie Ryan took over as manager and Clyde went back to being assistant to Eddie Robinson. During that winter the Atlanta Braves were sold to Mr. Ted Turner. He hired a new general manager, and Clyde remained with the Braves until September of 1976. Gabe Paul and Cedric Tallis got permission from the Braves to talk to Clyde about going to the New York Yankees. This was about the same time we were building our new house and the Yankees were in a pennant race.

We had been in the National League for 32 years and joining the Yankees meant changing leagues. Clyde phoned Gabe and told him that he would be honored to be in the Yankees organization. He packed his bags and went to New York, and I did not see him again until the World Series against the Reds. It was truly exciting and thrilling to be in the World Series again. I planned to watch the World Series at home, but Clyde called and told me that he had tickets for me. I booked a flight, packed my bags, and was off to New York.

Mr. George Steinbrenner, the Yankees owner, was very active and involved in the operation of his team. His aim and desire was to win a World Series and he was always working to make his team the best. Clyde got to work closely with him and was on the go on various assignments. We moved into our new home August 10, 1977, and Clyde came home long enough to move us in and everyone stayed over that first night. It was a real family experience.

In 1977 the Yankees were again in a World Series against the Dodgers, only this time the games were coast-to-coast. Mr. Steinbrenner always provided the best for his "baseball family" and made it a joy to be a part of the organization. He and his wife, Joan, were so gracious, and we enjoyed being with them for the celebration that would follow the World Series victory.

After the deaths of my parents, we decided that we would start our own tradition of Christmas with our family at our house. We continue this tradition, and now our family fills two long pews at church on Christmas Eve. We had higher ceilings in our new house and were able to have a bigger Christmas tree. We have a curved stairway, and we always gather there and sing happy birthday to Jesus. That comes first! That Christmas, Janet's boyfriend, Johnny Peacock, was spending the holidays with us. He had put a gift under the tree for her. When she opened it, she found a silver bell and inside the bell, tied with red ribbon, was a diamond ring. A wedding date was set for August 26th, and we started planning another wedding.

Spring training for the Yankees was in Fort Lauderdale. When Tommy John came to play for the Yankees, he and Sally introduced us to Dr. O. S. Hawkins, pastor of First Baptist Church. We found a church family there and it became a part of our lives and meant so much to us. What a great preacher and what a friendship. We made many friends and later on went on a trip to Israel with O.S., his wife Susie, and a group from the church.

Clyde was working hard, but he was able to get free for Janet and Johnny's wedding. Johnny's father had been an attorney and his mother a teacher—both were deceased. Being a Goldsboro boy, he had family and many friends to help make this another beautiful and memorable wedding.

The Yankees won the playoffs in 1978 and on June 4, 1978, Elizabeth Graham Blackman was born. We were so anxious to see our precious little granddaughter. Clyde had not been home since the wedding in August and was excited to see Elizabeth.

The season of 1979 brought tragedy to the Yankees when their catcher, Thurman Munson, was killed in a plane accident. More sadness came that fall when Jack Butterfield, the farm director, was killed in an automobile accident. It was a difficult year for all and especially for Mr. Steinbrenner. He cared, and he was always there for his Yankees family.

The years that Clyde worked for the Yankees were a challenge for me. My life was sometimes complicated by Clyde's schedule and change of jobs. I remember driving to Baltimore, checking into a hotel to be there when Clyde would arrive early the next morning. About midnight the phone rang, and it was Clyde calling to tell me that Mr. Steinbrenner wanted him to go on another mission. Of course, I was disappointed and so was Clyde, but I had no intention of making it harder for him, so I told him that I would simply drive home the next day. When Mr. Steinbrenner asked how I had taken the change in plans, Clyde told him, and he said to tell me that he would make it up to me, and he certainly did. He was very sensitive to our needs and many times made it possible for me to travel with Clyde to Boston, Chicago, or wherever Clyde would go.

Several times when Mr. Steinbrenner would have Clyde go back in uniform to help with the pitching, Clyde would stay with Ralph and Ann Branca at Westchester Country Club in Rye. They did so much to help us during those years. Finding a place to live for a short time wasn't easy!

Doug Melvin, who did a variety of jobs with the Yankees, lived in Connecticut and would sometimes give Clyde a ride to and from the stadium. They talked a lot of baseball. We became good friends with Doug and his wife, Ellen. Later, when Clyde became general manager, he hired Doug as the director of scouting.

The Yankees had a very successful season in 1980, winning 103 games, but they lost to Kansas City in the playoffs. Princie and Douglas Jackson Evans were married on January 10, 1981. All our family events were planned around Clyde's schedule. Ralph Branca sang, as he always did, "Daddy's Little Girl" at the wedding reception and let me say Ralph has a beautiful voice. Now all three daughters had graduated from college and we were thrilled to have given them nice weddings. All three were married to eastern North Carolina boys and were truly blessed.

There was a baseball strike in 1981 and many changes were made, and the Yankees won the pennant but lost to the Dodgers in the World Series. During the 1982 season, Mr. Steinbrenner asked Clyde to manage the team for August and September. Clyde enjoyed managing and succeeded in restoring some stability to the team. It was also a thrill to arrange for our grandson Jay, to be the batboy for one day. The game just happened to be on national television and Clyde was a little nervous, but all went well and Jay made his granddaddy proud. Normie taped the game, so Jay can one day show it to his kids.

The winter meetings were in Honolulu that December. Clyde and I were included in the Yankees delegation. It was a reunion for me. By this time my circle of friends included both the National and American leagues. The men were always busy with meetings and baseball talk. Joan Steinbrenner and I, as well as other baseball wives, entertained ourselves.

During the spring of 1984 Mr. Steinbrenner began talking to Clyde about being general manager. This was such a prestigious position. It would mean living in New York all the time, but it would also involve a demanding work schedule. Clyde had come to know Mr. Steinbrenner well and I told Clyde, when he asked me my opinion, that whatever he decided I would support. Clyde accepted the position, and we found a condominium at Water's

Edge in Rye, New York. It was the perfect place for the children to come for visits.

The hours were long when the team had night games, but when they were on the road, we had a normal lifestyle. This job was a change in lots of ways. It was a different relationship with the players, but Clyde made the transition quickly and smoothly. The next three years were interesting—Clyde did enjoy, and thrived, on the challenges of his job. Some days were rocky, but most were smooth. I can remember one day he came home and said that the next day he might not have a job—then went to bed and slept like a baby. His faith was never shattered. It was, and is, always strong. Sometimes we would sit on a bench by the water and enjoy the cool of the evening. If the Yankees were playing on the road that night, we would take a radio and listen to the game. I'm so glad that I had a love for baseball and for this one special baseball man—my husband.

Ann Branca was my best friend. Her daughter Mary was married to Bobby Valentine, and when he was named manager of the Texas Rangers, Mary rented their house to us, and we lived there during the years that Clyde was general manager. By this time Doug and Princie had our second granddaughter Blythe. This house was perfect for us, and it was great to have room for our family and friends to visit.

After Clyde went back to his job as special advisor, we spent the next summer in a hotel apartment in the city. Bobby Murcer and his wife Kay lived there and recommended it. I was so happy and was never afraid when Clyde was away. I could walk everywhere during the day. It was an ideal location for shopping, theater, restaurants, and the subway. Clyde and I had time to do things together, and it was the most carefree, relaxed, and enjoyable summer that I spent during our baseball career.

Clyde was at the stadium every day, and I went to almost every game. Watching the games was a big part of his job! I also enjoyed being with friends. Charlotte Witkind, Charm Freund, Emily Kraft, and Marion Merrill were there regularly and were dedicated fans— Marion always kept score! One of my biggest thrills was standing beside Robert Merrill, the opera star, and listening to him sing the national anthem. Every day we listened to Eddie Layton play the organ and Bob Shepard introduce the starting lineups. They are such a great part of Yankees tradition! Through the years I have gotten to know most of the great Yankees players at Old Timers' games and other events. I have treasured memories and reflect on these days often. Clyde worked with good people, especially his assistant,

Woody Woodward, whom he had great respect for. We enjoyed a great relationship with Woody, Pam, and their children. We also made many wonderful friends outside of baseball, including Bob and Barbara Elmo, who made their Greenwich house a home away from home for us.

Clyde was never sick nor did he ever miss a day's work until 1989, when he fell out of the tree house that he and our sons-in-law were building for the grandchildren. By this time Princie and Doug had given us Blythe, Miranda, and Sam. Janet and Johnny had Mary Clyde, Hadley, and Mallory Lee. Jay and Egie were older, but just as excited to see us. Clyde always likes to make sure that coming to Ma Ma's and Pa Pa's (that's what they call us) house would be fun and a happy experience. We provided bikes, miniature cars, swings, a basketball goal, a place to skate, and a tree house where they could spend the night. What I think we provided that was more important than anything else to our grandchildren was "ourselves." Clyde loves to play with the grandchildren, and those Wiffle ball games at family gatherings are fierce! How they love it! Our sons-in-law, Jesse, Doug, and Johnny, worked together well and later built Clyde a clubhouse. Watching our grandchildren grow and mature is pure pleasure, and we spend as much time with them as possible. We try to attend every piano and dance recital, band concert, drama production, and athletic event, whether it be soccer, basketball, or baseball games. All are honor students! We're continually amazed by their talents and accomplishments. Clyde is enjoying some of the activities that he had to miss when our girls were in school.

We celebrated our 50th wedding anniversary on November 29, 1996, taking a trip to Europe with our good friends Betty and Bill Kemp, who are seasoned travelers. We spent six weeks traveling by plane, train, boat, and car seeing the sights of nine countries. Betty and Bill made sure that we didn't miss anything!

Everywhere we have been in his baseball career, Clyde has had a fair and honest relationship with the news media, and we are grateful. The request for speaking engagements, appearances for charities, golf tournaments, fan mail, and many worthwhile causes keep him busy. It's nice to be remembered, and he does all that he can work into his schedule. As Clyde has become less involved in the day-to-day operations of baseball, he still enjoys scouting during spring training and doing special assignments. We absolutely love attending spring training at Legends Field in Tampa, and Clyde enjoys the scouting travels to other cities such as Sarasota, Lakeland, Dunedin,

Port Charlotte, Bradenton, Kissimmee, Baseball City, St. Petersburg, and Clearwater.

It's also great to be with former players and their wives who are good friends, like Susie and Jeff Torborg, and all the Yankees personnel and families who mean so much to us.

Baseball wives have contributed so much to the game of baseball, and I have been privileged to call so many of them my friends.

Baseball has had many changes since I first met Clyde. It has been so much a part of my life. Money has made such a difference in society's lifestyle and values. My hope and prayer is that present-day baseball players invest and use their money wisely and have the deep feeling and concern for each other that was so prevalent among players of our day.

We're still going to games, watching on television, and enjoying this sport together. Once baseball gets in your blood, it's there forever!

Appendix A

Timeline of Clyde King's Career

May 23, 1925	Born, Goldsboro, North Carolina
1942–46	Attended University of North Carolina at Chapel Hill
June 1944	Signed professional baseball contract with the Brooklyn Dodgers
June 1944	Major League pitching debut for the Brooklyn Dodgers at Ebbets Field
1953	Finished professional playing career pitching for the Cincinnati Reds
1955–56	Managed Atlanta Crackers; won Southern Association pennant; Manager of the Year Award in 1956
1957	Manager of the Hollywood Stars in the Pacific Coast League
1958	Manager of Columbus Jets in the International League
1959–62	Manager of the Rochester Red Wings in the International League
1963–64	Roving pitching instructor for the St. Louis Cardinals
1965–67	Major-league coaching career began as pitching coach for the Pittsburgh Pirates
1968	Manager of the Phoenix Giants, the San Francisco Giants' AAA club in the Pacific Coast League
1969–70	Major league managerial debut for the San Francisco Giants
1971–72	Manager of the Richmond Braves in the International League
1972–73	Assistant general manager of the Atlanta Braves
1974–75	Manager of the Atlanta Braves
1976–present	New York Yankees—positions have included scout, pitching coach, manager, general manager, special advisor to George M. Steinbrenner III
1983	Inducted into the North Carolina Sports Hall of Fame

Appendix B
Scouting Report on Baseball's Bests

From A to Z in the Broadcast Booth

MEL ALLEN: A graduate of the University of Alabama, an attorney, and a real Hall of Famer. Mel coined the famous phrase, "How 'bout that!" and it is still legendary. He was just a great guy to talk baseball to before the game. I felt saddened by his passing. He meant so much to the Yankees and their fans. We were all fans of Mel. Mel attended my North Carolina Hall of Fame induction ceremony, and I was always grateful for his attendance.

RED BARBER: He had a voice that made him easy to listen to, and he made you feel like you were at the game and in the ballpark even if you were at Brighton Beach. That's why the beaches in Brooklyn were filled with sunbathers and portable radios blasting out Dodgers baseball.

MARTY BRENNAMAN: He never misses a play. He can talk about any phase of the game. He's also a great basketball announcer and a UNC alumnus. He does a great job for the Reds.

JACK BUCK: He pays attention to the game and doesn't miss a play on the field. Another Hall of Famer in every respect. He's always doing something nice for somebody. Jack is another treasure of the broadcast booth. His trademark "That's a winner!" is known throughout the baseball world and the wider sports world. Jack always wanted to help people and I'm glad to see his son broadcasting on Fox network and carrying on the tradition. Jack really is one of my all-time favorites in the booth, and I liked his Mark McGwire 60th home-run call.

HARRY CARAY: A fan's announcer. He was great for the game of baseball. He really was an ambassador for the game in every sense. His rendition of "Take Me Out To The Ball Game" is still legendary in Chicago, and he just loved being around the fans. He liked talking baseball and everyone appreciated him. I'm glad to see his grandson Chip Caray carrying on the tradition in Chicago and getting to call the 60th Sammy Sosa home run.

JOE GARAGIOLA: Having been a player, Joe really knows the insides of the game, and he brought that insight to his broadcasts. He is certainly a detail person and if you were in your home, without a television, listening to Joe on radio, you would have enjoyed the beautiful pictures he painted with his voice of that summer game. On a personal note, he was the broadcaster when my grandson Jay was a batboy, so I guess I'm a little partial toward him.

MILO HAMILTON: Gets an A+ in every area of announcing a baseball game! He is always two or three plays ahead and two or three innings ahead. He has the ability to know what a manager is thinking and what he is apt to do with regard to managerial moves. He is extremely accurate in his announcing, and he has a good, easy-going voice. He won't let you go to sleep. He's one of my favorite people and a true Hall of Fame announcer. I tried to get him to come to New York when I was GM. Mr. Steinbrenner gave me permission to talk to him about coming to New York, but he just couldn't. It would have been fun to have Milo around me at Yankee Stadium. I will always remember those lunches at Gallagher's in New York and our favorite restaurants across the country. Milo is one of my closest friends in the game and I really treasure our friendship.

ERNIE HARWELL: He was easy to listen to and he did his homework. Another great ambassador for the game of baseball. Ernie is a legend in Detroit. Tiger baseball and Ernie Harwell go together. To have a fan following as big as Ernie's is a testament to his character and love of the game. Ernie's a good friend, a great person, and a fine Christian gentleman.

RUSS HODGES: The thing I remember about him is his call "The Giants win the Pennant, the Giants win the Pennant" four times. He was an icon in San Francisco, and his broadcasts were filled with character.

JON MILLER: I just like to listen to him on ESPN *Sunday Night Baseball*, as I did when he was the voice of the Baltimore Orioles. The Orioles made a big mistake by losing him. He is easy to listen to because of his entertaining and informative style of broadcasting a ball game. He's a great young voice in this era of baseball broadcasting.

BOB PRINCE: I remember he bought a long hot dog and called it the "green weenie" and it was the good luck charm for the Pirates. He could say things about a player that would really make you laugh yourself silly. He was a real joy to listen to, and he was the protégé of popular Pirate announcer Rosey Rowswell. He was also a good friend of mine in Pittsburgh, and I'll never forget the many restaurant experiences that we shared together.

PHIL RIZZUTO: Holy cow. He mentioned all of his friends at least once, ate canoli on the air, and was driving across the George Washington Bridge by the seventh or eighth inning. Phil is a terrific person and always has time for you! He can make baseball a fun game to listen to, and it is not often that someone of his stature can be as down to earth as he is.

VIN SCULLY: On a scale of 1 to 10, he's a 9 in my book. Vin is just the symbol of the Los Angeles Dodgers. He taught the game of baseball to all of Southern California, and he raised an entire generation on his calls. He's just a great treasure of the broadcast booth and a true gentleman. He got his start with the Brooklyn Dodgers.

LON SIMMONS: He had a great, deep voice and knew the game. He loved to broadcast the games. He was the kind of guy who came down on the field during batting practice before the game, and he always asked me questions about the pitching rotation. He always talked about the players' families on the radio and he was just beloved by all. I enjoyed my tenure as manager of the Giants, and he made the pregame shows fun for me. He was truly great.

CHUCK THOMPSON: The man with the golden voice for the Orioles. He had such a great voice. Chuck was on top of every play and was an excellent interviewer. He brought things to you over the radio that you just couldn't get from any other announcer. I just loved him.

JEFF TORBORG: The best young announcer coming along. He adds color and excitement to every game. He's going to go a long way.

BILL WHITE: He gave you the inside aspects of baseball and explained plays well. No one knows the game better than Bill. Fans miss his broadcasting.

Baseball's Bests on the Field

This is my "best" list that covers my playing days and managerial days. Excluded are present-day players because I haven't worked closely enough with them to really have an opinion on them. I've scouted them in spring training, but that is different than seeing them perform during the year day in and day out. That's why I hope that you all take my list in stride because it represents just the players I've worked with. Disclaimers for hurt feelings aside, here we go.

On the Hill

BEST RELIEF PITCHERS: Rich "Goose" Gossage of the Yankees and Jim Konstanty of the Phillies.

MOST RAW TALENT AS A PITCHER: Rex Barney. Although many fans knew him as the public-address person for the Orioles, he was some pitcher. He had a fastball that was something else; and he pitched a no-hitter against the Giants. With his untimely death I, as a former teammate, will miss him.

THE PITCHER WITH THE BEST MOVE TO FIRST BASE: Warren Spahn had such a good move to first base that you could be a base runner on first and stand on the bag and pat your foot and he'd pick you off between pats. That's how good he was. I often tell people that there was a time when there was a runner on first and a runner on third and he needed a double play to end the game and it was getting dark quickly. The ball was hard to see and the players were complaining to the umpires about how dark it was in the park. He came set and threw to first and the first baseman caught the ball and tagged the runner out and the batter swung at the air and it was strike three and the game was over. I made that story up. But, it shows you just how good his move was.

MOST COMPLETE PITCHER I SAW OR MANAGED: Warren Spahn. He could do it all. He was masterful on the mound and with his glove. He had a good move to first base. He was a good hitter. He could even run the bases well and was very durable, lasting for 21 years in baseball.

BEST KNUCKLE BALL PITCHERS: Hoyt Wilhelm and Phil Niekro.

PITCHER WITH THE BEST FASTBALL: Steve Dalkowski.

BEST 3–2 COUNT PITCHER: Robin Roberts.

BEST FIELDING PITCHER: Bobby Shantz.

BEST PITCHERS IN THE POST-SEASON: Lefty Gomez and Sandy Koufax.

TOUGHEST PITCHER IN A TIGHT SITUATION: Sal Maglie.

On the Base Paths

BEST BASE STEALERS OF ALL TIME: Rickey Henderson, Lou Brock, and Maury Wills.

SMARTEST BASE RUNNER OF ALL TIME: Jackie Robinson. No question about it in my mind.

MOST EXCITING BASE RUNNERS I'VE EVER SEEN: Jackie Robinson and Pete Reiser.

BEST AT STRETCHING A SINGLE INTO A DOUBLE: Jackie Robinson. No question about it. He could stretch a single into a double, day in and day out.

At the Plate

BEST PURE HITTERS IN THE GAME: Stan Musial and Ted Williams. You just threw the ball and prayed. Stan was truly Stan "The Man." He beat up on us Dodgers real well over the years. Ted might very well have been the "toughest out" in all of baseball. I can't ever remember seeing him swing at a bad ball with a 3–2 count on him.

BEST 3–2 COUNT HITTER: Eddie Stanky. He got over 100 bases-on-balls with a full count.

MOST CONSISTENT HOME RUN HITTER (YEAR IN AND YEAR OUT):   Hank Aaron. He always gave you well over 40 home runs year in and year out. He was just awe-inspiring to watch.

LONGEST HOME RUNS: Frank Howard and Mark McGwire.

BEST BUNTERS IN THE GAME: Phil Rizzuto (American League) and Richie Ashburn (National League).

In the Field

BEST DOUBLE-PLAY TANDEMS: Bill Mazeroski at second base and Gene Alley at shortstop. Jackie Robinson at second and Pee Wee Reese at shortstop. Bobby Richardson at second and Tony Kubek at shortstop.

BEST ARMS IN THE OUTFIELD: Roberto Clemente, Rocky Colavito, and Carl Furillo.

BEST OUTFIELDER AT THROWING MEN OUT AT THIRD BASE: Rocky Colavito.

BEST HUSTLER IN THE OUTFIELD: Roberto Clemente.

MADE THE HARD PLAYS LOOK EASY: Joe DiMaggio.

MOST GRACEFUL IN THE OUTFIELD: Joe DiMaggio.

At the Ballparks

WINDIEST CITY IN BASEBALL: Chicago

HOTTEST CITIES: St. Louis, Kansas City, and Cincinnati. I can remember some 106-degree days in St. Louis. I never felt so hot in my life as during some of those doubleheader days.

FAVORITE BASEBALL PARKS: Ebbets Field, Wrigley Field, Fenway Park, Yankee Stadium, and Polo Grounds. I love all of these old ballparks. I like the modern ballparks such as Bank One Ballpark, Camden Yards, and Turner Field, but no stadium of today evokes the same memories as the old ones did years ago because, for me, the older parks represent my young career and the best baseball memories for me.

Today's Game

CONGRATULATIONS TO: Mark McGwire and Sammy Sosa for breaking both Ruth's record and Maris's record. They are both fine young men and they have rejuvenated baseball.

MOST LIKELY TO WIN MORE BATTING TITLES THAN ANYONE ELSE: Tony Gwynn.

MOST LIKELY TO WIN A TRIPLE CROWN: Ken Griffey Jr. and Barry Bonds.

HARDEST THROWERS IN THE GAME: Randy Johnson and Roger Clemens.

BEST FIELDING PITCHER IN TODAY'S GAME: Greg Maddux.

BEST MOVE TO FIRST BASE IN TODAY'S GAME: Andy Pettitte.

MOST COMPLETE PITCHER TODAY: Greg Maddux.

Appendix C
My All-Time Roster—
American and National League

THESE LINEUPS REPRESENT THE PLAYERS WHOM I PLAYED OR MANAGED in my more than 50 years in baseball. The lineups do not include today's stars because I would need an additional lineup for each league to be fair to today's greats. The lineups do not include those who I did not see, such as Babe Ruth, so don't yell at me when you don't see his name in right field. These rosters only include those players whom I had the privilege to play against or manage against in the late 1940s through the 1970s. Disclaimers for hurt feelings aside, here we go again!

The National League

MANAGER: Leo Durocher.

PITCHERS: (R) Bob Gibson, (L) Sandy Koufax.

CATCHER: Johnny Bench.

FIRST BASE: Willie McCovey.

SECOND BASE: Jackie Robinson.

SHORTSTOPS: Pee Wee Reese and Ernie Banks. I felt I had to choose both of them. I just can't pick one. They were the best I've seen, and they're in the same league as far as ability is concerned.

THIRD BASE: Mike Schmidt.

OUTFIELD: (L) Stan Musial, (C)Willie Mays, (R) Hank Aaron and Roberto Clemente.

The American League

MANAGER: Casey Stengel.

PITCHERS: (R) Jim Palmer, (L) Whitey Ford.

CATCHER: Yogi Berra.

FIRST BASE: Hank Greenberg.

SECOND BASE: Bobby Richardson.

SHORTSTOP: Phil Rizzuto.

THIRD BASE: Brooks Robinson.

OUTFIELD: (L) Ted Williams, (C) Joe DiMaggio and Mickey Mantle, and (R) Frank Robinson.

Extra Innings

Every ball team needs a good closer, and I would like to close by saying thanks to the following key people:

My lovely wife, Norma, for her efforts in creating Chapter 23

My daughters, Normie, Princie, Janet

My wonderful grandchildren

My wonderful son-in-law Johnny Peacock, who helped me in editing Chapter 17

My good friend Mike Rouse, editor of the *Goldsboro News-Argus*, for his much appreciated support in spending hours reviewing the manuscript for me. I could not have finished this book without him. Thank you, Mike, and thanks to Billie, his wife, for allowing Mike to help me

My good friends Ralph and Ann Branca for their encouragement, support, and cooperation

My good friends Carmen and Yogi Berra, who wrote the foreword to this book

My good friends Dottie and Pee Wee Reese for their support

My good friends Ollie and Betsy Toomey for their encouragement and support

My good friends Marlene and Larry Rocks for their encouragement and patience; "Marle" for suggesting this book's title and Larry for his long hours of poring over page after page with me

My entire family, who encouraged me to write this book so that I could leave something for my children, grandchildren, and great-grandchildren

Ken Samelson, for his patience and understanding

My many friends across the country who kept asking me "when are you going to write a book?"

And finally, to God, who has sustained me through many years

—*Clyde King*

First and foremost, thanks to Norma King—a dear family friend without whose invaluable help this project would not have come to fruition, and whose constant encouragement and prayers while I was at school brought much joy to my life.

I wish to thank Carmen and Yogi Berra for their tireless work in writing the special foreword to this book, and for their encouragement and support.

Special thanks to Ralph and Ann Branca, who gave me invaluable anecdotal information.

I wish to thank baseball Hall of Famer Ralph Kiner and his wife DiAnn, family friends, who have constantly given me encouragement and support. Ralph, my baseball mentor, has given me insight into labor issues and broadcasting, as well as home-run support throughout my school years.

I also wish to thank Ernie Harwell. Ernie, a legend behind the microphone, is a special person as well. He and his wife Lulu are also family friends, and I'll always have Ernie to thank for my desire to write on the subject of baseball.

Jon Miller is another good friend I wish to thank for his constant encouragement and support throughout my school days. Thanks to Joe Angel, my good friend in Miami, who has always given me trust and constant encouragement. Thanks to Buck O'Neil, baseball legend and friend, who always took time to give me a few encouraging words during my school years.

I wish to thank former Boston Red Sox equipment manager Don Fitzpatrick, who gave me my first glimpse of behind-the-scenes baseball one sunny day at Fenway Park in 1990. I also want to thank Rob Antony of the Minnesota Twins for getting me started by arranging that first credential. A special thanks to Hall of Famer Duke Snider, who let me interview him at age 13. Thanks also to Hall of Famer Bob Feller for his insight into this great game.

I want to thank the following: Jim Schultz—VP of Public Relations for the Atlanta Braves; Dick Bresciani—VP of Media Relations for the Red Sox; Chuck Wasserstrom—Cubs PR Director; Jay Horwitz—Director of Media Relations for the Mets; Sharon Pannozzo; and Hall of Fame public relations director Jeff Idelson.

I wish to thank Kirby Puckett, Tony Gwynn, Mark Grace, Nolan Ryan, Greg Gagne, Andre Dawson, and Paul Molitor for making my first baseball interviews (at age 19) positive experiences that I'll never forget. These men gave me a sense of confidence and accomplishment. They may not have known what effect they had on me before; hopefully they do now.

I want to thank John Peacock, president of the Wayne County Chamber of Commerce, Goldsboro, North Carolina, as well as the Evans, Blackman, and Peacock families for their much appreciated support throughout this endeavor. Thanks Normie, Princie, and Janet!

A baseball book such as this one needs statistics and information that could only be found in a very special place—The National Baseball Hall of Fame in Cooperstown, New York. My good friend Tim Wiles, research director at the Hall of Fame, and his invaluable staff deserve much praise for their diligent efforts. To know Tim and to work with him is to truly appreciate him.

Milo Hamilton was my unofficial directory for phone numbers. Milo, I couldn't have reached so many former ballplayers without your help. Let it be known that you have the best memory of anyone for restaurants, especially where to find the best ice cream.

Thanks to Giants general manager Brian Sabean, manager Dusty Baker, Sally O'Leary of the Pittsburgh Pirates Alumni Association, Joe L. Brown, Mary Pellino of the Yankees, and Yankees general manager Brian Cashman.

Special thanks to Barry Halper of the New York Yankees for his constant encouragement.

Thanks to Phil Niekro, Branch Rickey III, Robert and Marion Merrill, former Yankee general counsel William F. Dowling, Boog Powell, and especially Hall of Fame announcer Jack Buck and Bishop Bevel Jones for their much appreciated praise and anecdotes for this book. Thanks to Hall of Fame sportswriter Bob Broeg for his encouragement.

Thanks to Vince Attard and Bob Ondrush at the Stony Brook Post Office in New York. Benjamin Franklin would be proud of you.

Thanks to family friends, Dr. Santiago Wong and family, Dr. Fred Mehlhop's family, Dr. Paul Stavrolakis, Anna Kless, and Theresa Bannon.

I wish to thank literary agent Jack Scovil for always believing in this book.

Thanks to good friend and editor Ken Samelson at NTC/Contemporary Publishing, who made this endeavor enjoyable and possible, as well as to project editor Julia Anderson, for her tireless work on this project.

—Burton Rocks